D0778830

ESSAYS on the CONSTITUTION of the UNITED STATES

Kennikat Press
National University Publications
Multi-disciplinary Studies in the Law

General Editor
Rudolph J. Gerber
Arizona State University

ESSAYS on the CONSTITUTION of the UNITED STATES

HENRY J. ABRAHAM WALTER F. MURPHY
DAVID FELLMAN C. HERMAN PRITCHETT
LOUIS HENKIN MARTIN SHAPIRO
ALPHEUS T. MASON HERBERT J. STORING

edited by
M. JUDD HARMON

National University Publications
KENNIKAT PRESS // 1978
Port Washington, N. Y. // London

Manufactured in the United States of America

Published by
Kennikat Press Corp.
Port Washington, N.Y./London

Library of Congress Cataloging in Publication Data
Main entry under title:

Essays on the Constitution of the United States.

(Multi-disciplinary studies in the law) (National University Publications)
Bibliography: p.
Includes index.
1. United States–Constitutional law–Addresses, essays, lectures. I. Harmon, Mont, Judd.
KF4550.A2E8 342'.73 78-6445
ISBN 0-8046-9210-6

CONTENTS

This volume is dedicated to Emma Eccles Jones, whose generosity was a major factor in making possible the Bicentennial Lecture Series upon which these essays were based.

ESSAYS on the CONSTITUTION of the UNITED STATES

ABOUT THE CONTRIBUTORS

Henry J. Abraham has been an active participant and leader in a great variety of academic and civil affairs and is a member of some twenty-five professional societies and associations. He has written nine books and dozens of scholarly articles. He is presently Henry L. and Grace Doherty Memorial Foundation Professor in Government and Foreign Affairs at the University of Virginia.

David Fellman, Vilas Professor of Political Science at the University of Wisconsin, is a teacher, scholar, author and civil servant. He has written numerous books and articles and has written the annual review of the Supreme Court for the *American Political Science Review.*

M. Judd Harmon is Professor of Political Science at Utah State University in Logan, Utah, and received his Ph.D. from the University of Wisconsin in 1953. He is the author of books and articles in the field of political science.

Louis Henkin was an officer of the United States Department of State for ten years before entering academic life. He is currently Hamilton Fish Professor of International Law and Diplomacy and Professor of Constitutional Law at Columbia University. His publications include an extensive list of articles in professional journals and books and monographs.

Alpheus T. Mason, Emeritus McCormick Professor of Jurisprudence at Princeton University, is widely recognized as the country's leading judicial biographer. He retired from the faculty of Princeton in 1968 after forty-three years of service. In addition to many scholarly articles Dr. Mason has written twenty books.

Walter F. Murphy is McCormick Professor of Jurisprudence at Princeton. He was a member of the New Jersey Advisory Committee to the U.S. Civil Rights Commission and the Board of Trustees of the Law and Society Association, among other public service organizations. He has written a large number of articles for professional journals of law and political science as well as several books.

C. Herman Pritchett has long been recognized as one of the leading authorities on the Constitution of the United States. He is a past president of the American Political Science Association and was a member of the American Bar Association Commission on Electoral College Reform in 1966. He has written many articles and is the author or co-author of numerous books. He was formerly Chairman of the Department of Political Science at the University of Chicago and is presently at the University of California, Santa Barbara.

Martin Shapiro has achieved an enviable reputation as a constitutional lawyer. He has written many articles on the courts and judicial process. He is the author and editor or co-editor of numerous books. He is currently a member of the faculty of the School of Law at the University of California at Berkeley.

Herbert J. Storing has been a member of the Political Science Department at the University of Chicago since 1956. His principal scholarly interests are in the areas of the American founding, constitutional law, black American political thought, and public administration theory. He has written many articles and edited and co-authored several books on these subjects.

M. JUDD HARMON

INTRODUCTION

The celebration of America's Bicentennial was, above all, a salute to our forebears, who won our independence as a nation and established the institutions that still govern the nation. Those institutions and the principles underlying them have, of course, altered. But the alterations are less striking than their continuity and durability. It is an historical fact of some consequence that we are, after two hundred years, still pointing with pride to the origins of our system. That system has, on occasion, been threatened, sometimes seriously, but it has survived and flourished, and it has done so on the basis of the consent of its citizens. Few other political societies can make such a claim.

Stability, standing alone, is no virtue. It is, however, one requirement for the good life, as Aristotle said. And there is no doubt that the great majority of Americans believe that, compared to most other peoples of the world, they live a good life. While maintaining a strong and probably healthy skepticism concerning those who are responsible for operating it, they also believe in the governmental system which helped produce it. Only a short time ago the traumas of Vietnam and Watergate created widespread doubts in the minds of Americans concerning their system, but this pessimism had largely vanished by the time the Bicentennial year began.

When we speak of the "system" and its "principles," we are referring mainly to those outlined in the Constitution of the United States, adopted thirteen years after the nation had declared its independence. Thus, it was fitting that a celebration of the Bicentennial should have included a consideration of our fundamental document of government. Americans have been debating its meaning, purpose, and value ever since the Philadelphia Convention of 1787. But it was particularly appropriate to do so on such an occasion as the Bicentennial because it gives an historical perspective to analysis that is often absent at other times. It is one thing to engage in a debate over the wisdom of a particular constitutional decision and quite another to consider the value of the Constitution over the long haul. Thus, although there may be public dissatisfaction with a specific issue of constitutional interpretation, it appears presently that most Americans are not only satisfied with the working of their Constitution but they are also enthusiastic and proud about its long-term success.

If this were true only with regard to the masses of average citizens, whose knowledge of the history and even the content of the Constitution is sketchy to say the least, it might be dismissed as a matter of little importance, a transitory phenomenon engendered by the holiday spirit of the Bicentennial. This, however, does not appear to be the case. Among the "experts," the scholars, the legal practitioners, and others who are both knowledgeable and directly interested, there seems to be a greater respect for the Constitution and confidence in its capacity to resolve problems than has existed for many years, perhaps greater than has ever existed.

It would be difficult to prove such an assertion, and I make no attempt to do so here. What follows is primarily a personal assessment based upon observations extending over a period of some thirty years. I do not pretend that those observations have led to unassailable conclusions, but my professional contemporaries will know what I am talking about.

I must admit that I had given little thought to this matter until it became my responsibility to provide an introduction to the eight essays which comprise this volume. These essays are based upon a series of lectures on the Constitution of the United States given during the Bicentennial year.* The authors, eight of the country's most distinguished constitutional scholars, were invited to speak and write on any aspect of the Constitution in which they had greatest interest. Surprisingly, there was no need to alter subject matter to prevent duplication; the authors selected topics that were quite diverse. Such diversity, however, made the task of writing an introduction much more difficult than would have been the case had the essays focused on one specific problem.

It was only after several readings and approaching despair over the possibility of finding something to tie them together that I saw a glimmer of light. It was faint at first, but the more I concentrated on it the brighter it became. It was a simple fact, so simple that I did not initially conceive its significance, although considering that Alpheus T. Mason had pointed clearly to it in his introductory essay I am appalled at my obtuseness. The common thread is that not one of these eminent constitutional authorities

*The Milton R. Merrill Bicentennial Lectures, Utah State University, 1975–76.

found fault with or criticized the fundamental principles of the document about which they were writing. To be sure, there was ample criticism, but it was directed toward persons–judges, public officials, and others–who had "misinterpreted" the Constitution or misused it. For the Constitution itself, for its basic principles and qualities, there was, implicitly if not always explicitly, a respect as sincere if not as flamboyant as that expressed during the Bicentennial celebration. It is most obvious in Mason's essay, but it is there in all of them.

The fact is worthy of consideration, for it represents a significant shift in academic opinion. I cannot conceive that a comparable collection of essays published, say, twenty-five or thirty years ago would not have included some which raised serious questions concerning federalism, separation of powers, checks and balances, legislative supremacy, judicial review, and other constitutional principles.

I do not suggest that there were no supporters of the Constitution in Academe at that time. I suspect that Professor Mason was saying then what he is saying now and that many agreed with him. But my generation, as students, were marching to different drummers–J. Allen Smith, Charles A. Beard, Vernon Louis Parrington, and their disciples, whose views were scarcely calculated to instill among their followers confidence in and admiration for the Constitution and the men who framed it.

According to this critical school, the Constitution was the handiwork of Americans who profoundly distrusted the democratic spirit which had carried us through the Revolution and the establishment of the Articles of Confederation. The Constitution, they argued, was designed to halt the developing movement toward equality and majority rule–euphemisms, they believed, for mob rule–and make the country safe for economic privilege disguised in the robes of "liberty." To be sure, the strategy did not enjoy unqualified success. The democratic trend was too powerful to block, but it was severely curbed through the judicious use of various devices, such as federalism and judicial review, which the Constitution provided. Thus, worthwhile progress could be made only by overcoming the obstacles placed in its path by the Constitution. To this end the Constitution was amended and interpreted, political parties were organized to overcome the handicaps of separation of powers, presidents were popularly elected (or nearly so) and wrested power from congressional representatives of special interests, and so forth. Only by neutralizing its enemy, the Constitution, could the American ideal be achieved.

These arguments did not fall on deaf ears. To a generation of students who bore the scars of depression and war they had a powerful appeal. We were aware that other views existed, those of E. S. Corwin and Charles Warren, for example, but these were less appealing. The hardships resulting from the Great Depression demonstrated the need for a greater measure of economic and social equality. That Fascism and Nazism were the enemies of democracy proved that democracy, based upon majority rule and equality, was the only morally acceptable governmental system. The New Deal, which sought both a greater degree of economic equality and the defeat of Nazism-Fascism, received the support of the vast majority of political scientists, students and teachers alike.

Typically, the critics of the Constitution praised the British system of government for its responsiveness to the popular will, a responsiveness untrammeled by such undemocratic restraints as federalism and judicial review. And although there were few who seriously suggested that the United States should move to a unitary and parliamentary system, there were many who were convinced that it was unfortunate such a move was impractical, for only by doing so could the United States make swift progress toward its egalitarian destiny.

I suggest that these critical views are not nearly so widespread today as they were twenty-five years ago—or twenty, fifteen, or ten years ago—and that the present trend is toward a new and greatly increased respect both for the Constitution and for the wisdom and foresight of the men of the Philadelphia Convention. Those who have engaged in this reappraisal do not all agree upon the reasons for their conclusions, and surely there is room for additional scholarly effort here. But that their conclusions are harmonious seems significant.

In a provocative essay published on the eve of the Bicentennial, Martin Diamond[1] harshly attacked the school of Smith, Beard, and Parrington, which argued that the Constitution was a betrayal of the Declaration of Independence and the Revolution, in the name of liberty but in the spirit of privilege. In fact, Professor Diamond wrote, the Declaration took its stand for *liberty*, for it was liberty, not democracy, in which eighteenth-century Americans were interested. And it was the *Constitution* which established democracy, a form of government appropriate to the achievement and defense of liberty. Those who have seen the Constitution as anti-democratic make the mistake of equating democracy with equality, which they regard as a "political good" superior to liberty. The framers of the Constitution were too much under the influence of Montesquieu to permit the establishment of *any* form of government in which power went unchecked, for unrestrained governmental power would violate the principle of liberty. Thus, the framers believed that devices which impose limits upon the powers of the majority were necessary if democracy were to succeed. In modern times, however, Professor Diamond continues, ideas of equality have become inflated. The older idea of "equal political liberty" has given way to an ideology which demands equality in all respects. This, of course, was neither the objective of the revolutionaries who produced the Declaration nor that of the framers of the Constitution.

On the other hand, in his introductory essay Professor Mason asserts that it was not democracy that the framers of the Constitution intended but "free government," a system which recognizes that human nature contains elements of both good and evil and provides devices designed to encourage the good and restrain the evil. For Mason the revolutionary quality of the Declaration was twofold: first, an assertion of equality, not in each and every respect, but in the possession of rights to life, liberty, and the pursuit of happiness; second, the assumption that government rests upon consent rather than fear. "Free government" does not make majority rule impossible; indeed, it has countenanced a "series of limited revolutions." But it assumes that tyranny can be imposed by a majority as well as by a minority and guards against both by providing institutional restraints that impede precipitous action.

It is, I believe, an increased awareness of and appreciation for this last point, among those who formerly were most critical of the Constitution, that accounts for the shift in opinion to which I have previously alluded. That the Constitution has imposed restraints upon the movement toward equality is obvious. But just as obviously that movement has continued. It is hard to imagine that even the wildest-eyed of the eighteenth-century radicals would have advocated all the policies, designed to advance the cause of equality, which have become the law of the land. Even Jefferson spoke of the desirability of government by a "natural aristocracy." If it had been the essential purpose of the Constitution to block the path to the achievement of equality, one can only conclude that it has failed. This is not to say, of course, that we have established complete political, economic, social, and racial equality in the United States of America. But that major progress in that direction has been made cannot be doubted.

Coupled with this awareness that the Constitution has permitted, if not facilitated, steady progress toward equality is, I believe, a growing and uneasy suspicion that perhaps too much progress in this direction has already been made. On this point I detect a distinct air of apprehension among liberals. Many of those who were enthusiastic supporters of the New Deal, for example, now openly express doubt about the wisdom of extending the welfare state and voice concern over the decline of the spirit of "enterprise." No less a New Dealer than William O. Douglas felt it necessary a decade ago to remind us that "the purpose of the Constitution and the Bill of Rights, unlike more recent models promoting a welfare state, was to take government off the backs of people."[2]

The widespread defections from the ranks of the Democrats in the presidential election of 1972 has generally been attributed to the belief among the defectors that George McGovern, the Democratic candidate, was an altogether too fervid proponent of the expansion of social and economic equality. And while there were many reasons for the nomination victory of Jimmy Carter in 1976, it is certainly the fact that he was widely regarded as much more moderate on this issue than McGovern had been four years previously. In the Republican Party the strongly conservative platform adopted in 1976 and the near-victory of Ronald Reagan provided further evidence of anxiety over this matter, an anxiety generally expressed in terms of fear of "creeping" or "galloping" socialism. That the deeply conservative Gerald Ford could be seriously regarded by many as a leftist, or, at best, soft on "socialism," bears eloquent witness to the strong feelings within the vocal and influential right wing of the Republican Party. But, although the majority of American voters reject the extreme position of the Republican (and Democratic) right, it is apparent that they are paying more attention to the issues upon which that faction has been harping for many years. That the right favors the status quo ante and moderates the status quo, or at least slower progress beyond it, does not alter the fact that both are apprehensive that equality is being extended at the cost of diminishing liberty.

The dean of American television editorialists, Eric Sevareid, recently commented that the fundamental philosophic disagreement in American politics is between those who believe that the poor support society and those who believe that society supports the poor. It would appear that the ranks of the latter faction are growing. This, of course, is simply another way of saying that a great many Americans believe that we have gone far enough, or too far, in using government to achieve social and economic equality.

Corollaries of the extension of the principle of equality from the political to the economic and social spheres have been the expansion of governmental powers, especially those of the national government, and an impressive increase in the size of government and in the cost of operating it. The transformation of the United States from a simple rural, agricultural society to a complex urban, industrial society and the growth of the nation's population would themselves have accounted for a large part of these developments. But it is also the fact that a society committed to equality is bound to require more government and more powerful government than one whose primary concern is liberty. This is not to suggest that a government committed to liberty is necessarily small and impotent. Liberty may be threatened not only by government but also by individuals, organizations, and foreign enemies. One of the justifications of government is that it provides protection, and it must be large and powerful enough to do so. However, a government whose essential function is the protection of the individual will not compare in size and power with one which additionally provides the vast array of services associated with the welfare state and administers the legislation designed to achieve a greater degree of social equality.

Just as many liberals of the older school now worry that the principle of equality has been overextended, so too do they express misgivings over the expansion of governmental size and power. It is a view which has had significant political consequences, for it provides one basis for the current phenomenon of "anti-Washingtonism" which formed a part of Carter's strategy to gain the Democratic nomination for the presidency and very nearly enabled Ronald Reagan to capture the Republican nomination from an incumbent Republican president.

A successful society demands that a decent balance of the often conflicting principles of liberty and equality be maintained. Quite aside from the fact that a simple humanitarianism requires attention to the plight of the less fortunate, it is also true, as Aristotle wrote long ago, that a polity in which differences in the holding of wealth are too great is inherently unstable, and that in such a situation the property and privileges of the wealthy themselves are threatened. On the other hand, equality achieved by governmental intervention necessitates limitations upon the liberties of the individual. Under "free government" there is bound to be constant struggle between the advocates of these two principles, and indeed that has been the case throughout the history of the American republic. That neither side has achieved permanent dominance is a victory for the principles of free government—for the Constitution.

The conventional wisdom among liberals of the New Deal school was, as stated above, that the Constitution was an enemy to be overcome because it had been used by executive, legislative, and judicial officers (especially the latter) to defeat majority demands for equality. There was little or no concern that the achievement of equality would create a larger and more powerful government which might threaten the liberties of the people. The new attitude of respect for the Constitution among those who were until recently its critics can be explained by not only the realization that the Constitution has countenanced a substantial expansion of equality but also that it may be useful in curbing further progress in the same direction.

For whichever direction public policy takes, toward liberty or equality, the Constitution assures that it cannot move too rapidly. It requires that "sober second thought" which is often annoying and frustrating but which, the record demonstrates, has proved its value. The Constitution could, of course, be altered to remove the obstacles to immediate achievement of its purposes. If a sufficiently large majority wished to do so, it could even require the calling of another constitutional convention wherein a new document, more amenable to the majority will, could be forged. That such a demand has not been made is, on the face of the matter, somewhat of an anomaly. It is likely, however, that most Americans, or at any rate most of those who think about the issue, understand that there are no permanent majorities and that they may, on any given occasion, be as supportive of a minority as they are of the majority position. In short, the majority itself accepts the principle that majorities, as well as minorities, cannot always be trusted—precisely the view of the authors of the Constitution. It does not seem unreasonable to suggest that one explanation for the present esteem accorded the Constitution is an awareness that the purposes it was intended to serve are wise and in the general interest.

Criticism of the Constitution will, of course, continue. Support for and opposition to the document, its interpretations, and applications have always been based, in large part, upon the personal feelings engendered by the consequences of those interpretations and applications. Supporters of the New Deal thought that civil liberties were inadequately protected by the Constitution whereas economic liberties were overly protected. Their opponents later railed against a constitutional interpretation which accorded civil liberties a preferred position. That the Constitution can be so construed as to permit the busing of public school students to achieve racial balance gratifies some and infuriates others. Countless similar examples could be cited. We have long since learned that tranquility is not an inevitable consequence of constitutionality.

A reasonable degree of stability has, however, been a consequence of the system of governmental institutions outlined by the Constitution. That complex array of checks and counterchecks discourages precipitate action and encourages deliberation. In the short run speed often seems desirable and deliberation's delay vexatious. In the long run, however, it is essential to liberty under the law that men think before they act in the name of an entire people. If the Bicentennial did no more than remind us of this connection between reasoned deliberation and intelligent, principled choice, its celebration was worthwhile.

1 ALPHEUS T. MASON

AMERICA'S POLITICAL HERITAGE
Revolution and Free Government–A Bicentennial Tribute

In 1974, two years before the Bicentennial of America's birth as a nation, free government experienced a crisis comparable only to the Civil War. Thoughtful Americans gravely wondered whether there would be anything to celebrate in 1976. Confronted with unprecedented betrayals, the institutions of free government–press, Congress, and courts–responded. Without loss of a drop of blood, America ousted from the highest office in the land a rebellious conspirator to obstruct justice.[1] To rid themselves of Britain's tyrannical rule, the colonies resorted to revolution. Thanks to the Founding Fathers' constitutional handiwork, that was not necessary on the eve of America's Bicentennial.

No happenstance, this timely tribute to the resilience of eighteenth-century institutions was the result of careful planning. James Madison, "Father of the Constitution," boasted that the American people "accomplished a revolution which has no parallel in the annals of human history. They reared the fabrics of government which have no models on the face of the globe. They formed the design of a great Confederacy which it is incumbent on their successors to improve and perpetuate."[2]

Madison's unqualified acclaim seems parochial, self-serving, even more so when one takes into account the fact that these exalted pronouncements were published in a newspaper article circulated during the heated campaign to win support for the proposed Constitution. Ratification was uncertain; America's constitutional future was clouded in doubt. Circumstances put a high premium on hyperbole. How do Madison's lofty claims measure up in the light of nearly two centuries of history?

Reprinted from *Political Science Quarterly* 91 (summer 1976): 193-217 by permission.

REVOLUTION WITHOUT PARALLEL

Nowadays few words are bandied about more freely than "revolution." For most it evokes images of violence, disruption, and anarchy. Yet the right of revolution, historically and logically, has high claim as the focus of America's Bicentennial. How can Americans denigrate contemporary models and celebrate 1776? In his classic formulation Jefferson made revolution seem glorious, noble, Heaven-sent.

> We hold these truths to be self-evident, that all men are created equal, that they are endowed by their Creator with certain unalienable rights. That among these are Life, Liberty and the Pursuit of Happiness. That to secure these rights, Governments are instituted among men, deriving their just powers from the consent of the governed. That whenever any Form of government becomes destructive of those ends, it is the Right of the People to alter or to abolish it, and institute a new Government, laying its foundations on such principles and organizing its powers in such form, as to them seem most likely to effect their safety and happiness.[3]

The Declaration of Independence is our national birth certificate. Our first state constitutions, some of them prefaced with the Declaration, denounced the doctrine of nonresistance against arbitrary power and oppression as "absurd, slavish, and destructive of the good of mankind."[4] Lincoln called the people's "*right* to rise up, and shake off the existing government, and form a new one that suits them better–a most sacred right–a right, which we hope and believe, is to liberate the world."[5] In 1953 Arthur Schlesinger, Sr., listing America's ten contributions to civilization, accorded top rank to the right of revolution.[6] At no time in our history could we reasonably or gracefully turn our backs on it. Nor can we do so in 1976.

"If there be a principle," James Madison commented in 1793, "that ought not to be queried within the United States, it is that every Nation has a right to abolish an old government and establish a new one. . . . It is the only lawful tenure by which the United States hold their existence as a Nation."[7] "It is in vain," Madison wrote in *Federalist* no. 41, "to oppose constitutional barriers to the impulse of self-preservation. It is worse than in vain, because it plants in the constitution itself necessary usurpations of power, every precedent of which is a germ of unnecessary and multiplied repetitions." Although not always in agreement with his *Federalist* collaborator, Alexander Hamilton called revolution "an original right of self-defense, paramount to all positive government."[8]

The right of revolution has an honorable heritage. In immortalizing it Jefferson drew ideas and phraseology from John Locke's *Two Treatises of Government*. Locke had proclaimed: "Should either the executive or the legislative, when they have got power in their hands, design or go about to enslave or destroy them, the people have no other remedy than this, as in all other cases when they have no judge on earth, but to appeal to Heaven"[9]–apparently a euphemism for revolution.

A staunch conservative, Locke held that the "end of civil society is civil peace." Wary of its disruptive possibilities, he argued that rebellion is not likely to occur. With both ruler and ruled in mind, he suggested that "the properest way to prevent the evil is to show them the danger and injustice of it who are under the greatest temptation to run into it." Rulers would be more inclined to remain on good behavior, and the people, aware of the consequences, would be willing to suffer "slips of human frailty" until evils become insufferable. Thus, for Locke, revolution seemed not so much a right to be asserted as a recipe for its avoidance.

Locke's constitutionalism is marked by the absence of any worldly authority for resolving conflicts between unabashedly tyrannical government and palpable grievances. "*Who shall* be Judge whether the Legislative act contrary to their Trust? To this I reply, *The People shall be Judge*. . . . But this cannot mean that there is no judge at all. For where there is no Judicature on Earth to decide controversies amongst Men, *God* in Heaven is *Judge*."

Omission of a common power over all in Locke's system seems more extraordinary in light of the fact that under his theory men left the state of nature and entered civil society to enjoy the advantage of such an arbiter.[10] Yet for individuals and minorities in his civil society, the "Appeal to Heaven" would seem to be an empty declamation:

> The right of resisting, even Manifest Acts of Tyranny, will not suddenly, or on slight occasion, disturb the Government. For if they reach no further than some private Men's rights, though they have a right to defend themselves, and to recover by force what by unlawful force is taken from them; yet the right to do so, will not easily engage them in a contest, wherein they are sure to perish.

Belying Locke's expectations, the American colonies rebelled. Against incalculable odds they invoked force against force. Locke's *Second Treatise of Government* justified their Appeal to Heaven: "The use of force without authority always puts him that uses it into a State of War, as the aggressor, and renders him liable to be treated accordingly." Ironically, the rationale Locke used to uphold the supremacy of Parliament, Jefferson asserted to repudiate it.

Locke's theory had been working itself into the minds of the colonists long before 1776. The real revolution being, as John Adams said, "in the minds and hearts of the people," it was "effected before the War commenced."[11] Furthermore, as we shall see, the revolution continued after the war ended.

In the prerevolutionary controversy, lawyers and law-minded leaders played a prominent role. Arguing their case against Britain in constitutional terms, the colonists deplored denial of representation, rejected parliamentary supremacy, and proclaimed a theory of higher law which, though advocated in England by the eminent Lord Coke, was never sanctioned in the mother country. In denouncing the infamous Writs of Assistance, James Otis, challenging the supremacy of Parliament, claimed for the executive courts power to declare "the act of a whole Parliament void."[12]

The constitutional argument ended ultimately in an impasse. Parliament asserted its supremacy; in rebuttal the colonies asserted their own. Want of a common power over all, as in Locke's *Two Treatises,* to resolve conflicting claims, led to the most forbidding of all political monsters—*imperium in imperio*—many sovereigns in the same community.

Inspired, finally, by the vision of "a great country, populous, and mighty" (Franklin's language), even the lawyers shifted ground, deepening the base of their grievances. "To what purpose," James Otis asked, "is it, to base the colonists' argument on the cases of Manchester and Sheffield? If those, now so considerable places are not represented, they ought to be."[13] This moral approach became the fundamental premise of the call for revolution and independence.

As formulated in the Declaration of Independence, the right of revolution, a moral rather than a legal or constitutional imperative, was both conservative and radical. Jefferson's animating purpose, like Locke's, was conservative. The colonists revolted, not so much to initiate a completely new order as to reestablish British rights and liberties on this side of the Atlantic.[14] We have taken up arms, the Continental Congress explained, July 6, 1775, "in defense of the freedom that is our birthright, and which we ever enjoyed til the late violation of it."[15]

Edmund Burke, symbol of conservatism, warmly endorsed the American revolution, and harshly denounced the French. The French began inauspiciously, he commented, "by despising everything that belonged to them."[16] The Americans, on the other hand, exhibited unswerving devotion to liberty according to British ideas and experience. Parliament, not the colonies, exercised power contrary to the British constitution.

America never had a revolution comparable to the upheavals in France and Russia. The Revolution of 1776 did not wipe the constitutional slate clean. In the modern European sense of the word, the momentous step taken in 1776 was hardly a revolution at all.[17] Tocqueville noted "the great advantage of the Americans." They arrived at a condition of liberty without rejecting their inherited principles.[18]

The Declaration of Independence is also radical. It sanctioned the belief, extreme even by present-day standards, that all men, regardless of race, color, or creed, are endowed by their Creator with certain unalienable birthrights. Endorsed is the potentially subversive doctrine that just governments can safely rest on reason and consent rather than on fear and coercion.

"Fear, the foundation of most governments," John Adams wrote in 1776, "is so sordid and brutal a passion, and renders men in whose breasts it predominates so stupid and miserable, Americans will not be likely to approve of any political institution which is founded on it."[19] Although "the capacity of mankind for self-government" had yet to be demonstrated, Madison singled out this "honorable determination" as the motivating force in "all our political experiments."[20]

Reason is among the most fragile, the most uncertain ingredients in the lexicon of statecraft. When rationalism was in its heyday, a contemporary of the Founding Fathers, Dr. Samuel Johnson, cautioned in *Rasselas:* "Of the uncertainties in our present state, the most dreadful and alarming is the uncertain continuance of reason." Small wonder Jefferson called the decision of 1776 "the bold and doubtful election we then made for our country."[21] "Experience must be our only guide," John Dickinson cautioned the Philadelphia Convention delegates in 1787. "Reason may mislead us."[22] Not until our own time, barring the Civil War, has this country experienced in full measure the precarious dimensions of the epochal decision of 1776.

Henry Steele Commager declares that the Declaration of Independence is more subversive than the *Communist Manifesto.*[23] Marx's apocalyptic vision precludes further revolution.[24] For Jefferson it is a continuing political phenomenon, as inescapable as it is desirable. With reference to Shays's Rebellion in Massachusetts, he exclaimed: "God forbid we should be twenty years without such a rebellion. . . . "[25] Commager suggests that "ardent conservatives who fear revolution everywhere might logically start by banning the Declaration from schools and textbooks."

Jefferson's rationalization of revolution includes negative and positive aspects. It asserts the natural right of people to alter or abolish tyrannical government, and affirms their right to establish a new government more in keeping with their safety and happiness. Thus, the Declaration of Independence and the Constitution are parts of one consistent whole.[26] For both, liberty and justice were the animating principles. The negative phase, elimination of arbitrary power, was relatively easy; establishing a free government was far more difficult. "The generation which commences a revolution," Jefferson noted, "rarely completes it."[27]

Our revolutionary fathers were dissenters; we are the descendants of dissenters. Unlike some of the modern breed, they did not proclaim the rottenness of their entire heritage, and urge its destruction, root and branch. After throwing off the British yoke, the victorious revolutionaries knew that a more difficult task lay ahead—that of building a constitutional order in which man's destructive impulses could be brought within the framework of civility, rationality, and law. If the American Revolution had been merely destructive dislodgment of lawless government, it would not have been justified. If "the precious blood of thousands" had been spilt, Madison declared, so that "the government of the individual states . . . might enjoy a certain extent of power . . . ," it would not have been worthwhile. The only justification for revolution was the replacement of Britain's tyrannical rule with a government capable of advancing "the real welfare of the great body of the people."[28]

By 1783 the revolutionaries of 1776 were triumphant. The American states had achieved independence not only from Great Britain, but also from each other. One problem was solved only to create another. In the sense of want of a common power over all, the states after 1776 were in a Lockean state of nature. Because separation from Britain would place states, like Locke's individuals in his imaginary precivil society, in a position of independence with respect to each other, Loyalists Daniel Leonard and Samuel Seabury resisted revolution. "Two supreme or independent powers cannot exist in the same state," Leonard warned. "It would be what is called *imperium in imperio,* the height of political absurdity."[29] Although a forerunner of independence, John Adams, anticipating the conditions that made American political life so critical in the 1780s, declared: "Two supreme and independent authorities cannot exist in the same state any more than two supreme beings in one universe."[30]

By declaring that "each state retains its sovereignty, freedom and independence," the Articles of Confederation created precisely the political absurdity Leonard and Adams had foreseen and condemned. "They still seem to cherish with blind devotion," Hamilton commented derisively, "the political monster of an *imperium in imperio.*"[31] Enforcement difficulties arose from the fact that the articles operated on states in their corporate capacity instead of on individuals. Deploring gross inadequacies, John Quincy Adams observed:

> The work of the founders of our independence was but half done. For these United States, they had formed no *Constitution.* Instead of resorting to the source of all constituted power [the people], they had wasted their time, their talents, . . . in erecting and roofing and buttressing a frail and temporary shed when they should raise the marble palace of the people to shelter the Nation from the Storm.[32]

Yet the Articles performed invaluable service. The Confederation Congress waged war, made peace, and kept alive the idea of union when it was at its lowest ebb.

In 1783 the war was over, the Revolution unfinished.

"There is nothing more common," Dr. Benjamin Rush declared in 1787, "than to confound the terms of the *American Revolution* with those of the *late American War.* The American war is over; but this is far from being the case with the American Revolution. On the contrary, nothing but the first act of that great drama is closed. It remains yet to establish and perfect new forms of government." Underscoring his sense of urgency, Dr. Rush appealed to "Patriots of 1774, 1775, 1776–heroes of 1778, 1779, 1780. Come forward! Your country demands your services! The Revolution is not *OVER.*"[33]

Dr. Rush's call was heeded. In 1787 delegates from the various states (not including Rhode Island) assembled in Independence Hall, Philadelphia, the same place where, eleven years earlier, the Declaration of Independence had been signed. In 1776 reason and consent had been solemnly proclaimed as viable foundations of government. In 1787 these supports were subjected to a severe test. Hamilton posed the crucial issue: Could political communities called states through "reflection and choice" be transformed into "a union under one government"?[34]

The Constitution, like the Declaration of Independence, highlights the role of reason in statecraft. The convention began auspiciously, Jefferson commented, "by assembling the wise men, instead of the armies."[35] America, he said, "set the world an example of the formulation of political institutions by reason alone without bloodshed."[36] James Wilson boasted:

> America now exhibits to the world a gentle, a peaceful, a voluntary, and deliberate transition from one constitution of government to another. In other parts of the world, the idea of revolutions in government is connected with the ideas of wars and all the calamities attendant on wars. But happy experience teaches us to view such revolutions in a very different light: to consider them as progressive steps in improving the knowledge of government, and increasing the happiness of society and mankind.[37]

A century later John W. Burgess denounced the Constitutional Convention as counterrevolutionary, designed to turn back the democratic tide unleashed in 1776. "What they [the convention delegates] actually did, stripped of all fiction and verbiage," Burgess wrote in 1890, "was to assume constituent powers, ordain a constitution of government and of liberty, and demand the *plebiscite* thereon, over the heads of all existing legally organized powers. Had Julius [Caesar] or Napoleon committed these acts, they would have been pronounced coup d'état."[38]

Burgess's indictment seems extreme. The convention continued the revolution Jefferson adumbrated in 1776. It was, however, revolutionary both technically and substantively. In mandating that the document be ratified by nine rather than all the state conventions, it violated a provision in the Articles of Confederation which required unanimity. The Constitution was revolutionary, as Madison conceded, in deriving all authority not from states but from people. Confessing irregularities, Madison explained that these proceeded from "an irresistible conviction of the absurdity of subjecting the fate of twelve states to the perversion or corruption of a thirteenth." In the end he grounded his justification in the right of revolution, in "the great principle of self-preservation," in the "transcendent and precious right of the people to abolish or alter their government as to them shall seem most likely to effect their safety and happiness."[39]

The right of revolution, a legitimizing concept in 1776, remained so in 1787. "Supreme, absolute, and uncontrollable authority *remains* with the people," James Wilson declared on 4 December 1787. "I recollect no constitution founded on this principle: but we have witnessed the improvement, and enjoy the happiness, of seeing it carried into practice. The great and penetrating mind of *Locke* seems to be the only one that pointed towards even the theory of this great truth."[40]

FREE GOVERNMENT IN THE MAKING

Since revolution was, as Madison recognized, "the only lawful tenure by which the United States hold their existence as a Nation," it was incumbent on the Founding Fathers to institutionalize, legitimize, and domesticate it—bring it within the four corners of the Constitution—to fill the yawning hiatus in Locke's constitutional system.

Louis Hartz declares that Locke "dominates American thought as no thinker anywhere dominates the political thought of a nation."[41] Jefferson's appraisal was less categorical. For him, "Locke's little book on government is perfect so far as it goes."[42] Jefferson's quarrel with Locke concerned "practice" rather than "theory." In 1787, as in 1776, *Two Treatises of Government* was an arsenal of ideas. On the institutional side it was of limited usefulness. Apart from the basic notion that all just governments derive their power from the consent of the governed, the functioning of America's political institutions differs as fundamentally from Locke's as it does from the British system today. Locke's concern for liberty and property is reflected in his stress on natural law and natural rights. But his constitutionalism boils down to political limits on government—those imposed at election time, plus the faith that rulers and ruled alike would be guided by considerations of justice and common sense. The idea of a constitution limiting and superintending the operations of government forms no serious part of Locke's system. It has been said that Locke was "unreasonable only in his faith in reason."[43]

The artless "Appeal to Heaven" posed a challenge for our constitution makers. Needed were terrestrial procedures and forums that would reduce the occasions for revolution to the minimum. Madison articulated the crucial question: How could "the mild and salutary *coercion* of *magistracy*" be substituted for the "destructive *coercion* of the sword"?[44]

As Madison envisaged it, the problem was twofold: to enable government to control the governed and oblige government to control itself. Dependence on the people was recognized as the "primary control," but experience demonstrated the need for "auxiliary precautions."[45]

The Constitution's framers were inspired by profound suspicion of any and all power holders. "The truth is," Madison remarked, "all men having power ought to be mistrusted." Jefferson concurred: "It would be dangerous delusion were a confidence in the men of our choice to silence our fears for the safety of our rights: Confidence is everywhere the parent of despotism–free government is founded in jealousy, and not in confidence."[46]

Trying experience under the Articles of Confederation and the new state constitutions had brought democracy into question, including its primary tenet, majority rule. Disillusioned by the actual working of these hastily constructed institutions, the delegates convened at Philadelphia in 1787 realized that "the temple of tyranny has two doors"–monarchy and democracy. One has been bolted by proper restraints, the other left open, thus exposing society to "the effects of our own ignorance and licentiousness."[47] Both history and experience made democracy suspect. "Remember," John Adams warned, "democracy never lasts long. It soon wastes, exhausts, and murders itself. There never was a democracy yet that did not commit suicide."[48]

What the framers established was not "democracy the most simple" but "the most complicated government on the face of the globe."[49] They called their creation *free government.* More easily described than defined, it involves a complexus of controls designed to temper together into one consistent work the sometimes opposite, sometimes complementary, elements of liberty and restraint.[50] Madison stated the Founding Fathers' objective in *Federalist* no. 37: "To combine the requisite stability and energy in government with inviolable attention to liberty and the republican form." This goal could be achieved only by a constitutional arrangement setting interest against interest, ambition against ambition, power against power.

"In questions of power," Jefferson admonished, "let no more be heard of confidence in man [power holder], but bind him down from mischief by the chains of the Constitution."[51] Besides the right of revolution, these constitutional shackles include government under law, separation of powers, federalism, the Bill of Rights, and judicial review.

GOVERNMENT UNDER LAW

Locke's legislature, though avowedly supreme, was supposed to keep within the bounds set by natural law as well as "promulgated established law." But these limitations, like the right of revolution, were parchment barriers. The American Constitution makes the idea of higher law a truly operative principle. Madison cited "the distinction, so well understood in America, but little understood in any other country, . . . between a constitution established by the people and unalterable by government and a law established by government and alterable by government." He noted that: "Even in Britain where the principles of political and civil liberty have been most discussed, it is maintained that the authority of the parliament is transcendent and uncontrollable."[52] Not so in America.

"Superiority of the Constitution," James Wilson declared, means "control in *act*, as well as right." "To control power, and conduct of legislatures, by an over-ruling constitution," Wilson told the Pennsylvania ratifying convention, "was an improvement in the science and practice of government reserved for the American states."[53] For Oliver Ellsworth, third chief justice of the United States, the Philadelphia Convention's signal achievement was the substitution of "coercion of law" for the "coercion of arms."

For the first time in history two levels of law were recognized and put into practical effect: the higher law of the Constitution, which the people alone could make and unmake; and statutory law, to be made and unmade within limits imposed by the Constitution. Locke had hinted at this idea, as had Lord Coke. It had been broached in the early 1760s by James Otis and others on this side of the Atlantic. But in not one state, following independence, did a constituent assembly meet and establish a new government. None of the new constitutions was an act of constituent power, in accord with the idea Jefferson adumbrated in the Declaration of Independence.

"There was never any sovereign government in America,"[54] Woodrow Wilson said. Government under law was not a new idea. Aristotle, universal wise man of all time, had anticipated it. Among others, he had the idea. Article 6, paragraph 2, embodies this concept. To be recognized and accepted as "the supreme law of the land," the laws of the United States and of the states must be passed "in pursuance of" the Constitution.

SEPARATION OF POWERS

No man, no government official, high or low, can escape the Constitution's limitations. Written restrictions, though important, do not suffice. "You may cover whole skins of parchment with limitations," John Randolph said, "but power alone can limit power."[55]

By 1787 experience had demonstrated that the primary control—"dependence on the people," the ballot—was not enough. Noting that "the science of politics," since 1776, had "received great improvement," Hamilton listed as "wholly new discoveries the regular distribution of power into distinct departments of government, the introduction of legislative balances and checks, the institution of courts composed of judges holding their offices during good behavior, the representation of people in the legislature by deputies of their own election."[56]

A mutually checking arrangement governs the legislative branch. The Senate acts as an "impediment against improper acts of legislation" in the House of Representatives and vice versa. The president's veto provides a barrier against oppressive legislation by both houses. Though often restrained from engaging in "unjustifiable pursuits" by "apprehension of congressional censure," the president is also subject to impeachment. Hamilton proudly pointed to this provision as a vast improvement over the British system where "the person of the King is sacred and inviolable." He is "amenable to no constitutional tribunal, no punishment without involving the crisis of a national revolution."[57] America runs no such risk. The president may be impeached and removed from office and thereafter be liable to prosecution and punishment in the ordinary courts of law. Hamilton praised the provision for impeachment (until 1974 considered more or less moribund) as substituting "the mild magistracy of the law for the terrible weapon of the sword."

In support of this realistic approach the framers invoked Montesquieu's *Spirit of the Laws* and his key to liberty—separation of powers. "Every man invested with power," the French nobleman had written, "is apt to abuse it. . . . There can be no liberty where the legislative and executive powers are united in the same person or body of magistrates."[58] For Madison, no "principle" was of "greater intrinsic value." Subscribing to it, he wrote:

The great security against a gradual concentration of the several powers in the same department consists in giving to those who administer each department the necessary means and personal motive to resist encroachments of the others. The provision for defense must in this, as in all other cases, be commensurate to the danger of attack. Ambition must be made to counteract ambition, . . . supplying by opposite and rival interests the defect of better motives.

Separation of powers is a misnomer. The Constitution separates organs of government; it fuses functions and powers. Montesquieu's principle, Madison explained, does not mean that various departments ought to have "no partial agency or no control over the acts of each other." The three departments must be "connected and blended." Otherwise the "degree of separation which the maxim requires, as essential to free government, can never in practice be duly maintained." This "sacred maxim of free government" is "subverted" where "the *whole* power of one department is exercised by the same hands which possess the *whole* power of another department."[59]

Montesquieu's "political truth," sanctioned with "the authority of countless patrons of liberty" (Madison's words), was incorporated in the Constitution. The idea was not new. America institutionalized it.

FEDERALISM

Federalism, America's nearest approach to a unique creation, is another device for obliging government to control itself. It is a dual system in which two authorities, nation and states, govern the same territory and the same people, each supreme in its own sphere, neither supreme within the sphere of the other. Just as the states would naturally resent encroachments by national authority, so the central government would protect the people from the tyranny of their own state governments. Citing the provision of the Constitution which guarantees each state a republican form of government, Madison echoes a Lockean refrain: "Existence of a right to intervene will generally prevent the necessity of exerting it."[60] But there is always the possibility that encroachments may be carried so far as to provoke an "Appeal to Heaven." Anticipating this eventuality, Hamilton wrote:

The State legislatures, who will be not only vigilant but suspicious and jealous guardians of the rights of the citizens against encroachments from the federal government, will constantly have their attention awake to the conduct of national rulers, and will be ready enough, if anything improper appears, to sound the alarm of the people, and not only to be the voice, but if necessary, the *Arm* of their discontent.[61]

Hamilton faced up to the possibility of violent conflict, but played it down, arguing that countervailing forces alone would suffice to preclude resort to force: "The extreme hazard of provoking the resentments of the state governments, and a conviction of the utility and necessity of local administrations for local purposes, would be a complete barrier against oppressive use of such a power."

In light of profound concern among Antifederalists, Madison and Hamilton's reassurances, even then, must have seemed strained. Yet Hamilton bore down on the point: "It may safely be received as an axiom of our political system, that the State governments will, in all possible contingencies, afford complete security against invasions of public liberty by the national authority."[62] The Civil War tragically belied these confident expectations.

BILL OF RIGHTS

As the Constitution came from the hands of the framers, the powers of the national government were enumerated but not defined. Without specification or definition, other powers were reserved to the states or to the people. The Constitution was drafted, submitted to state conventions, and ratified without a Bill of Rights. While the states pondered ratification, Jefferson urged specific restraints on national authority. Arguing that "a bill of rights is what the people are entitled to against every government on earth," he insisted that natural rights "should not be refused or rest on inference."[63]

Alexander Hamilton and James Wilson demurred. Both contended that a bill of rights was unnecessary. Why make exceptions to power not granted? "In a government of enumerated powers," Wilson declared, "such a measure would not only be unnecessary, but preposterous and dangerous." For Hamilton, bills of rights "would sound much better in a treatise on ethics than in a constitution of government."[64]

Thanks to Jefferson, these arguments did not prevail. Insisting on curbs over and beyond structural checks, he advocated "binding up the several branches of the government by certain laws, which when they transgress their acts become nullities." This would "render unnecessary an appeal to the people, or in other words a rebellion on every infraction of their rights."[65] When a reluctant James Madison[66] yielded to Jefferson's plea for a bill of rights, and deduced supporting reasons, Jefferson singled out the argument of "great weight" for him—the legal check it puts in the hands of the judiciary.[67]

Once again, America owed a heavy debt to the past. The idea of natural rights was not new. It came to America most directly from Locke. These fundamental maxims of a free society gained no greater moral sanction by incorporation in our basic law, but individuals and minorities could thereafter look to courts for their protection. Rights, formerly natural, became civil.

JUDICIAL REVIEW

For peaceful resolution of controversies, whether among the three branches of the national government or between the central authority and the states, Hamilton and Madison, and the Founding Fathers generally, relied on the Supreme Court. "One court of supreme and final jurisdiction," Hamilton observed, is a "a proposition . . . not likely to be contested." In a flash of remarkable foresight, he suggested that discharge of its responsibilities would "have more influence upon the character of our governments than but few may imagine."[68] Madison considered judicial review helpful in warding off conditions that might lead to rebellion. "Some such tribunal is clearly essential," he declared, "to prevent an appeal to the sword, and a dissolution of the compact; and that it ought to be established under the general, rather than under the local governments is a position not likely to be combated."[69]

It was not to be supposed, Hamilton observed, "that the Constitution could intend to enable the representatives of the people to substitute their *will* to that of their constituents." Accordingly, courts "were designed to be an intermediate body between the people and the legislature, in order, among other things, to keep the latter within the limits assigned to their authority."[70]

John Marshall, destined as fourth chief justice of the United States to enforce Hamilton's ideas as the law of the land, had envisioned judicial review as an alternative to revolution. "What is the service or purpose of a judiciary," he inquired in the Virginia Ratifying Convention, "but to execute the laws in a peaceful, orderly manner, without shedding blood, or creating a contest, or availing yourselves of force? . . . To what quarter will you look for protection from an infringement on the Constitution, if you will not give the power to the judiciary? There is no other body that can afford such a protection."[71]

Judicial review is the most conspicuous weapon in the arsenal of devices for substituting "the mild magistracy of the law" for "the terrible weapon of Force." Not expressly authorized by the Constitution, an auxiliary of all other "auxiliary precautions," it was taken for granted in 1787 and for nearly a century thereafter. For the framers of the Constitution judicial review rested "upon certain general principles [government under law, separation of powers, federalism, Bill of Rights] which in their estimation made specific provisions for it unnecessary."[72] Not until after 1890, when judicial *review* became judicial *supremacy,* did the legitimacy of judicial review become a topic for scholarly research.

Distrust of government in all its branches and at all levels is free government's dominant characteristic. Courts are the only apparent exception. "No one says anything against judges," Edmund Randolph commented in the Virginia Ratifying Convention.[73] "Were I to select a power which might be given with confidence," Madison observed in the same forum, "it would be judicial power."[74] As a member of the First Congress, Madison, introducing the Bill of Rights amendments, declared that courts would be "an impenetrable bulwark against every assumption of power in the Legislative or Executive."[75] Jefferson, later Chief Justice Marshall's arch-critic, initially believed that the courts, "if rendered independent . . . merit confidence for their learning and integrity."[76]

But the judiciary, like other organs of government, is limited and sometimes the target of distrust. From Justice Stone, a knowledgeable and sophisticated jurist, comes one of the most astonishing comments in the annals of the Supreme Court. In an otherwise trenchant dissenting opinion, he wrote: "While unconstitutional exercise of power by the executive and legislative branches of the government is subject to judicial restraint, the only check upon our own exercise of power is our own sense of self-restraint."[77] There are, in fact, various restraints on the judiciary, formal and informal, including impeachment and threat of court packing. When its restraining power affects vital issues of the day, as under Jefferson, Lincoln, the two Roosevelts, and Lyndon Johnson, the Supreme Court falls under criticism and control as defying the all-important element in our constitutional tradition–distrust of power as such.

On occasion the Supreme Court as an alternative to Locke's "Appeal to Heaven" has been disappointing. In 1857 a sharply divided Court outlawed the Missouri Compromise,[78] and thus helped to precipitate the Civil War. In the late 1960s and early 1970s, several unsuccessful efforts were made to test the constitutionality of the Vietnam War. Justices Douglas and Stewart protested the Court's denial of certiorari in a case which might have dealt with the president's power to wage an undeclared war. Three soldiers had rejected duty in Vietnam, contending that the war was illegal and immoral. Said Justice Stewart: "These are large and deeply troubling questions. . . . We cannot make these problems go away simply by refusing to hear the case of three obscure Army privates. I intimate not even tentative views upon any of these matters, but I think the Court should squarely face them by granting certiorari and setting this case for argument."[79] In 1970 Massachusetts went to extraordinary lengths to obtain a judicial ruling on a war neither initially authorized nor subsequently ratified by Congress, except by the Tonkin Gulf Resolution. Proceeding as *parens patriae,* the state passed a law designed to protect its citizens from forced participation in combat or support of combat troops in Vietnam. Acting under this statute, Massachusetts sought leave to file a bill of complaint against Secretary of Defense Laird in the Supreme Court's original jurisdiction. Against the objections of Justices Douglas, Harlan, and Stewart, the Supreme Court denied the motion.[80]

Deeply disturbed, Justice Douglas expressed his concern in *Points of Rebellion,* published in 1970. No longer responsive to human needs, government had become, he argued, "a police state in which all dissent is suppressed or rapidly controlled." Drawing a dramatic parallel with 1776, Douglas concluded: "George III was the symbol against which our Founders made a revolution, now considered bright and glorious. . . . We must realize that today's Establishment is the new George III. Whether it will continue to adhere to its tactics [of suppression], we do not know. If it does, the redress, honored in tradition, is also revolution."

RIGHT OF REVOLUTION INSTITUTIONALIZED

Neither the Declaration of Independence nor the Constitution was designed to end the revolutionary cycle. The "exercise of an original right of the people," "a very great exertion not frequently to be repeated" (Chief Justice Marshall called it),[81] the Constitution was "intended to endure and to be adapted to the various crises in human affairs."[82] American constitutionalism can be fairly viewed as a series of limited revolutions. Besides the doubleheader 1776 and 1787, there is the "Revolution of 1800," so labeled by Jefferson himself. It was "not effected by the sword," he observed, "but by the rational and peaceful instrument of reform, the suffrage of the people."[83] Other revolutions followed: the Jacksonian revolution, the constitutional revolution of the 1890s, when judicial *review* became judicial *supremacy,* the Roosevelt revolution, the Warren Court revolution.[84]

For James Iredell of North Carolina "One of the greatest beauties of the American system was revolution by Amendment. Without it, the people would have to bring about amendments more or less by civil war."[85] Recognizing the inevitability of social and economic transformation, sometimes of revolutionary dimensions, Madison declared in *Federalist* no. 41: "A system of government, meant for duration, ought to contemplate these revolutions, and be able to accommodate itself to them." With one exception—the Civil War—all occurred without violence, within the bounds of law.

The *Federalist*'s authors did not close their eyes to the possibility of "mortal feuds," "conflagrations through a whole nation," which "no government can either avoid or control."[86] "It is a sufficient recommendation of the federal Constitution," Madison argued, "that it diminishes the risk of a calamity, for which no possible constitution can provide a cure."[87]

The Constitution demonstrates the power of reason in statecraft. The Civil War proved its limitations. By 1860 it became clear that the framers' most significant creation—federalism—carried within it an irreconcilable ambiguity. Madison had fashioned federalism's blueprint six weeks before the Philadelphia Convention assembled. Anticipating, on April 8, 1787, that "some leading propositions would be expected from Virginia," he wrote Governor Edmund Randolph:

> I hold it for a fundamental point, that an individual independence of the States is utterly irreconcilable with the idea of an aggregate sovereignty. I think, at the same time, that a consolidation of the States into one simple republic is not less unattainable than it would be inexpedient. Let it be tried, then, whether any *middle ground* can be taken, which will at once support a *due supremacy* of the national authority, and leave in force the local authorities so far as they can be *subordinately useful.*[88]

An architect would hesitate to begin construction of a house with drawings so imprecise as Madison carried to the Constitutional Convention. But the delegates were in Philadelphia not to build a house but to erect a federal system of government—union without unity. Their handiwork, though in close accord with the Madisonian model, proved inadequate.

Just as years of debate preceding independence proved powerless to resolve the issue of sovereignty between Britain and the colonies, so decades of discussion on the political platform, in Congress, on the hustings, and in the Supreme Court were unable to tame *imperium in imperio.*

AMERICA'S "APPEAL TO HEAVEN"

In *Federalist* no. 22 Hamilton had denounced as "gross heresy" the notion that "a party to a *compact* has a right to revoke that *compact.*" Nullification and secession—state sovereignty asserted in its boldest form—proclaimed the heresy Hamilton deplored. The constitutional response was the Civil War amendments, particularly the Fourteenth. Framed in the most sweeping terms by a radical Republican Congress, the latter was designed, apparently, to clip the wings of state sovereignty, once and for all. Directed explicitly to the state, that Amendment declares that "no state shall make or enforce any law which shall abridge the privileges and immunities of citizens of the United States, nor shall any state deprive any person of life, liberty, or property without due process of law, nor deny to any person within its jurisdiction equal protection of the laws." The apparent intention was to make the first eight amendments binding on the states and enforceable by Congress and the federal courts.

Yet in the first case[89] involving this amendment, the Supreme Court emasculated its major provisions—"privileges and immunities," "due process," "equal protection." For a majority of six, Justice Miller's explanation borders on apology:

> The argument we admit is not always the most conclusive which is drawn from the consequences urged against the adoption of a particular construction of an instrument. But when, as in the case before us, these consequences are so serious, so far-reaching and pervading, so great a departure from the structure and spirit of our institutions; when the effect is to fetter and degrade the state governments by subjecting them to the control of Congress, in the exercise of powers heretofore universally conceded to them of the most ordinary and fundamental character; when, in fact, it radically changes the whole theory of the relations of the State and Federal governments to each other, and both of these governments to the people; the argument has a force that is irresistible, in the absence of language which expresses such a purpose too clearly to admit of doubt.[90]

Justice Miller's sensitivity to a theory of federal-state relations, presumably established in 1789, is such that despite the amendment's all-embracing injunctions against state power vis-à-vis individual rights, he shrinks from the belief that the Congress, which framed the Fourteenth Amendment, intended to alter that relationship. Any such change, even by amendment, seemed suspect. In a vehement dissenting opinion Justice Field charged that the Court's restrictive interpretation reduced the Fourteenth Amendment to "a vain and idle enactment, which accomplished nothing."[91]

When the Civil War was over, the Supreme Court was confronted with the practical question—whether during that conflict Texas was out of the Union. Chief Justice Chase replied in the negative, fashioning a theory of federalism that practically restates the Madisonian formula of 1787: "The preservation of the States, and the maintenance of their government, are as much within the design and care of the Constitution as the preservation of the Union and the maintenance of the National government. The Constitution, in all its provisions, looks to an indestructible Union of indestructible States."[92]

By judicial fiat, if not by constitutional amendment, America's "Appeal to Heaven" left federalism virtually intact. A theory of the Union which reason could not establish was won by resort to force. What John Quincy Adams said of the Constitution was equally applicable to the

Union. It had to be "extorted from the grinding necessities of a reluctant nation."[93] Justice Holmes, himself a soldier in Lincoln's army, understood the subtleties involved:

When we are dealing with words that are also a constituent act like the Constitution of the United States, we must realize that they [the framers] have brought into life a being the development of which could not have been foreseen completely by the most gifted of its begetters. It was enough for them to realize or to hope that they had created an organism; it has taken a century and has cost their successors much sweat and blood to prove that they created a nation.[94]

A FLEXIBLE CREATION FOR FALLIBLE MEN

We return to Madison's boast: revolution without parallel; fabrics of government without a model. The father of the Constitution was right on both scores. That twofold effort established free government. Its meaning, strength, and inescapable risk are rooted in human nature. "Man's capacity for Justice," theologian Reinhold Niebuhr observed, "makes democracy possible, but man's inclination toward injustice makes it necessary."[95] Society is torn not only by conflict between men of good will and mutual assistance, on the one hand, and the vicious and degenerate on the other, but also by a more baffling struggle raging within each individual. "For the good that I would I do not: but the evil which I would not, that I do" (Romans, 7:19). The Constitution reflects this dualism. It grants and limits power.

The Founding Fathers did not postulate goals obtainable only if men were sinless. "If angels were to govern men," Madison commented, "neither external nor internal controls on government would be necessary."[96] Hamilton warned that "the supposition of universal venality is little less an error in political reasoning than the supposition of universal rectitude."[97] The major objective was to fashion a constitutional system in which both aspects of man's nature could find expression.[98]

Not even unqualified majority rule is a safe guardian of the inextricably related values, liberty and restraint.[99] Without ignoring ends the Constitution stresses means. The framers endorsed the seemingly fatalistic view that free government "is a method of finding proximate solutions for insoluble problems."[100]

In 1787 Hamilton applauded the "great improvements" made in "the science of politics."[101] Among other things, he noted the distribution of powers among the various organs and agencies of government. But Madison cautioned that "no skill in the science of government" had been able "to discriminate or define with sufficient certainty the different provinces of government."[102]

Constitutional lines of demarcation, whether between national government and state, among president, Congress, and Court, or that most precious barrier circumscribing power at all levels vis-à-vis individual rights, are not drawn with mathematical exactness. For Madison it was "a melancholy reflection" that liberty would "be equally exposed to danger whether the government have too much or too little power, and that the lines which divide these extremes should be so inaccurately defined by experience."[103] The imponderable nature of politics and the ever-present imperatives time and circumstance suggest that the effort to draw precise constitutional dividers would have been fruitless, even if tried. The framers knew the "dangers of delusive exactness."

"The lines of politics," Edmund Burke declared, "are not like the lines of mathematics. They are broad and deep as well as long. They admit of exceptions; they demand modifications. No lines can be laid down for civil or political wisdom. They are a matter incapable of exact definition."[104] Distribution of powers among distinct departments and levels of government, along with the fusion of power and functions, creates tension—"vibrations of power," Hamilton called it, "the genius of our government."[105]

The enduring lesson of American history is that opposition, freedom to disagree, protest, dissent, built into the organization and structure of our constitutional system, are its lifeblood. Criticism of official conduct, Madison said, "is the duty as well as the right of intelligent and faithful citizens." Society is entitled to the advantage of such criticism, and so are would-be usurpers of power. Divergence of opinion quickens our notion of the common interest. "If there were no different interests," Rousseau commented, "the common interest would barely be felt, as it would encounter no obstacles; all would go of its own accord, and politics would cease to be an art."[106] Enemy lists, ruthless elimination of opposition and dissent, are less demanding than the art of bringing differing minds into constructive accord. Adlai Stevenson gloried in the "discordant symphony" of a free society.

Justice Holmes, declaring that the best test of truth is the power of thought to get itself accepted in the competition of the market of ideas, identified this as "the theory of our Constitution."[107] Earlier he had denied that the Constitution "is intended to embody a particular *economic* theory, whether of paternalism and the organic relation of the citizen to the state or of *laissez faire.*" Anticipating the *political* theory enunciated many years later, he declared: "It is made for people of fundamentally differing views, and the accident of our finding certain opinions natural and familiar, or novel, and even shocking, ought not to conclude our judgment upon the question whether statutes embodying them conflict with the Constitution of the United States."[108] It may be, as Holmes said, that the "ultimate kingship"[109] belongs to the man who initiates fundamental ideas, but even these need to be tested by contact with others, especially by those inclined to disagree with them.

Like all ideas, political truth–justice–is unattainable. Consensus cannot be ranked as an ultimate. Truth and justice are goals to be striven for with the tacit understanding that they may not be reached.[110] "Sometimes new truth," Niebuhr remarked, "rides into history upon the back of an error."[111]

Essential to the successful operation of free government are mutual respect, accommodation, tolerance. The "healing balm of our Constitution," Jefferson warned, is that "each party should shrink from all approach to the line of demarcation, instead of rashly over-leaping it, or throwing grapples ahead to haul to hereafter."[112] With rare exceptions, Jefferson's recipe for avoiding an impasse between nation and state, among the various organs of our tripartite system, and between government at all levels and individual rights, has been followed. Confrontations, as in the Civil War and 1974, are the exception rather than the rule.[113]

Constitutions, structural checks, bills of rights–none of these safeguards nor all combined will render free government secure. In the Virginia Ratifying Convention of 1788, Madison warned: "To suppose that any form of government will secure liberty or happiness without virtue in the people is a chimerical idea."[114] In various ways and on many occasions, Jefferson pointed to its ultimate reliance–character and spirit of the people.

2 *HERBERT J. STORING*

THE CONSTITUTION AND THE BILL OF RIGHTS

The foundation of the American constitutional system was not completed, it is widely agreed, until the adoption of the first ten amendments in 1791. The absence of a bill of rights from the original Constitution had of course been a major item in the Antifederalist position. "No sooner had the Continental Congress laid the proposed Constitution before the people for ratification," Irving Brant writes, "than a great cry went up: it contained no Bill of Rights."[1] According to Robert Rutland, whose book *The Birth of the Bill of Rights, 1776-1791* is the major history of these events, "The Federalists, failing to realize the importance of a bill of rights, miscalculated public opinion and found themselves on the defensive almost from the outset of the ratification struggle."[2] Another scholar, Bernard Schwartz, says: "Here, the Antifederalists had the stronger case and their opponents were on the defensive from the beginning. It was, indeed, not until the Federalists yielded in their rigid opposition on Bill of Rights Amendments that ratification of the Constitution was assured. On the Bill of Rights issue, it is the Antifederalist writings which are the more interesting and even the more influential."[3]

So, as the story is generally told, the Federalists gave us the Constitution, but the Antifederalists gave us the Bill of Rights. Moreover, it seems quite plausible today, when so much of constitutional law is connected with the Bill of Rights, to conclude that the Antifederalists, the apparent losers in the debate over the Constitution, were ultimately the winners. Their contribution to the scheme of American constitutional liberty seems to be a more fundamental one. Rutland puts this point well: "The facts show that the Federal Bill of Rights and the antecedent state declarations of rights represented, more than anything else, the sum total of American experience and experimentation with civil liberty up to their adoption."[4]

We all have a tendency to look at the past through the glass of our present concerns and presuppositions. That is altogether understandable; it can be given a plausible justification; it is sometimes said to be the only thing we can do. The result, however, is that we tend to speak to the past rather than to let the past try to speak to us. I want to try to reconstruct some of the debate over the Bill of Rights in a way that will enable it to speak to us. I think the result will be to show that the common view that the heart of American liberty is to be found in the Bill of Rights is wrong. That view rests, I think, on a misreading of the events of the American founding and reflects and fosters a misunderstanding of the true basis of American constitutional liberty.

To begin, we need to remind ourselves of some of the central facts about the way the Constitution was ratified. On 17 September 1787 the convention sitting in Philadelphia finished its business and sent its proposed constitution to Congress for transmittal to the states, there to be considered in conventions specially elected for that purpose. The Federalists in several states moved quickly to secure ratification. The Pennsylvania legislature began discussing the calling of a convention, even before the the Constitution had been acted upon by Congress, and provided for a convention to meet on 21 November. Delaware was, however, the first to ratify, on 7 December, followed by Pennsylvania on 12 December. The Pennsylvania ratification was accompanied by charges of steamrolling and unfair tactics; the opposition remained unreconciled and demanded a second national convention. There followed ratification in rapid succession by New Jersey, Georgia, and Connecticut. By the middle of January 1788, however, no major state had ratified except Pennsylvania, where the opposition was still strong.

The Massachusetts convention met on 14 January, and the evidence suggests that there was probably a majority against the Constitution or at least that the Antifederalists were very strong. The Massachusetts convention saw intensive debate, accompanied by equally intensive parliamentary and political maneuvering. Finally, for reasons that will always be debated, John Hancock, the hitherto absent president of the convention, made an appearance and proposed that along with ratification the convention recommend a series of amendments to "remove the fears and quiet the apprehensions of many of the good people of the commonwealth, and more effectually guard against an undue administration of the federal government. . . ."[5] This proposal, supported by Samuel Adams, secured ratification in Massachusetts on 6 February by the still close vote of 187 to 168. Indeed, it is scarcely too much to say that this formula secured the ratification of the Constitution; for some version of it was used in every state that ratified after Massachusetts, with the exception of Maryland but including the crucial and doubtful states of Virginia and New York. The Constitution was ratified, then, on the understanding that an early item on the national agenda would be the consideration of widely desired amendments.

The story is completed in the First Congress. When the new government began functioning in 1789, James Madison introduced in the House of Representatives a series of amendments which, after consideration there and in the Senate, were framed as twelve proposed amendments and sent to the states for ratification. Two of these amendments (of minor importance) were not ratified by the states.[6] The others were ratified in 1791 and became the first ten amendments to the Constitution–our Bill of Rights.

The reader of the debates of the First Congress can hardly avoid being struck by the persistence with which Madison pressed his proposals and the coolness with which they were initially received. The House of Representatives was hard at work getting the government organized and underway. It was engaged in establishing the executive departments and providing for a national revenue system; the Senate was working on a bill to establish the federal judiciary (where several of the main questions raised in proposals for amendment would have to be faced). It seemed sensible to most of Madison's colleagues to concentrate on getting the government well launched, to acquire some experience in it, and to avoid a premature reopening of the divisive debate over ratification. It is true that Madison had explicitly committed himself to the position that the First Congress should propose amendments to be submitted to the states; "amendments, if pursued with a proper moderation and in a proper mode, will be not only safe, but may serve the double purpose of satisfying the minds of well meaning opponents, and of providing additional guards in favour of liberty."[7] Nevertheless, Madison could have explained, altogether plausibly, to his Virginia constituents that he had introduced amendments as promised, but that they had been postponed until the House could finish the obviously more pressing business of launching the new government. Yet in the face of resistance from political friends as well as foes, Madison pressed forward. Why?

Madison's insistent sponsorship of amendments has to be seen, I think, as the final step in the strikingly successful Federalist strategy to secure an effective national government. I do not claim that this strategy was conceived at the beginning of the ratification debate–it developed as events emerged–or that all Federalists were parties to it; if they had been, Madison would not have had the opposition he did at the outset of the debate on amendments. But I think it is fairly clear that Madison knew what he was doing: he meant to complete the Federalist ratification victory, and in fact he did so.

Madison's proposals were designed primarily to prevent two things from happening. The first aim was to thwart the move for a general convention to consider amendments under the authority of Article V of the Constitution. A second convention was a favorite plan of the Antifederalists; the Federalists feared that such a convention might be—was indeed, intended to be—a time bomb that would destroy the essentials of the Constitution. The second and related aim was to snuff out the attempt to revise the basic structure and powers of the new federal government, which was the main thrust of Antifederal opposition. All the state ratifying conventions that proposed amendments included suggestions to strengthen the states and limit the powers of Congress relating to such crucial matters as federal elections, taxes, military affairs, and commercial regulation. Madison made clear that he had no intention of proposing, or accepting, any amendments along these lines. "I should be unwilling to see a door opened for a reconsideration of the whole structure of Government—for a reconsideration of the principles and the substance of the powers given; because I doubt, if such a door were opened, we should be very likely to stop at that point which would be safe to the Government itself."[8] Madison's strategy was to seize the initiative for amendments, to use the Federalist majority in the First Congress to finish the unavoidable business of amendments in such a way as to remove from the national agenda the major Antifederalist objections—and incidentally to secure some limited but significant improvements in the Constitution, especially in securing individual rights.

Thus, on 6 June Madison offered his proposals, mustering all his remarkable influence to urge on the friends of the Constitution the prudence of showing their good faith and tranquilizing the public mind by putting forward amendments "of such a nature as will not injure the Constitution" and yet could "give satisfaction to the doubting part of our fellow-citizens." He urged also that "it is possible the abuse of the powers of the General Government may be guarded against in a more secure manner than is now done, while no one advantage arising from the exercise of that power shall be damaged or endangered by it." "We have," he said, "in this way something to gain, and, if we proceed with caution, nothing to lose."[9]

Secure in the knowledge of a large majority back of him (once he could get it to move), Madison proposed amendments designed to correct minor imperfections in the structure of government, which I pass over here,[10] to secure traditional individual rights, and to reserve to the states powers not granted to the federal government. These proposals were recast by the House, but little of substance was added or taken away. A comparison of Madison's original proposals and the first ten amendments of the Constitution shows both the value of a serious and thoughtful deliberative process in improving the original language and the dominance of Madison's impulse.

The crucial fact is that none of the amendments regarded by the opponents to the Constitution as fundamental was included.

Indeed, in one of his proposals Madison tried to turn the table on the Antifederalists by using the Bill of Rights momentum to make what he regarded as a substantial improvement in the constitutional design. He proposed that "no state shall violate the equal right of conscience, or the freedom of the press or the trial by jury in criminal cases." Admitting that many state constitutions already had such provisions, Madison saw no reason against double security. And he shrewdly observed that

> nothing can give a more sincere proof of the attachment of those who opposed this Constitution to these great and important rights, than to see them join in obtaining the security I have now proposed; because it must be admitted, on all hands, that the State Governments are as liable to attack these individual privileges as the General Government is, and therefore ought to be as cautiously guarded against.[11]

This amendment, which Madison thought "the most valuable amendment in the whole list,"[12] was eventually rejected by the Senate, as perhaps he expected it would be. It reflected, nonetheless, Madison's long-standing view that the chief danger to American liberty lay in the incapacity, instability, and injustice of state governments.

Madison's proposals were first referred to the committee of the whole house; later, after a good deal of controversy about how to proceed, they were referred to a select committee of eleven, on which Madison sat. To this select committee were also referred, pro forma, all the amendments proposed by the state ratifying conventions. But the committee reported out Madison's amendments only. The majority had now committed itself to action, and Madison's proposals were briskly moved through the House, over some objections of unseemly haste, echoing similar briskness and similar complaints in the early stages of the ratification of the Constitution itself. Attempts by Antifederalists such as Aedanus Burke and Elbridge Gerry to secure consideration of the more fundamental amendments proposed by the state ratifying conventions were courteously but firmly and quickly turned aside.

The objective of amendments, Madison had said, was to "give satisfaction to the doubting part of our fellow-citizens." But they did not give satisfaction. Burke spoke for most of his fellow Antifederalists when he contended that Madison's amendments were "very far from giving satisfaction to our constituents; they are not those solid and substantial amendments which the people expect. They are little better than whip-syllabub, frothy and full of wind, formed only to please the palate; or they are like a tub thrown out to a whale to secure the freight of the ship and its peaceable voyage." Samuel Livermore thought Madison's amendments were "no more than a pinch of snuff; they went to secure rights never in danger."[13] And when later the amendments went to the states the main opposition to their ratification came not from the friends but from the former enemies of the Constitution, whose opinion the amendments were supposed to placate. Their view, generally speaking, was that expressed by Samuel Chase to John Lamb of New York. "A declaration of rights alone will be of no essential service. Some of the powers must be abridged, or public liberty will be endangered and, in time, destroyed."[14] Of course, Madison knew that his amendments would not satisfy the hard-core Antifederalists. His strategy was rather to isolate them from the large group of common people whose opposition did rest, not on fundamental hostility to the basic design of the Constitution but on a broad fear that individual liberties were not sufficiently protected. By conciliatory amendments, he told Jefferson, he hoped "to extinguish opposition to the system, or at least break the force of it, by detaching the deluded opponents from the designing leaders."[15] However little the Antifederalist leaders ultimately relied on the absence of a bill of rights, too many reams of paper and hours of speaking had been devoted to it to make it now very plausible for them to dismiss a Federalist-sponsored bill of rights as mere froth. Bristling (pleasurably, one supposes) at accusations from the Antifederalists of lack of candor, Madison could ask "whether the amendments now proposed are not those most strenuously required by the opponents of the Constitution?" Have not the people been "taught to believe" that the Constitution endangered their liberties and should not be adopted without a bill or rights?[16] And by whom had they been taught? That liberty had never been in serious danger under the Constitution is what the Federalists had claimed; but under Madison's prodding they were now moderately yielding to their opponents' sensibilities. Those opponents could not expect to make much headway by admitting that the Federalists had been right on the bill of rights issue all along. "It is a fortunate thing," Madison solemnly declared in the house, "that the objection to the Government has been made on the ground I stated; because it will be practicable, on that ground, to obviate the objection, so far as to satisfy the public mind that their liberties will be perpetual, and this without endangering any part of the Constitution, which is considered as essential to the existence of the Government by those who promoted its adoption."[17] The Antifederalist leaders objected to what Madison had *not* included in his amendment, but they had been neatly boxed in.

In September 1789 Edmund Pendleton wrote to Madison:

> . . . I congratulate you upon having got through the Amendments to

the Constitution, as I was very anxious that it should be done before your adjournment, since it will have a good effect in quieting the minds of many well meaning Citizens, tho' I am of opinion that nothing was further from the wish of some, who covered their Opposition to the Government under the masque of uncommon zeal for amendments and to whom a rejection or a delay as a new ground of clamour would have been more agreeable. I own also that I feel some degree of pleasure, in discovering obviously from the whole progress, that the public are indebted for the measure to the friends of Government, whose Elections were opposed under pretense of their being averse to amendments.[18]

My argument thus far is that the primary significance of the Bill of Rights is seen most clearly in what it does not include. Madison's successful strategy was to finish the debate over ratification by pushing forward a set of amendments that almost everyone could accept and that excluded all the Antifederalists' fundamental proposals. There is also a more positive and substantial significance. To consider this we need to understand first why there was no bill of rights in or attached to the Constitution as originally drafted. The most obvious answer is that it was only after the convention in Philadelphia had spent three months constructing a government that it occurred to anyone to attach a bill of rights to it. By the time Mason and Gerry did propose a bill of rights on 12 September, it was clear to almost everyone that the convention needed to finish its business and put its proposal to the country. It seemed likely, moreover, despite Mason's contention to the contrary, that the drafting of a bill of rights would turn out to be a long and difficult business.

But why was a bill of rights not considered earlier? And why, even admitting that it might be difficult to draw up, could it be dispensed with? There is a bewildering diversity of arguments made by defenders of the Constitution to explain why a bill of rights was undesirable or unnecessary. These are not always consistent or very plausible; but at bottom there are a couple of powerful and, I think, deeply compelling arguments.[19] The most widely discussed argument against a federal bill of rights was made by James Wilson in his influential "State House" speech on 6 October 1787. Wilson pointed to the fact that the general government would possess only specifically enumerated powers, unlike the state governments, which possessed broad, general grants of authority. Thus, in the case of the states, "everything which is not reserved is given," but in the case of the general government "everything which is not given is reserved." Once this distinction is understood, the pointlessness of a federal bill of rights emerges:

for it would have been superfluous and absurd to have stipulated with a federal body of our own creation, that we should enjoy those privileges of which we are not divested, either by the intention or the act that has brought the body into existence. For instance, the liberty of the press, which has been a copious source of declamation and opposition—what control can proceed from the Federal government to shackle or destroy that sacred palladium of national freedom?[20]

Wilson articulated here a fundamental principle of the American Constitution, that the general government possesses only enumerated powers. It is, however, open to the objection that enumerated powers must imply other powers (an implication strengthened by the necessary and proper clause) and that a train of implied powers may lead to encroachments on state prerogatives. Madison made a kind of concession to this argument by proposing in one of his amendments that "the powers not delegated by this Constitution, nor prohibited by it to the States, are reserved to the States respectively." Attempts to insert "expressly" before "delegated," thus restoring the language of the Articles of Confederation and more tightly restraining federal authority, failed (though the ubiquitous "expressly" proved extremely difficult to eliminate from American political debate). Indeed, the House accepted Charles Carroll's motion to add "or to the people," which was presumably meant to narrow the states' claim to reserved powers.[21] Thus emerged what is now the Tenth Amendment. But this amendment was quite rightly seen by the Antifederalists as no substantial concession at all. It merely stated the obvious in a coldly neutral way: that what was not granted was reserved.

Losing the battle of "expressly delegated" was merely the sign of the Antifederalists' loss of the battle over the basic character of the Constitution. They threw up, however, a second, less than best, defense against the possibility of unjust enlargement of federal powers, and that was the campaign to give specific protection to especially important or exposed individual rights. This was part of the serious argument for a bill of rights; and Madison's response here was more substantial, as we have seen. The result is the prudent and successful scheme of limited government that we now enjoy in the United States, with both its Constitution and its Bill of Rights. Security is provided at both ends: limited grants of power; protection of individual rights. This scheme is well known enough to require from me little in the way of either explanation or praise. Perhaps a view from the founding might caution us, however, not to exaggerate its benefits. Justice Black to the contrary notwithstanding, it is impossible in any interesting case to define the rights protected in the amendments with sufficient exactness to permit their automatic application. A bill of rights cannot eliminate the need for political judgment, and therewith the risk of abuse. James Iredell, in his reply to George Mason's "Objections" to the Constitution, displayed the ambiguity, for example, of "cruel and unusual punishments" and at the same time the impossibility of exhaustive particularization.[22] Alexander Hamilton defied anyone to give a definition to "liberty of the press" "which should not leave the utmost latitude for evasion." "I hold it to be impracticable; and from this, I infer that its security, whatever fine declarations may be inserted in any constitution respecting it, must altogether depend on public opinion, and on the general spirit of the people and of the government. And here, after all . . . must we seek for the only solid basis of all our rights."[23]

It is interesting to consider what our constitutional law would be like today if there had been no Bill of Rights. Its focus would presumably be to a far greater extent than it is today on the powers of the government. We might expect a more searching examination by the Supreme Court of whether federal legislation that seems to conflict with cherished individual liberties is indeed "necessary and proper" to the exercise of granted powers. We might expect a fuller articulation than we usually receive of whether, in Marshall's term, "the end" aimed at by given legislation "is legitimate." Might this not foster a healthy concern with the problems of *governing*, a healthy sense of responsible self-government?

Doubtless a jurisprudence without a Bill of Rights would also have to find ways of scrutinizing the impact of legislation on the individual. How could that be done? Could the individual "take advantage of a natural right founded in reason," one Antifederalist asked; "could he plead it and produce Locke, Sydney, or Montesquieu as authority?"[24] Perhaps he could. One Federalist said that while there was no way to predict in advance what laws may be "necessary and proper," "this we may say—that, in exercising those powers, the Congress cannot legally violate the natural rights of an individual."[25] Another insisted that "no power was given to Congress to infringe on any one of the natural rights of the people by this Constitution; and, should they attempt it without constitutional authority, the act would be a nullity, and could not be enforced."[26] Such views have found expression in the Supreme Court by men who would rest their findings of governmental usurpation squarely on the inherent purposes and limitations of all legitimate, free government. "I do not hesitate to declare," Justice Johnson said in *Fletcher v. Peck,* "that a state does not possess the power of revoking its own grants. But I do it on a general principle, on the reason and nature of things: a principle which will impose laws even on the Deity."[27] And Justice Chase, in *Calder v. Bull*, insisted that

> there are certain vital principles in our free Republican governments, which will determine and overrule an apparent and flagrant abuse of legislative power; as to authorize manifest injustice by positive law; or to take away that security for personal liberty, or private property, for the protection whereof the government was established. An act of the Legislature (for I cannot call it law) contrary to the great first principles of the social compact, cannot be considered a rightful exercise of legislative authority.[28]

Of course, government *does* "violate" the natural rights of the indi vidual, at least in the sense that it legitimately prevents him from enjoying the fullness of his rights. The question that always has to be asked is whether individual rights have been unnecessarily or unreasonably abridged. Such questions are not easy to answer, with or without a bill of rights. Any formulation of the standard of natural rights is problematical and obscure. But is it much more cloudy or contingent than "cruel and unusual punishment," "excessive bail," or "freedom of the press?" Would the nationalization of civil rights which Professor Fellman has discussed in this series have been less well guided by something like Cardozo's standard of "implicit in the concept of ordered liberty"[29] than it has been by the tortuous reasoning induced by preoccupation with the issue of "incorporation?" Without a bill of rights our courts would probably have developed a kind of common law of individual rights to help to test and limit governmental power. Might the courts thus have been compelled to confront the basic questions that "substantive due process," "substantive equal protection," "clear and present danger," etc., have permitted them to conceal, even from themselves? Is it possible that without a bill of rights we might suffer less of that ignoble battering between absolutistic positivism and flaccid historicism that characterizes our constitutional law today?

I stray from my principal concern, though not, I think, from the spirit of the argument I am examining. The basis of the Federalist argument was that the whole notion of a bill of rights as generally understood is alien to American government. It was derived from Britain where there was no written constitution and where individual liberties were secured by marking out limits on royal prerogative. Here the Constitution itself is a bill of rights, the Federalists often argued, meaning that it was derived from the people themselves, that it provided for a sound system of representation, and that it granted limited powers to a balanced government. Quoting from the opening of the preamble, *Publius* said, "Here is a better recognition of popular rights than volumes of aphorisms which make the principal figure in several of our State bills of rights and which would sound much better in a treatise of ethics than in a constitution of government."[30] This argument shows the redundancy of any declaration of the right of people to establish their own government, but it does not reach the chief problem of popular government, which is majority tyranny. Protecting individuals and minorities against unjust action by the majority, or the government reflecting the wishes of the majority, is a major benefit of a bill of rights in the Antifederalist view. Like most Federalists, Madison never denied this, but he did not think it very reliable. The solution has to be found at a deeper level, in the functioning of a large, differentiated commercial society. And so far as the possible dangers from government are concerned, protection must be found in the very constitution of that government. Thus, Thomas McKean told his Pennsylvania colleagues that although a bill of rights "can do no harm, I believe, yet it is an unnecessary instrument, for in fact the whole plan of government is nothing more than a bill of rights—a declaration of the people in what manner they choose to be governed."[31] In the words of another Federalist:

> Where the powers to be exercised, under a certain system, are in themselves consistent with the people's liberties, are legally defined, guarded and ascertained, and ample provision made for bringing condign punishment to all such as shall overstep the limitations of the law—it is hard to conceive of a greater security for the rights of the people.[32]

But admitting that a bill of rights was not necessary, what harm could it do? "A bill of rights may be summed up in a few words," Patrick Henry told his fellow Virginians. "What do they tell us?—That our rights are reserved. Why not say so? Is it because it will consume too much paper?"[33] By 1789 Madison conceded this; he told Congress that we have nothing to lose and something to gain by amendments to secure individual rights. Why not concede the point earlier? Madison admitted that "some policy had been made use of, perhaps, by gentlemen on both sides of the question."[34] On the Federalist side, an unyielding resistance to a bill of rights is to be explained by a fear that it would divert the campaign for ratification of the Constitution into what surely would have been a long and circuitous route to amendments, a route along which the essentials of the Constitution would have been extremely difficult to protect. As long as the Constitution remained unratified, Madison wrote to George Eve in 1783, "I opposed all previous alterations as calculated to throw the States into dangerous contentions, and to furnish the secret enemies of the Union with an opportunity of promoting its dissolution."[35]

There was also, I think, a deeper and more positive reason for what appears to many scholars a rigid and defensive opposition to a bill of rights. The Federalists were determined that Americans not be diverted, in a more fundamental sense, from the main task of providing themselves with effective government. Jefferson, writing from France, admitted to Madison that bills of rights have an occasional tendency to cramp government in its useful exertions; but he thought that such inconvenience was short-lived, moderate, and reparable.[36] The friends of the Constitution, on the other hand, feared that an undue concern with rights might be fatal to American liberty. "Liberty may be endangered by the abuses of liberty," *Publius* warned, "as well as by the abuses of power, and the former rather than the latter is apparently most to be apprehended by the United States."[37] James Iredell saw in the old state bills of rights evidence that "the minds of men then [were] so warmed with their exertions in the cause of liberty as to lean too much perhaps toward a jealousy of power to repose a proper confidence in their own government."[38] The Federalists feared that

Americans were all too wont to fall into easy and excessive criticism of all proposals for effective government. They saw in the arguments against the Constitution a tendency to drift into the shallow view that Americans could somehow get along without government—without the tough decisions, the compulsion, the risk that government must always involve. The main political business of the American people, they thought, was and would continue to be not to protect themselves against political power but to accept the responsibility of governing themselves. The Federalists did not deny that government, once established, may need protecting against, but they tried to make sure that that would always be seen for the secondary consideration it is. The lesson that the furor over a bill of rights threatened to obscure was, in Edmund Pendleton's words, that "there is no quarrel between government and liberty. The war is between government and licentiousness, faction, turbulence, and other violations of the rules of society, to preserve liberty."[39]

It was altogether appropriate, from this Federalist point of view, that the Bill of Rights should have emerged from a separate set of deliberations, occurring after the Constitution had been framed and accepted and its government set in motion. Even at this point, however, the Federalist concession was less than might at first appear. We have seen that by taking the initiative for amendments Madison confined discussion to a bill of rights (plus a few, noncontroversial changes) and excluded that whole set of major Antifederalist proposals that would limit the powers of the general government or otherwise change the basic design of the Constitution. We must now see that Madison also took a narrow view of the meaning of a bill of rights as such, with the aim of preserving not only the constitutional scheme but also the vigor and capacity of government.

In their extraordinary exchange of views between 1787 and 1789, Thomas Jefferson pressed on Madison his opinion in favor of a bill of rights.[40] But the significant fact is not that Madison came to favor a bill of rights—he said truthfully that he had always favored it under the right circumstances. What is significant is the time he chose to move for a bill of rights, the kinds of rights protected, and the form the Bill of Rights took.

> I will own that I never considered this provision [of a bill of rights] so essential to the Federal Constitution as to make it improper to ratify it, until such an amendment was added; at the same time, I always conceived, that in a certain form, and to a certain extent, such a provision was neither improper nor altogether useless.[41]

Jefferson repeatedly described the kinds of protection he wanted in terms like the following: "a bill of rights providing clearly and without the aid of sophisms for freedom of religion, freedom of press, protection against standing armies, restriction against monopolies, the eternal and unremitting force of the habeas corpus laws, and trials by jury in all matters of fact triable by the law of the land and not by the law of Nations."[42] Three of these amounted to substantial restrictions on the power of government to act—the restrictions on monopolies, standing armies, and the suspension of habeas corpus; Jefferson clearly thought that they were vital barriers against governmental tyranny. It is equally clear that Madison consistently opposed all such amendments as obstacles to effective government. He did not include them in his original proposals (though there had been such proposals from the state ratifying conventions), and he and the Federalist majority beat down all attempts to secure such amendments.

There is moreover a deeper stratum in Madison's concern to prevent bills of rights from inhibiting government. The Antifederalists' advocacy of a bill of rights was concerned with more than specific protections; their overriding concern here was to make sure that government was rooted firmly in natural rights and justice. One of the confusions to the modern ear in the debate over the Bill of Rights and in the language of the old state bills of rights is the jumbling together of natural rights, civil rights, basic principles of justice, maxims of government, and specific legal protections. The state bills of rights were full of "oughts" and general principles. The Virginia Declaration of Rights of 1776 provides, for example: "That all men are by nature equally free and independent, and have certain inherent rights, of which, when they enter into a state of society, they cannot, by any compact deprive or divest their posterity; namely, the enjoyment of life and liberty, with the means of acquiring and possessing property, and pursuing and obtaining happiness and safety." Again, "Government is, or ought to be, instituted for the common benefit, protection, and security of the people, nation or community." The legislative and executive powers "should be separate and distinct from the judiciary"; "elections . . . ought to be free"; jury trial in civil cases "is preferable to any other, and ought to be held sacred."

Bills of rights were often described by their advocates as having as their purpose "to secure to every member of society those unalienable rights which ought not to be given up to any government."[43] Yet bills of rights, as we know them today, do not protect natural rights. And there seems to be something empty in the declarations of natural rights in a Constitution. That was the Federalist view. Thus, the acerbic Dr. Rush praised the framers for not disgracing the Constitution with a bill of rights: "As we enjoy all our natural rights from a pre-occupancy, antecedent to the social state," it would be "absurd to frame a formal declaration that our natural rights are acquired from ourselves."[44] The Antifederalists insisted, on the contrary, that the main purpose of a bill of rights is to provide an explicit set of standards in terms of which a government can be judged and, when necessary, resisted. A good bill of rights is a book in which a people can read the fundamental principles of their political being. "Those rights characterize the man, essentially the true republican, the citizen of this continent; their enumeration, in head of the new constitution, can inspire and conserve the affection for the native country, they will be the first lesson of the young citizens becoming men, to sustain the dignity of their being. . . ."[45] This is what explains the affirmation of natural rights, the "oughts," the unenforceable generality of the state bills of rights and of many of the Antifederalists' proposals. In Patrick Henry's words:

> There are certain maxims by which every wise and enlightened people will regulate their conduct. There are certain political maxims which no free people ought ever to abandon—maxims of which the observance is essential to the security of happiness. . . .
>
> We have one, sir, *that all men are by nature free and independent, and have certain inherent rights, of which, when they enter into society, they cannot by any compact deprive or divest their posterity.* We have a set of maxims of the same spirit, which must be beloved by every friend to liberty, to virtue, to mankind: our bill of rights contains those admirable maxims.[46]

This was the reason that the state bills of rights preceded their constitutions and could be described as the foundation of government. Edmund Randolph put it as well as anyone in his comment on the Virginia bill of rights:

> In the formation of this bill of rights two objectives were contemplated: one, that the legislature should not in their acts violate any of those cannons [*sic*]; the other, that in all the revolutions of time, of human opinion, and of government, a perpetual standard should be erected around which the people might rally, and by a notorious record be forever admonished to be watchful, firm and virtuous.
>
> The corner stone being thus laid, a constitution, delegating portions of power to different organs under certain modifications, was of course to be raised upon it.[47]

The problem with a bill of rights as a "perpetual standard" or a set of maxims to which people might rally is that it may tend to undermine stable and effective government. The Virginia Declaration of Rights asserted that free government depends on "a frequent recurrence to fundamental principles." The Federalists doubted that. Recurrence to first principles does not substitute for well-constituted and effective government. In some cases, it may interfere. Does a constant emphasis on unalienable natural rights foster good citizenship or a sense of community? Does a constant emphasis on popular sovereignty foster responsible government? Does a constant emphasis on a right to abolish government foster the kind of popular support that any government needs? The Federalists did not doubt that these first principles are true, that they may be resorted to, that they provide the ultimate source and justification of government. The problem is that these principles, while true, can also endanger government. Even rational and well-constituted governments need and deserve a presumption of legitimacy and permanence.[48] A bill of rights that presses these first principles to the fore tends to deprive government of that presumption.

For this reason, I think, Madison drastically limited the kind of standard-setting, maxim-describing, teaching function of bills of rights that the Antifederalists thought so important. In the hands of Madison and the majority of the First Congress, the Bill of Rights became what it is today: not the broad principles establishing the ends and limits of government, not "maxims" to be learned and looked up to by generations of Americans, not statements of those first principles to which a healthy people should, according to the Virginia Declaration of Rights, frequently resort; but specific protections of traditional civil rights.

With two exceptions, all the "oughts," all the statements of general principle, were excluded from Madison's original proposals–and these two were themselves eliminated before the House of Representatives finished its work. One of Madison's amendments would have declared that the powers delegated by the Constitution "are appropriated to the departments to which they are respectively distributed" so that no department shall exercise powers vested in another.[49] This was rather weakly defended by Madison in the House, where it was accepted; but it was rejected by the Senate, and no one seems to have regretted its loss. The second and most important residue of the old maxims was Madison's first proposal, which was a statement that all power derives from the people, that government ought to be instituted for the benefit of the people, and that the people have a right to change the government when they find it adverse or inadequate to its purposes.[50] This proposal was later reduced by a committee (on which Madison sat) to a brief and ill-fitting preface to the preamble ("Government being intended for the benefit of the people, and the rightful establishment thereof being derived from their authority alone, We the People of the United States . . . "). It was finally dropped altogether as a result of the acceptance of Sherman's proposal to have the amendments added at the end of the Constitution. It is hard to imagine that Madison was sorry to see these proposals rejected. Indeed, it is curious how poorly they fit into the Constitution. The separation of powers amendment was to be given a separate article of its own, a clear breach of the economy of the Constitution; yet there was no other place for it. Even more striking is the awkward placing of Madison's first proposal prior to the preamble and the intolerable grammatical cumbersomeness of the Committee of Eleven version. Both these drafting inelegancies derived from Madison's determination to fit all of the amendments into the existing text of the Constitution.

Virtually all the advocates of a bill of rights assumed that it should come at the head of the Constitution; Madison wanted it in the body; it came finally at the tail.[51] Madison's argument was that "there is a neatness and propriety in incorporating the amendments into the Constitution itself; in that case the system will remain uniform and entire. . . . " He wanted to avoid a form that would emphasize the *distinction,* common in the states, between the Constitution and the Bill of Rights. On the other hand, Roger Sherman, who was far from keen on having amendments at all, argued that to try to interweave the amendments with the Constitution was to mix brass, iron, and clay; "The Constitution is the act of the people and ought to remain entire." George Clymer supported Sherman; the amendments should be kept separate so that the Constitution "would remain a monument to justify those who made it; by a comparison the world would discover the perfection of the original and the superfluity of the amendments." Madison sought to secure his amendments against the possibility of their being held merely redundant and ineffective; he wanted them to "stand upon as good a foundation as the original work." When he said that a separate set of amendments would "create unfavourable comparisons," he was concerned to avoid a denigration of the amendments. But neither did he wish to elevate them to a distinct, primary position. His proposed form was designed to secure protection for the most widely agreed rights that would be both authoritative and inconspicuous. Sherman had his way, for reasons that do not fully emerge from the report of the debate. Ironically, the result seems to have been exactly the opposite of what Sherman intended, and yet to have gone beyond what Madison wanted. Separate listing of the first ten amendments has elevated rather than weakened their status. The over-all result is a Bill of Rights that is much less than the broad, preambular statement of basic principles that the enthusiastic proponents of bills of rights had in mind. At the same time it is—or has in this century become—rather more significant (not less, as Sherman and his friends wanted) than scattered protections of individual rights inserted into the Constitution would have been.

What can we say in conclusion in answer to our original questions? What is the significance of the absence of a bill of rights from the original Constitution and of its subsequent addition?

First, the basic justification for the absence of a bill of rights was that the main business of a free people is to establish and conduct good government; that is where the security of freedom must be sought. For the Americans in the 1870s, still warm with the ultimate truths of natural rights and revolution, the rhetoric of bills of rights might serve as a delusive substitute for the hard tasks of self-government.

Yet, second, bills of rights are an appropriate second step. Governments do tend to abuse their powers; and while the main protections are to be found in representation and social and political checks, a bill of rights can provide useful supplemental security.

Third, the initiative seized by Madison in the First Congress enabled the Federalists to complete their ratification victory by using amendments to better secure individual rights as the vehicle for decisively (if not finally) laying to rest the major Antifederal objections to the powers of the general government.

Fourth, the traditional notion of a bill of rights was drastically narrowed by largely eliminating the usual declarations of first principles, frequent resort to which Madison thought caused serious harm to government by disturbing that healthy crust of prejudice needed to support even the most rational government.

At the same time, however, and finally, the civil rights that were secured by the new Bill of Rights were limited and defined enough to be capable of effective (though not unproblematical) enforcement. The oft-described transformation of the moralistic "ought nots" of the old bills of rights into the legal "shall nots" of the United States Bill of Rights *is* a true and important part of the story. But I hope it is now clear that that transformation was possible only as a result of a drastic narrowing and lowering deliberately intended to secure the central place for the establishment and conduct of free government as the main business of a free people.

Yet there is still in our Bill of Rights an echo of the earlier declarations of natural rights and maxims of well-constituted free governments. This is especially true of the First Amendment, which might be described as a statement in matter-of-fact legal form of the great end of free government, to secure the private sphere, and the great means for preserving such a government, to foster an alert and enlightened citizenry. In the form of a protection of civil liberties, then, the First Amendment echoes the great principles of natural liberty and free government that played so large a role in the state bills of rights.[52] The preamble contains a similar echo of the basic principle of human equality and popular sovereignty. The Bill of Rights provides a fitting close to the parenthesis around the Constitution that the preamble opens. But the substance is a design of government with powers to act and a structure arranged to make it act wisely and responsibly. It is in that design, not in its preamble or its epilogue, that the security of American civil and political liberty lies.

3 *DAVID FELLMAN*

THE NATIONALIZATION OF AMERICAN CIVIL LIBERTIES

The most elemental and inescapable fact about the American Constitution is that it provides for a federal system of government. The basic pattern of the American system is federal in character not because the powers of government are divided between the central and the local governments—which we happen to miscall states—but because the division of authority is made in a particular way. After all, except for a few historical little oddities like Monaco and Andorra, modern nations are so large and populous that they cannot be governed from a central point. Thus, the world over, in almost all nations there are local as well as national governmental institutions. Some are unitary in style and others are federal, and the distinction between them is a product of constitutional law.

The fact that the English system is unitary does not mean that Great Britain is without local governmental institutions. The English counties, county boroughs, boroughs, urban and rural districts, are by no means museum pieces. On the contrary, they exercise considerable authority, levy and collect taxes, and perform significant functions. What puts the English constitution in the category of unitary systems is a purely legal fact, namely, that the institutions and powers of the local governments of the country are defined by the national government, that is to say, by Parliament. Accordingly, local institutions and powers are subject to alteration, enlargement, abridgement, or even abolition at the will of Parliament, acting without the concurrence of the local governments. In a purely legal sense, it may be said that local governmental institutions and powers are at the mercy of Parliament. I stress the "purely legal" character of this arrangement, because I would not want to leave the impression that local governments in Britain are in any danger of imminent extinction. The British people are strongly attached to their local institutions, and they also have the power to vote for members of Parliament, and I am confident that any M. P. who would openly espouse the total abolition of local government would become an ex-M. P. at the next election. He might also end up in a booby hatch.

In contrast with unitary systems, the American pattern of government is federal because the division of powers between the central government and the states is not formally defined by the central government, but is provided for in a Constitution which cannot be altered formally by the national government acting alone. The amending process involves action on the part of at least two-thirds of the members of Congress and three-fourths of the states. It follows that it is important to know how a constitution may be amended, since that tells us whether the system is federal or unitary. Since Parliament is sovereign, it may do anything that can be done through law. Thus, a Swiss writer, Jean Louis DeLolme, in a rather famous eighteenth-century book on the English constitution, wrote: "It is a fundamental principle with the English lawyers that Parliament can do everything except making a woman a man or a man a woman."[1] Of course, this observation was made before the art of surgery reached its present state of sophistication. Perhaps the elegant Blackstone phrased the idea of parliamentary supremacy more felicitously when he said of Parliament, in his *Commentaries*, that it "can, in short, do everything that is not naturally impossible. . . ."[2]

On the other hand, in our federal system the powers of the national government are specified or enumerated in the Constitution, and the Tenth Amendment declares that all powers not delegated to the central government are reserved to the states.[3] Thus, so far as the United States Constitution is concerned, the reserved powers of the states are not enumerated; the states look to that Constitution only to find out what they may not do, since the Constitution, from the very beginning, has imposed various limitations upon them. In our scheme of things, however, the states perform many important functions: they collect many taxes, such as property, sales, and income taxes, spend enormous sums of money, enact and enforce most criminal laws, create and regulate most corporations, regulate most public utilities, maintain most elements of the public educational system, and exercise most aspects of the police power in the interest of protecting public health, safety, convenience, and morality. Furthermore, as a distinguished scholar has written:

> The fields that consume most domestic expenditures—education, highways, welfare, health, natural resources, public safety—are funded with a combination of Federal grants or loans and state and local taxes or service charges, and they are staffed partly by the personnel of national, state, and local

government. This means that national and local authorities must take account of state preferences in virtually all major policy decisions.[4]

It is undeniable, of course, that over the years the powers of the national government have grown considerably by a process of broad construction of the provisions of the Constitution, though several formal amendments have also enlarged national power. A quick glance at the rate of growth of the federal budget furnishes eloquent testimony to the fact that the national government has been an expanding system. From the earliest days of the republic, the Supreme Court has been committed to the proposition that in addition to its specifically delegated powers, the federal government has all implied powers which are "necessary and proper"[5] to carry delegated powers into execution, and this leads it to read the power-granting provisions of the Constitution broadly and not with niggardly narrowness.[6] Furthermore, it should never be forgotten that since the Supreme Court is a wholly national institution, not responsible in any way to the states, it is understandable that over the years it has, on the whole, taken a national position in constitutional interpretation. *As a matter of law*, if Congress enacts a statute, and the president signs it, and in appropriate litigation the Supreme Court upholds it, there is nothing the states can do about it. Of course, the growth of national power is not always or necessarily at the expense of state power. The plain fact is that as we move into the third century of our existence as an independent nation, the powers and responsibilities of government have been increasing at all levels of authority, and roughly at about the same rate. We simply have more government of all kinds today as compared to the situation which existed when the Constitution went into effect in the spring of 1789.

The pattern of power distribution in our federal system is reflected in the history of American civil liberties. When the Philadelphia Convention of 1787 drafted the Constitution, the delegates neglected to include a bill of rights of the sort which had already become a well-known feature of most, though not all, state constitutions. Actually, the authors of the Constitution did not ignore the subject altogether, since they wrote into the original document provisions guaranteeing jury trial in criminal cases,[7] freedom from both federal and state ex post facto laws and bills of attainder,[8] freedom from state laws impairing the obligation of contract,[9] and the enjoyment of "the Privilege of the Writ of Habeas Corpus," except where the public safety requires its suspension "in Cases of Rebellion or Invasion."[10] But what were missing were clauses protecting such traditional rights as freedom of religion, liberty of speech and press, protection against unreasonable searches and seizures, compulsory self-incrimination, cruel and unusual punishments, and the like. The absence of such a bill of rights was a principal point of contention on the part of those who opposed ratification of the Constitution, and the Federalists, who championed ratification, recognized that they had made a serious strategical political error, an error which they promised to rectify as soon as possible. Accordingly, the first session of the very first Congress drafted and sent to the states, on 25 September 1789, a Bill of Rights taking the form of a series of amendments, ten of which were promptly ratified by the requisite number of states by 15 December 1791.

In the celebrated case of *Barron v. Baltimore*,[11] decided by the Supreme Court in 1833, Chief Justice John Marshall made it very clear that the restrictions of the federal Bill of Rights applied only to the national government, and not to the states. In refusing to hear an appeal from the Maryland courts in which the Fifth Amendment guarantee of just compensation for private property taken for public use was invoked, the Court noted that those who wrote and ratified the Bill of Rights intended to apply its restrictions only to the new, untested national government, to allay the fears of those who were worried about its dimensions. The chief justice also observed that wherever the Constitution imposes limitations on the states, it does so in express terms. Furthermore, Marshall pointed out that if the people desired additional safeguards against the state governments, they had available to them the easier method of merely amending their own state constitutions. What Marshall neglected to point out—and how he missed the point is still a great mystery to me—is that the First Amendment begins with the phrase "*Congress shall make no law* respecting an establishment of religion . . . ," etc., and surely this would be curious language indeed if the intention had been to apply the Bill of Rights to the states.

It followed that prior to the Civil War there was no way to appeal to the United States Supreme Court from the state courts on the basis of any of the guarantees of the federal Bill of Rights. On such serious matters as freedom of speech or press, or the rights of the accused, aggrieved parties could not get beyond state courts. For example, in 1845 the Supreme Court refused to take an appeal from a decision of the City Court of New Orleans which had sustained an ordinance which obviously raised serious questions concerning the violation of religious freedom.[12] Justice Catron simply pointed out that "the Constitution makes no provision for protecting the citizens of the respective States in their religious liberties; this is left to the State constitutions and laws; nor is there any inhibition imposed by the Constitution of the United States in this respect on the States."[13] Accordingly, during the first seventy-five years of our history under the Constitution, the scope and meaning of our civil liberties were, for the most part, determined by the states, with finality. Not only was there no appeal to the national judiciary from the state courts, but Congress rarely enacted legislation which involved basic liberties, with the notable exception of the short-lived Alien and Sedition Acts of 1798.

From the point of view of effective responsibility for defining and protecting our civil liberties, the legal picture changed drastically with the adoption in 1868 of the Fourteenth Amendment to the Constitution of the United States. Section 1 of this amendment provides that "no State shall make or enforce any law which shall abridge the privileges or immunities of citizens of the United States; nor shall any State deprive any person of life, liberty, or property, without due process of law; nor deny to any person within its jurisdiction the equal protection of the laws." In addition, the last section of the Fourteenth Amendment provides that "the Congress shall have power to enforce, by appropriate legislation, the provisions of this article." In addition, the Thirteenth Amendment, ratified in 1865, which abolished slavery, and the Fifteenth, adopted in 1870, which forbade denial of the right to vote on account of race, color, or previous condition of servitude, both authorized Congress to adopt appropriate legislation to enforce their provisions. On the basis of these fresh delegations of power, Congress adopted no fewer than seven major civil rights statutes between 1866 and 1875, adding up to a very considerable code of law designed to protect the basic rights of the newly freed black citizens of the country. Furthermore, since the Constitution is not merely a political document, but also a self-executing body of law—and the supreme law of the land—the Supreme Court may rule on constitutional questions arising under the Reconstruction amendments without the authority of statutes. That is to say, these amendments greatly expanded federal judicial power as well as legislative power.

Actually, the Reconstruction amendments got off to a very bad start in the decisions of the Supreme Court. In the very first case to reach it invoking section 1 of the Fourteenth Amendment, decided in 1873, the Court declined to hold that the right of a citizen to work at his trade was a federal right or privilege.[14] The Court declared that it was a state right or privilege, and hence not within the ambit of federal judicial power to protect. If such an ordinary, garden-variety right as the right to work for a living is to be regarded as a federal right, then, said Justice Miller, *all* man's rights are now federalized; that would constitute the Court "a perpetual censor upon all legislation of the states," and the effect of that would be "to fetter and degrade the state governments by subjecting them to the control of Congress, in the exercise of powers heretofore universally conceded to them of the most ordinary and fundamental character. . . ." This, he noted, would change radically "the whole theory of the relations of the state and Federal governments to each other and of both these governments to the people. . . ."[15]

That the Supreme Court was determined to limit the thrust of the Reconstruction amendments was underscored ten years later when, in a group of cases brought together as the *Civil Rights* cases,[16] it was decided that the legislative power of Congress to enforce section 1 of the Fourteenth Amendment was limited to actions by a state, and did not extend to ordinary relations between individuals. The Court fixed its attention upon the phrase "no State shall" in ruling unconstitutional a federal statute forbidding innkeepers, theater owners, and public conveyances to discriminate on grounds of race or color. Again, the Court argued that if Congress is free to legislate over "the whole domain of rights appertaining to life, liberty and property, defining them and providing for their vindication," then "that would be to establish a code of municipal law regulative of all private rights between man and man in society. It would be to make Congress take the place of the State Legislatures and to supersede them."[17]

The privileges and immunities clause of the Fourteenth Amendment has never recovered from the impact of the Court's decision in the *Slaughterhouse* case, and plays no role of any significance in contemporary constitutional law.[18] On the other hand, the history of due process and equal protection clauses has been quite different, though they acquired importance only in recent years.

A central question in American constitutional law during the past century has involved the meaning of due process of law. More specifically, does Fourteenth Amendment due process derive any of its content from the specific limitations on the central government which are spelled out in the federal Bill of Rights? The Supreme Court took a first hesitant step in the direction of incorporating provisions of the Bill of Rights into the due process clause of 1897, when it held that the Fifth Amendment requirement of just compensation for property taken for a public use applied to the states.[19] That is to say, if a state takes private property for a public use without giving just compensation, it has taken the property without due process of law. In this respect, very little happened until the Court decided the celebrated case of *Gitlow v. New York*[20] in 1925. Here the Court flatly asserted, without even arguing the point, that we may and do assume that freedom of speech and of the press–which are protected by the First Amendment from abridgement by Congress–are among the fundamental personal rights and "liberties" protected by the due process clause of the Fourteenth Amendment from impairment by the states."[21] Gitlow lost his appeal from a conviction in the New York courts for violating a state criminal anarchy law, but the long-run significance of the case lies in the fact that the Supreme Court was willing to take jurisdiction of the appeal. Since then, a state denial of liberty of speech and the press presents a federal question of constitutional law over which the Supreme Court will take jurisdiction.[22] In 1940 the Court read the liberty secured by the due process clause of the Fourteenth Amendment to include the First Amendment guarantee of religious freedom.[23] Today all parts of the First Amendment apply as federally enforceable limitations on the states.

The Supreme Court was, for many years, unwilling to review the decisions of state appellate courts in criminal cases. As recently as 1915 the Court declined to make an independent review of the facts where the appeal alleged mob domination of the trial, on the theory that if the state has an appeals court empowered to correct errors, a review by this court satisfies due process.[24] It was not until 1923, in the leading case of *Moore v. Dempsey,*[25] that the Supreme Court held that where a person convicted in a state court petitions for a writ of habeas corpus in a federal district court on the ground that the trial court had been dominated by overwhelming mob pressures, the district judge must make an independent evaluation of the facts, even though the state appellate court had reviewed the facts and upheld the verdict. This decision opened the door to a significant expansion of federal control over state criminal procedure through review by the Supreme Court on the basis of the due process clause. While some justices, such as the first Justice Harlan (1877-1911),[26] and later on Justices Black and Douglas,[27] as well as some scholars,[28] took the position that Fourteenth Amendment due process should be construed as nationalizing the whole Bill of Rights, a majority of the Court has to this day preferred to follow what may be described as a process of selective incorporation. Most of the provisions of the Bill of Rights have now been incorporated into the due process clause, but a few, which the Court does not regard as essential to justice, have not been applied to the states. For example, due process does not embrace the Fifth Amendment guarantee of indictment by grand jury,[29] or the Second Amendment right to bear arms, or the Third Amendment provision about quartering troops in private dwellings, or the Seventh Amendment guarantee of trial by jury in suits at common law which involve more than $20. Furthermore, there is as yet no square holding by the Supreme Court that the prohibition in the Eighth Amendment of excessive bail is federally enforceable as against the states.

In the field of criminal appeals the first significant breakthrough after *Moore v. Dempsey* came in 1932, in the celebrated case of *Powell v. Alabama,*[30] which first brought the Scottsboro case to the attention of the Supreme Court. Here the Court ruled for the first time that the Sixth Amendment guarantee of the right to the assistance of counsel in criminal prosecutions was binding upon the states as a requirement of due process, at least in capital cases. After considerable fumbling with a rule which would apply this guarantee to noncapital felony cases only where the absence resulted in injustice,[31] the Court finally adopted a per se rule in 1963, in the famous *Gideon* case,[32] in which the right to counsel in state courts was extended to all felony cases. Finally, in 1972 the Court applied the rule to all misdemeanor cases involving the possibility of any imprisonment at all.[33]

On the theory that they are fundamental requirements of just treatment and a fair trial, the Court has read into the due process clause of the Fourteenth Amendment most of the provisions of the federal Bill of Rights which are designed to protect the accused. Thus, the Fourteenth Amendment now applies to the states all the guarantees of the Sixth Amendment, which, in order of their appearance in that amendment, include the rights to a speedy trial,[34] to a public trial,[35] to an impartial jury,[36] to due notice of charges,[37] to confront (i.e., crossexamine) one's accusers,[38] to have compulsory process for obtaining witnesses in one's behalf,[39] and finally, the right to the assistance of counsel. The Fourth Amendment right of freedom from unreasonable searches and seizures, including the federal exclusionary rule,[40] which since 1914 has required federal judges to exclude illegally seized evidence from the trial, has been fully binding on the states since 1961.[41] The Fifth Amendment prohibition of double jeopardy was read into Fourteenth Amendment due process in 1969.[42] In addition, the Fifth Amendment rule against compulsory self-incrimination is now fully binding upon the states.[43] Indeed, to protect the privilege the Court went out of its way, in the *Miranda* case,[44] to spell out a fairly complete code of behavior which all police must observe in the course of interrogating persons who have been taken into custody. The Eighth Amendment prohibition of cruel and unusual punishments was incorporated into Fourteenth Amendment due process in 1962.[45] Some sort of climax was achieved by the Supreme Court when, in May 1968, it ruled that trial by jury was a due process right because a jury is "a protection against arbitrary rule."[46]

The expansion of the concept of due process, as creating federally enforceable limitations on the states, is not limited to incorporating selected portions of the Bill of Rights, since, as construed by the Court, it has an independent force outside the specific provisions of the Constitution. For example, in the famous *Mooney* case,[47] decided in 1935, the Court ruled that where the prosecution deliberately deceives the court and jury by presenting testimony known to be perjured, the state has denied due process. The Court said that this would be "as inconsistent with the rudimentary demands of justice as is the obtaining of a like result by intimidation."[48] Later on the Court extended the *Mooney* rule to include the suppression by the prosecution of evidence favorable to the accused.[49] Similarly, in 1960 the Court gave the due process concept added bite by setting aside a criminal conviction on the ground that there was no evidence in the record to justify the trial court's action.[50] In other words, the Court declared, in effect, that a state has committed a wholly arbitrary and unreasonable act in convicting a person without any evidence of guilt; this is a capricious act which cannot be squared with the due process commitment to justice. It is of interest to note that this rule was adopted just before the first peaceful "sit-in" cases began to reach the Court. In one appeal after another the Court set aside state convictions on the basis of the no-evidence rule.[51]

National control over criminal justice in the states has also been enlarged in recent years through a broadened interpretation of the federal habeas corpus act.[52] Federal habeas corpus is available to persons in state custody on two conditions: (1) the petitioner must show that he is in custody in violation of federal law; (2) he must first exhaust any remedies available to him in the state courts.[53] Subject to these two conditions, a person in state custody may pursue his claim to freedom in the federal courts. This remedy was greatly expanded in two important decisions rendered by unanimous votes in 1963 and 1968. In the first case the Court ruled that a state prisoner who has been placed on parole is "in custody" within the meaning of the federal habeas corpus statute, on the ground that the conditions of his parole imposed serious restraints upon his liberty.[54] In the second case the Court ruled that a federal habeas corpus court may entertain an application for the writ even though the petitioner's sentence had expired and he had been discharged from parole status.[55] The basis for this decision was the consideration that as a result of his conviction, the petitioner suffered from certain disabilities—e.g., as to eligibility for certain licenses, the right to be a trade union official, and the right to vote and hold office—as a result of the conviction he was attacking in his petition for habeas corpus. The Court thought that the persistence of these collateral disabilities gave the petitioner a substantial stake in the judgment of conviction which survived the satisfaction of the sentence. It was noted that the habeas corpus statute provides that "the court shall . . . dispose of the matter as law and justice require," and that Congress amended the statute in 1966 to authorize as relief "release from custody *or other remedy.*"[56] Thus, in the judgment of the Supreme Court, as Justice Black expressed the thought, the writ of habeas corpus does not supply "a static, narrow, formalistic remedy; its scope has grown to achieve its grand purpose—the protection of individuals against erosion of their right to be free from wrongful restraints upon their liberty."[57]

The exercise of federal judicial power over the states in the cause of protecting civil liberties has also taken the form, in recent years, of an unprecedentedly vigorous interpretation of the equal protection clause of the Fourteenth Amendment. Especially during the Warren years did the Supreme Court expand the concept of equal protection to spectacular proportions. In the field of public education, beginning with *Brown v. Board of Education*[58] in 1954, the Supreme Court initiated a veritable revolution in our social system by holding unconstitutional segregation in the public schools on grounds of race, as a denial of equal protection of the laws, although the Court recognized that the best that could be anticipated was progress towards the desired goal "with all deliberate speed."[59] By 1964 the Supreme Court announced that "the time for mere 'deliberate speed' has run out. . . . "[60] A second development in equal protection law occurred in 1962 in the landmark case of *Baker v. Carr,*[61] which inaugurated the one-man-one-vote revolution in our representative legislative bodies, including districting by the states with reference to the federal House of Representatives.[62] A third important new application of equal protection law was pronounced in 1956 in *Griffin v. Illinois,*[63] where the Court held for the first time that if a state denies a free transcript to an indigent who needs one to prosecute an appeal effectively, it denies this poor person his Fourteenth Amendment right to equal protection of the laws. This decision, as one might have anticipated, quickly led to others involving access of the poor to judicial remedies they could not afford to pay for.[64]

Speaking more generally, in roughly the past quarter of a century the Court has seriously modified the traditional canon of interpretation in deciding whether a statutory classification is valid, in terms of protection, bearing in mind that classification of some sort is inherent in most legislation. The conventional test has been that if the Court can think of any reasonable ground which would justify the challenged classification, it must be assumed that that was what the legislative body had in mind.[65] But the Warren Court departed from this deference to legislative discretion in cases involving what it regarded as fundamental constitutional rights, such as the right to vote,[66] or such "suspect" classifications as those based on race,[67] in respect to which it subjected the challenged statutes to very strict or rigid scrutiny. Unless it could be persuaded that such statutes were supported by a "compelling state interest," they were held violative of the equal protection principle.[68] According to this canon of constitutional interpretation, many statutes carry an unusually heavy burden of justification, and, of course, invite a more than customary exercise of judicial power in passing judgment on legislative choices.

Clearly, one of the most noteworthy aspects of our evolving federalism has been the steady growth of responsibilities assumed by the national government with respect to the definition and protection of civil liberties. The Supreme Court's ever-broadening construction of the due process and equal protection clauses in section 1 of the Fourteenth Amendment now provides remedies against the states which were completely unavailable a few years ago. Furthermore, while these two clauses are still limited to situations involving state action, the Court has broadened the concept of state action to the point that private parties fall within the concept if any sort of collaborative official action is also involved.[69] In addition, while the Court once construed the scope of the legislative power of Congress in enforcing the Thirteenth Amendment very narrowly,[70] in 1968 it opened the door to a vast expansion of federal legislative power by construing this amendment to extend beyond slavery, as such, to include what judges have called "the badges and incidents" of slavery, such as an ability to buy real estate on nondiscriminatory terms.[71] Similarly, while the Court in 1883 held a federal statute invalid which forbade discrimination by private owners of places or instruments of public accommodation, a 1964 statute to the same effect was promptly upheld by the Supreme Court as a valid exercise of the commerce power.[72] Indeed, one of the most remarkable legislative achievements of our times has been the great body of statutes which Congress has adopted since 1957, after a grim silence on the subject of civil rights for eighty-two years. Following the establishment of the United States Civil Rights Commission by the Civil Rights Act of 1957,[73] Congress adopted an impressive code of statute law dealing with such diverse matters as voting rights, invasion of federal rights by violence, discrimination in places of public accommodation, segregation in public facilities and public education, discrimination in federally assisted programs, equal employment opportunity, and fair housing, notably in the Civil Rights Acts of 1960,[74] 1964,[75] and 1968,[76] and the vitally important Voting Rights Act of 1965,[77] the life of which was recently extended. In addition, there has been in recent years a remarkable surge in the number of lawsuits filed in federal district courts under Sec. 1983 of Title 42 of the U. S. Code, which gives these courts the jurisdiction to provide civil remedies for denials of federal civil rights under color of state law.[78]

The increased availability in the federal courts of the writ of habeas corpus to persons convicted of state crimes has resulted in putting thousands of cases on their dockets. For example, in 1974, 7,626 petitions for habeas corpus were filed in the U.S. district courts by state prisoners, and the federal courts of appeals were called upon to review denials of the writ in 773 cases,[79] The burden on the federal district judge is not as staggering as these figures may suggest, since most of the work in connection with the handling of this flood of petitions is done by members of the judge's staff, especially the U.S. magistrate, the clerk of court, and the judge's law clerk, and most petitions are denied summarily, without evidentiary hearings. In fact, federal judges grant very few of these petitions. For example, 5,337 state prisoners applied for habeas corpus in the decade ending in 1955, and only 88, or 1.5 percent, were granted the writ, and not all of them were in fact released from confinement.[80] Most applications are completely unjustified or utterly frivolous, and federal judges actually devote little working time to them. In addition, they are understandably reluctant to overrule the state courts, especially in the states which have adequate postconviction remedies of their own.

In its famous and influential report *To Secure These Rights,* which President Truman's Committee on Civil Rights published in 1947, the major conclusion was that "the National Government of the United States must take the lead in safeguarding the civil rights of all Americans." It declared that "it is sound policy to use the idealism and prestige of our whole people to check the wayward tendencies of a part of them," and that "the American people have traditionally shown high national regard for civil rights, even though the record in many a community has been far from good."[81] In large measure the country has accepted this advice. On the basis of the due process and equal protection concepts, the U. S. Supreme Court defines the parameters of free speech, freedom of the press, freedom of religion, freedom of association, as well as many of the basic rights of persons accused of crime. For several millions of black Americans the right to vote is now under federal protection, a fact strikingly illustrated by the abatement of race baiting in those states where such tactics once paid handsome political dividends. We still look to the states to handle most litigation and to protect most of our rights, but when and if they falter there is now available a considerable array of corrective federal remedies. Supreme Court decisions are now followed in the states universally or instantaneously, and there has been no end of ill-tempered grumbling on the part of many state judges,[82] but in the long run the views of the Supreme Court, as the conscience of the nation as a whole, tend to prevail, though of course unevenly.

4 *HENRY J. ABRAHAM*

THE SUPREME COURT IN THE EVOLVING POLITICAL PROCESS

In order to comprehend the ebb and flow of the political struggle in the United States, it is necessary to keep in mind that the American democracy is based, at least institutionally, upon the concept of the *separation of powers,* duly modified by that of the attendant *checks and balances.* At times the former, and to a much lesser extent the latter, may be considerably more of a theoretical than a practical phenomenon; but the conjunction of the two represents an omnipresent, and not infrequently an omnipotent, aspect of the governmental process in the United States. It is one of the two or three cardinal characteristics of what to many an observer, domestic as well as foreign, have been the mysteries of American politics . . . mysteries which have prompted some to quote an Arthur Guiterman ditty:

> Providence, that watches over children, drunks and fools,
> With silent miracles and other esoterica,
> Continue to suspend the ordinary rules,
> And take care of the United States of America.

That, appealing and attractively facile as it is, is hardly a satisfactory explanation of the problem. The presence of the separation of powers, discounted by its checks and balances, however, is of its very essence. Indeed, the history of the United States has been characterized by a rather persistent and more or less continuous contest between the three "separated" branches, the executive, the legislature, and–to a somewhat smaller degree, the judiciary–to attain and maintain a position of independent power, if not of dominance, in the American political system. When the reference is to the judiciary, it is at once realistic and necessary to direct attention to the pinnacle of its power and authority, namely, the Supreme Court of the United States. But it is well to remember that that tribunal stands at the apex of a judicial structure in which the basic work is done below, indeed in fifty-one different judicial systems—which, however, do ultimately, and I say fortunately, converge on the highest court of all.

The chief weapon at the disposal of the Supreme Court in the separation-of-power-cum-checks-and-balances struggle or game has been its overriding power of *judicial review,* a power possessed by the judiciary of but a few other countries—normally those with a federal structure of democratic government, such as Australia, Canada, and India. It is a power utterly absent in such unitary democratic states as Britain—where the courts do, of course, have power to interpret and to adjudicate, but not to exercise a judicial *veto* over legislative or executive action. Briefly defined, judicial review signifies the power of any court of record, no matter how high or low, to hold unconstitutional, and hence unenforceable, any law, any official action based upon it, and any illegal action by a public official that it deems—upon careful, normally painstaking, reflection, and in line with the canons of the taught tradition of the law as well as judicial self-restraint—to be in conflict with the basic law, in the United States its written Constitution. In other words, in invoking the power of judicial review, a court applies the superior of two laws, which at the level of the federal judiciary of the United States signifies the Constitution instead of a legislative statute or some action by a public official allegedly or actually based upon either.

For reasons presently to be developed, the United States Supreme Court itself has rarely invoked this, its ultimate, power. It much prefers to resort to its penultimate power, that of statutory construction, which permits it to have its proverbial cake and yet eat it—a tactic not exactly viewed with particular favor by legislators! Of some 85,000 public and private laws passed to date by the United States Congress, the Supreme Court has struck down as unconstitutional only 122 provisions in 116 or 117 of these laws (depending upon one's count), often, yet certainly not always, the entire law. Some 1000 state and local laws and provisions of state constitutions, on the other hand, have run wholly or partly afoul of that judicial checkmate since 1789; but we are here primarily concerned with the problem on the national level. We should note that after the famous decision in *Marbury v. Madison*[1]—in which John Marshall, our fourth and generally regarded as our greatest and most influential chief justice, divined the doctrine of judicial review, no other federal legislation was declared unconstitutional by his Court, and only thirty-six state statutes during the remaining thirty-two of his long tenure of thirty-four and a half years (the third longest on the high bench, exceeded only by Mr. Justice

Douglas's incredible near thirty-seven and Mr. Justice Stephen J. Field's thirty-four and three quarter years).[2] And a mere year later Marshall made sure that judicial authority was equally applicable over the executive branch by ruling in the *Flying Fish* case[3] that President Adams had exceeded his authority in ordering the navy to seize vessels bound to or from a French port because Congress had authorized seizure of ships only going *to* French ports. Of course, regardless of its utilization of judicial review, the Marshall Court wielded immense power, coming on the heels of a very inauspicious beginning under three weak and/or disinterested leaders of a then lowly regarded and rather inactive Court, and, guided by the dominant figure of the assertive chief justice of the United States, did more than either of the two other branches to make the young United States a strong, vigorous, powerful nation, and its Constitution an effective, elastic basic law. Not until Mr. Chief Justice Taney's controversial decision in *Dred Scott v. Sandford*[4] in 1857, that was intended to stem the tide of the oncoming Civil War and had precisely the opposite effect, was another federal statute struck down by the Supreme Court. Of course, the greatest crisis evoked by the exercise of the Court's power did not arrive until, dominated by the four key doctrinaires among the so-called Nine Old Men of the Hughes Court—Associate Justices Sutherland, Van Devanter, Butler, and McReynolds—it declared unconstitutional no less than thirteen crucial New Deal laws between 1934 and 1936, many of them by five to four, laws heavily and overwhelmingly endorsed by both the executive and legislative branches. Since that time only forty provisions of Congressional statutes have fallen—all, in fact, since 1943. And we ought to observe at once that all those forty fell because they infringed personal rights and/or liberties safeguarded under the Constitution. Of them four involved procedures by the military authorities under sections of the post-World War II Uniform Code of Military Justice; five were sundry provisions of the immigration and nationality statutes; two, provisions of the Federal Firearms Act; one, a provision in the Pure Food and Drug Act of 1906, as amended; one, the Communist exclusion section of the Landrum-Griffin Act of 1959; one, a provision of the Gambling Tax Act of 1951; one, the entire Communist Propaganda Labeling Act of 1962; one, a provision of a federal statute regarding illegal still sites; two were sections of the Subversive Activities Control Act of 1950; one, a segment of the Lindbergh Kidnapping Act; one, a District of Columbia statutory provision that denied welfare assistance to residents of the District who had not lived within its jurisdiction at least one year immediately prior to an application for such assistance; two involved statutes concerning the possession and importation of marijuana; one was a provision of a federal statute that made it a crime for an actor in a theatrical production to wear a United States military uniform if the actor's portrayal was unfavorable to the service; one, the provision of the Voting Rights Act of 1970 extending the vote to eighteen-year-olds in state elections; two were mail block statutes; one, a provision of the Higher Education Facilities Act of 1963; one, the 1882 law banning all "unauthorized" demonstrations on the grounds of the United States Capitol; one, a section of the Social Security Act of 1935 that differentiated in the payment of benefits between illegitimate and legitimate children of the same wage earner; two were provisions of the Food Stamp Act of 1964, as amended, that were regarded as arbitrarily violating due process by their classification of "ineligibles"; two were provisions, in two separate statutes, that provided greater benefits for servicemen than for servicewomen; one, a provision of the Social Security Act of 1935 that barred benefits to illegitimate children of disabled workers just because they were born after the disability began; one was a provision of that statute which denied certain Social Security benefits to widowers with children in their care while granting them to widows; two provisions of the Federal Election Campaign Act of 1974; two provisions of the Fair Labor Standards Act of 1938, as amended; and two additional provisions of the Social Security Act of 1935, as amended.[5]

The relationship of struggle among the three branches has seen supremacy alternate from branch to branch; sometimes it has featured a quasi-alliance between two branches against a third—without necessarily successful results in the short run. A pertinent example here is the frustrating post-1933 effort of the closely allied New Deal legislature and executive, which on many major issues—in fact, on all major economic and social ones—had to wait for victory over the Supreme Court for fully four and a half years after having received a very clear popular mandate in the election of 1932 and an overwhelming one in that of 1936. Unlike Mr. Nixon and his ill-fated administration, whom fate gave four Supreme Court appointments in a year and a half, F. D. R. had to wait until, early in 1937, Mr. Chief Justice Hughes and Mr. Justice Roberts, impressed by the obvious handwriting on the wall of political reality, executed the famous "switch-in-time-that-saved-nine," followed in short order by the replacement of the retiring Mr. Justice Van Devanter by United States Senator Hugo Lafayette Black, Democrat of Alabama, who took his seat that fall.

In general, the tone of dominance has been set by the tenor and personality of the elected chief executive who, after all, is the sole individual in the American federal governmental process to have a nationwide constituency, and who, within generous limits, and they would appear to be ever-broadening ones, is in a position to interpret his powers narrowly or broadly as his judgment may dictate. In other words, whenever the president has been of the category commonly called "active" or "strong"—e.g.,

Washington, Jackson, Polk, Lincoln, Wilson, the two Roosevelts, and Lyndon Johnson–his branch, in the long run and sometimes in the short, has been able to acquire relative supremacy. Where he has been "passive" or "weak"; simply lacked sufficient support in Congress or by the people; or perhaps did not manifest sufficient concern for, or understanding of, or even interest in, the political process–e.g., John Quincy Adams, Pierce, Buchanan, Andrew Johnson, Grant, McKinley, Harding, Coolidge, Hoover, and Eisenhower–supremacy passed to Congress or, on occasion, to the Supreme Court. In several instances no clear-cut supremacy can be justifiably pinpointed. This is true, for example, of the presidencies of Madison, Monroe, Hayes, Cleveland, Taft, Truman, the end of the second Eisenhower term after the dismissal of Sherman Adams and the death of John Foster Dulles (there is no doubt at all about the presence of Congressional supremacy during the latter's first term in office), and of Kennedy's incumbency. Then it should be noted that during some presidencies, or at least portions thereof, the executive has tended to dominate in foreign affairs and Congress in internal matters–e.g., Truman, Eisenhower, and Kennedy.[6] We then have the contemporary example of the case of Richard M. Nixon, whose concededly innovative foreign policy initiatives were accompanied by an ever-accelerating thirst and quest for maximum executive power, based on the dangerous concept of a "plebiscitary presidency," that inexorably resulted in gross constitutional abuses and the subversion of the democratic process, and culminated in his resignation in August 1974 in the face of certain impeachment and conviction for high crimes and misdemeanors in office. The record seems to indicate that Ford, in turn, was not accorded a very "strong" rating. It is, of course, much too early to essay a fair judgment of President Carter in any direction. (See Appendix, Table 2.)

The United States Supreme Court, too, would seem to have sporadically challenged the authority of both president and Congress. Yet, despite three or four periods of tendencies toward judicial supremacy–Marshall's Court from 1801 to 1829; Taney's sporadically and, specifically, in 1857; Fuller's from 1888 to 1910 (his Court made a specialty of striking down practically every federal and state attempt in the realm of economic and social legislation on the grounds of laissez-faire violations of the alleged guarantees of substantive due process of the Fifth and Fourteenth Amendments[7]), and Hughes's from 1934 to 1936–the Court has never really actively bid for the role of dominant governmental agency in the land, despite contemporary assertions about the Warren Court, although a good case might be advanced for such a policy during the era of Mr. Chief Justice Marshall. In viewing the Marshall period, as well as the heyday of the Hughes anti-New Deal Court, one may conceivably speak of government by judiciary, or "judicial supremacy." Yet even then there was never any genuine likelihood that the Court would, in the final analysis, or in the long run, effectively dominate the executive and/or the legislature. When all is said and done, the United States Supreme Court does not possess the political power; the arsenal of potent weapons of government; the tools of or desires for the publicity media; or the strategic position in the government and in the body politic generally enjoyed by the other two branches. Even if the Court, from time to time, has brought about a temporary halt in the exercise of power in certain directions by the other two branches, when either of these two has chosen to fight back hard, the Supreme Court has generally failed in the long run to stop them permanently—and in the words of the late great Princeton professor of constitutional law Edward S. Corwin the run had better not be too long either! This has been especially true in its relationship with, and actions toward, the national legislature—although the Court, on significant occasions, has demonstrated its willingness to take on Congress[8] as well as the president.[9]

In any event, if not without considerable toil and trouble, the Supreme Court may be reversed in its decisions, or, either as a result of pressure from the other agencies of government or because of the influence of new personnel on the bench, it may reverse itself. While the decisions of the Court constitute without question the supreme law of the land, the Court, in effect, depends upon the power of persuasion. Purse and sword are in other hands—the legislature and the executive, respectively. Decisions running counter to the broad consensus simply do not last in the long run. If the Court is to thrive, it must, as Wallace Mendelson has said so well, "respect the social forces that determine elections and other major political settlements. No Court can long withstand the morals of its era."[10] The justices, in the observation of Alexis de Tocqueville of over a century ago, do indeed possess enormous power, "but it is the power of public opinion." While the Court is morally obligated to be its molder and leader on significant occasions, rather than merely its register—as the Warren Court's civil libertarian posture demonstrated—the Supreme Court is quite conscious of the over-all exhortation, well expressed by Francis Biddle, that "we must not get away too far from life, and should continually touch the earth for renewed vitality."[11] Nonetheless, it is essential that we do recognize the very considerable power, and, indeed, proven success of the Court's role as a teacher, a molder, an innovator, in the short run. Hence, it does not merely serve as a legitimater or negater—although it is in these capacities that we normally conceive of it, and quite justifiably so.[12]

On the other hand, the judicial alignment in the long run with the other two major branches on overriding policy matters may not follow axiomatically; but it does come very close to reality. Some observers of the scene have even contended that far from representing a dependable means of preventing "legislative tyranny," judicial review of national policy seems to have but marginal value.[13] Whatever the actual merits of this judgment may be, the judiciary is well aware of the limitations upon its powers. Mr. Justice Frankfurter, the conscience of the Supreme Court on this issue during most of his significant service of almost a quarter of a century, thus addressed himself to the issue of reversing the Supreme Court in his now well-known separate concurring opinion in the unanimously decided 1958 *Little Rock School* case, *Cooper v. Aaron,*[14] in which he quoted at length from his own concurring opinion in the *United Mine Workers* case of 1947:

> Even this Court has the last say only for a time. Being composed of fallible men, it may err. But revision of its errors must be by orderly process of law. The Court may be asked to reconsider its decisions, and this has been done successfully again and again throughout our history. Or, what this Court has deemed its duty to decide may be changed by constitutional amendment.[15]

He might have added that one of the major causes of revision and reconsideration is the inevitably changing composition of the Court.[16] Yet any recognition of that crucial element in judicial decision making must carefully guard against an all-too-often popular, often misinformed and/or uninformed and oversimplified, catch-all analysis of its significance. In any event, reversal of judicial action is possible, and it has frequently been, and will continue to be, effectuated.[17]

Among other fascinating aspects of my favorite branch of our government is one inevitably recurring question, always at once enigmatic and controversial: Does the Supreme Court, at the apex of the judiciary, merely *judge* each case on its intrinsic merit, or does it also *legislate*? In theory, all the members of any judicial tribunal do is to judge the controversies over which they have jurisdiction and arrive at decisions in accordance with the legal aspects of the situations at issue. Yet especially the nine justices of the United States Supreme Court are frequently charged with "legislating" rather than "judging" in handing down their decisions. This charge usually admits, and indeed grants, that the Court must of course possess the power to interpret legislation, and, if "absolutely justified" by the particular issue at hand, even strike down legislation that is unconstitutional beyond "rational question." The charge against the Court insists, however, that a line must be drawn between the imposition of judicial judgment and the exercise of judicial will. The latter is described as legislating, presumably the function of the legislature, and hence reserved to it.

But, no matter how desirable one may be in the eyes of a good many observers, is it possible to draw such a line?

It is, of course, impossible. As with every "line," questions arise at once as to how, where, when, and by whom it shall be drawn. Nor do the justices claim to have a ready-made answer to the problem, though Mr. Justice Owen Roberts, for one, attempted in the case of *United States v. Butler*[18] to draw that line once and for all in an often-quoted, yet hardly realistic, passage from his opinion for a majority of six, which declared the New Deal's Agricultural Adjustment Act of 1933 unconstitutional: "When an act of Congress is appropriately challenged in the Courts as not conforming to the constitutional mandate, the judicial branch of Government has only one duty–to lay the article of the Constitution next to the act and to decide whether the latter squares with the former."[19] In theory, this is a praiseworthy formula; in practice, it is invoked by judges who must decide the meaning of the all-important verb "to square." The response to the *Butler* decision–culled from contemporary press commentary–is illustrative of the enigma: "Bravo," applauded the opponents of the New Deal: "Great judicial statesmanship, proper and precise interpretation of the written Constitution!" Countered the proponents of the New Deal: "An unwarranted, outrageous assumption of legislative authority, an arrogant disregard of constitutional limitations of judicial power." And soon thereafter President Roosevelt moved to "pack" the Court with members who would read the Constitution *his* way.

The response to the *Butler* case is but one example of the ever-recurring problem. Another famous illustration of a set of diametrically opposite-in-reaction postures is that of the decisions in *Dred Scott v. Sandford*[20] and *Brown v. Board of Education,*[21] where friend and foe of racial equality may be found first on one, then on the opposite side of the scale of plaudits, depending upon the course of the decision and the commitment of the commentator! It would seem that, to a large extent, official as well as private reaction is more or less a matter of whose ox is being gored, to use Al Smith's happy phrase.

It is not, however, quite so simple, although unquestionably reactions to Supreme Court decisions are normally highly subjective. Nor is the key to the problem, in what Professor Alpheus T. Mason properly styled "an unrealistic dictum,"[22] the well-known, superficially logical statement by Mr. Chief Justice Stone, who was among the three dissenters in the aforementioned *Butler* decision, when he thus admonished the six adherents to Mr. Justice Roberts's majority opinion: ". . . while unconstitutional exercise of power by the executive and legislative branches of the government is subject to judicial restraint, the only check on our own exercise of power is our sense of self-restraint."[23] To be sure, the assertion does have the ring of truth and merit. Yet it too sweepingly glosses over the facts of political life, facts which have amply demonstrated the long-run power of the other two branches, especially that of the legislature. Moreover, it is but a short step from the Stone statement to a contentious pronouncement by Charles Evans Hughes, publicly voiced in 1907 while he was serving as governor of New York—and one he later grew to regret—that "we are under a Constitution, but the Constitution is what the judges say it is." This assertion goes considerably beyond that by Mr. Justice Stone, of course, for, being a campaign statement—although that of a future associate justice and later chief justice of the United States Supreme Court—it failed to point to the complexities inherent in such a facile pronouncement, complexities which do include, but are certainly not confined to, the very real sense of self-restraint that, to a greater or lesser degree, is always present on the bench.

It is obvious, however, that the judges do "legislate." They do make law. One of the most consistent advocates of judicial self-restraint, Mr. Justice Holmes, recognized "without hesitation" that judges do and must "legislate." But, he added significantly, they "can do so only interstitially; they are confined from molar to molecular motions."[24] Judges are human, as indeed all of us are; but they are also judges, which most of us are not. Being human, they have human reactions. "Judges are men, not disembodied spirits; as men they respond to human situations," in Mr. Justice Frankfurter's words. Mr. Justice McReynolds insisted that a judge neither can, nor should, be "an amorphous dummy, unspotted by human emotions." And Mr. Justice Cardozo spoke of the cardiac promptings of the moment, musing that "the great tides and currents which engulf the rest of men do not turn aside in their course and pass the judges by."[25]

But being human, as indicated, is not the sole factor in the judicial decision-making process. A jurist is also presumably a qualified and conscientious member of the tribunal; he or she is in no sense of the term a free agent, free to render a decision willy-nilly. There is a deplorable tendency on the part of many observers to oversimplify the judicial decision-making process. Judges are "rigidly bound within walls that are unseen" by the average layman. These walls are built of the heritage of the law; the spirit of the Anglo-Saxon law; the impact of the cases as these have come down through the years; the regard for stare decisis (although there are, of course, often several precedents from which to choose); for a genuine sense of historical continuity with the past, as Holmes put it, "is not a duty, it is only a necessity";[26] the crucial practice of judicial self-restraint;[27] in brief, *the taught tradition of the law.*

Moreover, to reiterate an earlier point, the judges are very well aware of at least two other cardinal facts of judicial life: that they have no power to enforce their decisions, depending, as they do, upon the executive for such enforcement; and that they may be reversed by the legislature, albeit with varying degrees of effectiveness and if not without some toil and trouble, as the case of the Crime Bill of 1968, with its three-pronged attack on the Court, demonstrates. To underscore an earlier Hamiltonian point, the Supreme Court's only power is its power to persuade. Purse and sword are in other hands. But not only do we often expect too much from the Court; we let it, or wish it to, settle policy matters that ought to be, yet for a variety of reasons are not, tackled by the other branches–witness such contentious issues as desegregation, reapportionment, redistricting, criminal justice, and separation of church and state. As Anthony Lewis has observed so perceptively, "Judicial intervention on fundamental issues is most clearly justified when there is no other remedy for a situation that threatens the national fabric–when the path of political change is blocked."[28] This was the case with the areas of endemic racial segregation and persistent legislative mal-, mis-, and non-apportionment. It was not the case with such contentious criminal justice decisions as *Miranda v. Arizona*:[29] there, by reading a particular code of police procedure into the general language of the Constitution, the Court overreached itself. Nor was it the case with the Court's recent highly questionable involvement with a host of nonjudicial and certainly nonjudicious aspects of the vexatious realm of abortion.[30] Nor, to point to a third realm, is it true of the Court's increasing involvement–some have styled it "meddling"–with matters of discipline in the public schools.[31] Our courts should not be viewed as wastebaskets of social problems, which does not mean, of course, that law does not play an efficacious role in social reform. It does, however, point to the inescapable fact that the other branches must do their jobs.

Reflecting upon these several considerations in the analysis of this power struggle, we may find the work of the Supreme Court plus the force and implications of its decisions in closer focus. At times the Court has clearly led the country (e.g., the Marshall era); at times it has deliberately stimulated social and economic progress (e.g., the post-1937 Court); at other times it has more or less held the line (e.g., the Chase-Waite era–with important qualifications); at others it has deliberately delayed (e.g., the Fuller Court). At times it has looked to majority sentiment, as it were, by following the election returns (e.g., the *Insular* decisions at the turn of the last century);[32] at others it has defied majority sentiment and even vilification (e.g., a good many of the 1956–57 term civil liberties decisions;[33] its mid-1960s decisions in the delicate and emotional realm of freedom of religion and the separation of state and church;[34] the Warren Court's controversial exhortations in the realm of criminal justice during the

1960s;[35] and the Burger Court's terpsichorean ventures into the "suspect"[36] categories and substantive issues of the due process of law[37] morass). At times its decisions have been seemingly motivated by "sectional" or "class" considerations (e.g., *Dred Scott*, the 1886 *Santa Clara* case, proclaiming corporations as "persons," and the 1954 and 1955, and 1969 and 1971 segregation/desegregation cases);[38] at other times they have been truly "national" in spirit and effect (e.g., the series of landmark Marshall decisions in the *Marbury, McCulloch, Martin,* and *Gibbons* cases, and the sundry reapportionment and redistricting decisions of the 1960s).[39] In a very real sense, the Court through the years has been the conscience of the country. In a measure it has represented the Rousseauist *volonté générale* of the land. It has done this through its decisions, speaking through its justices, who, almost always of a very high caliber, have interpreted the Constitution as they saw it, in line with the taught tradition of the law.

Of course, the Supreme Court of the United States is engaged in the political process, but, in Mr. Justice Frankfurter's admonitory prose, it is "the Nation's ultimate judicial tribunal, not a super legal aid bureau."[40] Neither is the Court, in the second Mr. Justice Harlan's words, "a panacea for every blot upon the public welfare, nor should this Court, ordained as a judicial body, be thought of as a general haven for reform movements."[41] Of course, the justices, who have been styled "inevitably teachers in a vital national seminar,"[42] consult their own policy preferences. But they do so in an institutional setting which forces responsibility upon them. They must meet and maintain high standards of integrity, intelligence, logic, reflectiveness, and consistency. They must demonstrate a sense of history, coupled with awareness of the realities and vagaries of public affairs, a task that has been aptly called "the hunch of intuition about the inner life of American democracy."[43] They have the exciting, yet delicate, task of heeding the "felt necessities of the time," in Mr. Justice Holmes's inspired phrase, while holding aloft the banner of constitutional fundamentals.

The Supreme Court of the United States, which Woodrow Wilson viewed as "the balance wheel of our whole constitutional system . . . a vehicle of the Nation's life . . . ," may indeed be perpetually steeped in controversy. It may not always have exercised its power, or exercised it wisely when it did; it may on occasion have gone well beyond its presumed function. It may not always have been able to make its decisions stick, and there may well be much room for improvement. No institution of government can be devised by human beings that will be satisfactory to all people at all times. The Court is much better at saying what the government may not do than in prescribing what the government must do and how it must go about doing it. Indeed, the Court should resolutely shun prescriptive policy making. It has quite enough to do in constitutional and statutory application and interpretation. To reiterate the second Mr. Justice Harlan's often-quoted admonition: "The Constitution is not a panacea for every blot upon the public welfare; nor should this Court, ordained as a judicial body, be thought of as a general haven for reform movements."[44] It may thus well be questioned whether the Court should be involved, as it has become increasingly, in such realms as economic, as distinct from political and legal, equality, and private, as distinct from public, morality. To paraphrase Professor Paul Freund of Harvard's law school, the question is not whether the Court can do everything, but whether it can do something, and do that in its proper sphere. Of course, these lines are often as brittle and elusive as they are vexatious, and the Court can escape neither controversy nor criticism, nor should it. In Mr. Justice Holmes's words: "We are very quiet up there, but it is the quiet of a storm center, as we all know." As an institution at once legal, political, and human, it possesses both the assets and liabilities that attend these descriptive characteristics.

When all is said and done, the Court is not only the most fascinating, the most influential, and the most powerful judicial body in the world; it is also the "living voice of [the] Constitution," as Lord Bryce once phrased it. As such, it is both arbiter and educator, and, in essence, represents the sole solution short of anarchy under the American system of government as we know it. It must act, in the words of one commentator, "as the instrument of national moral values that have not been able to find other governmental expression"[45]–assuming, of course, that it functions within its authorized sphere of constitutional adjudication. In that role it operates as the "collective conscience of a sovereign people."[46] And no other institution "is more deeply decisive in its effect upon our understanding of ourselves and our government."[47] In other words, through its actions the Court defines values and proclaims principles.

Beyond that, moreover, the Supreme Court of the United States is the chief protector of the Constitution, of its great system of checks and balances, and of the people's liberties. The Court may have retreated, even yielded to pressures now and then, but without its vigilance America's liberties would scarcely have survived. Within the limits of procedure and deference to the presumption of the constitutionality of legislation,[48] the Court–our "sober second thought"[49]–is the natural forum in American society for the individual and for the small group. It must thus be prepared to say "no" to the government–a role which Madison, the father of the Bill of Rights, fervently hoped it would always exercise. There are many citizens, indeed most, once they have given the problem the careful thought it merits, who will feel more secure in the knowledge of that guardianship, one generally characterized by common sense–not necessarily determined by political "consensus"–than if it were exercised primarily by the far more easily pressured, more impulsive, and more emotion-charged legislative or executive branches. All too readily do these two consensus-oriented bodies yield to the politically expedient and popular, for they are close, indeed, to what Judge Learned Hand once called "the pressure of public hysteria, public panic, and public greed." The Court, which thus often has had to act as a "moral goad" to the latter two, is neither engaged in, nor interested in, a popularity contest–its function is emphatically not one of counting constituents! Should that time ever arrive, the supreme judicial tribunal, as we now know it, will have lost its meaning.

Even if a transfer of that guardianship to other institutions of government were theoretically desirable, which few thoughtful citizens believe, it would be politically impossible. "Do we desire constitutional questions," asked Charles Evans Hughes, not then on the bench, in his fine book on the Court, "to be determined by political assemblies and partisan divisions?"[50] The response must be a ringing "no!" In the 1955 Godkin lectures which he was to deliver at Harvard University when death intervened, Mr. Justice Robert H. Jackson had expressed his conviction eloquently and ably: "The people have seemed to feel that the Supreme Court, whatever its defects, is still the most detached, dispassionate, and trustworthy custodian that our system affords for the translation of abstract into constitutional commands."[51] And we may well agree with Thomas Reed Powell that the logic of constitutional law is the common sense of the Supreme Court of the United States.

As a commentary on this point, that distinguished observer of Court and Constitution reported an incident that took place in a debate on the floor of the United States Senate after the turn of the century between Senators Spooner of Wisconsin and Tillman of South Carolina. At one juncture Tillman exclaimed: "I am tired of hearing what the Supreme Court says. What I want to get at is the common sense of the matter." Rejoined Senator Spooner, "I too am seeking the common sense of the matter. But, as for me, I prefer the common sense of the Supreme Court of the United States to that of the Senator from South Carolina."[52]

In the long run, common constitutional sense has always served the Court well in its ceaseless striving, as a voice of reason, to maintain the blend of continuity and change which is the sine qua non for desirable stability in the basic governmental process of a democracy. In that role it will–for it must–live in history.

5 *MARTIN M. SHAPIRO*

THE CONSTITUTION AND ECONOMIC RIGHTS

Perhaps the most important point to be made in a Bicentennial appraisal of the Supreme Court is that the dominant scholarly image of the Court is enjoying its forty-third, not its two hundredth, birthday. The New Deal of President Franklin Delano Roosevelt was instituted in 1933. Since that time almost all the scholarly treatments of the modern Supreme Court have been produced either by active proponents of and participants in the New Deal or by its intellectual and political allies and successors.[1] The first step toward accurately assessing the participation of the Supreme Court in modern American politics is to understand that nearly all the materials necessary to such an assessment have been created by political scientists, lawyers, and the justices who were engaged in extended defenses of a particular political movement distinguished by a high propensity to self-adulation and a peculiar uneasiness about its own legitimacy.

The scholarly wing of the New Deal exhibited this propensity and uneasiness in a number of ways, most notably in building out of the Roosevelt experience that wondrous intellectual structure "the strong presidency."[2] It is one of the great ironies of recent American political history that a Republican president, Richard Nixon, became the ultimate proponent of the Democratic theory of the strong presidency and was destroyed by his pursuit of that sweeping presidential power which New Deal writers had sanctified. It is one of the small ironies of American intellectual history that a number of the New Deal creators of the strong presidency, horrified by the dawning perception that from time to time a Republican might inhabit the house that they had built, have now begun the task of dismantling it.[3]

The task of scholarly New Deal commentators on the Supreme Court was somewhat more complex. In one sense, all they had to do was build the image of a "weak court" to complement their image of the strong presidency. Indeed, one wing of New Deal commentators concentrated on building up the proposition that the Supreme Court had reached its twilight by the 1930s and subsequently could and should do nothing at all except perhaps legitimate the new powers given to the presidency and its servants. This was the famous school of judicial self-restraint, or judicial modesty.[4]

One grave difficulty was encountered, however. The theory of the strong presidency proclaimed that the president was chief legislator as well as chief diplomat, chief administrator, and commander in chief. Thus, the proclamation of a strong presidency carried the automatic reciprocal of not only a weak Congress but of one that would follow the president's legislative leadership. Perhaps it is a testament to the strength of the Marshall tradition that not even the most abject scholarly servants of the presidency dared to proclaim the president chief justice as well as chief everything else. Thus, simply to proclaim a strong presidency and a weak Supreme Court would not properly enlist the Court as a faithful subordinate of the New Deal. Those who announced the doctrine of judicial self-restraint were content to neutralize a rival of the New Deal presidency. Others sought some doctrinal alternative to judicial self-restraint that would not only end judicial opposition to the New Deal but enlist the Supreme Court as its active and faithful follower.

The New Deal coalition included, among other elements, blacks, left-leaning intellectuals, and other assorted underdogs. Opposition to the New Deal emanated from, among other places, major corporate industry, and business more generally. What was needed, therefore, was a constitutional doctrine that would render the Supreme Court active in the defense of New Deal underdogs but trigger the judicial self-restraint syndrome when the New Deal's business enemies sought judicial protection for their interests.

PROPERTY RIGHTS AND PERSONAL RIGHTS

The key to the development of such a doctrine was the creation and popularization of a distinction between "property" rights and "personal" or "civil" rights. Such a distinction was not easy to incorporate into the Constitution. Most of the new civil and personal rights and liberties were to be based upon the Fourteenth Amendment. However, the amendment itself coupled life, liberty, and property as the essential bases for human personality. It was a commonplace of American intellectual and constitutional history that the protection of property had been one of the major considerations behind the writing of the Constitution and the creation of the federal union.

No matter how tenuous the distinction between property and civil rights might be in terms of our constitutional traditions, however, it was highly consonant with the social, economic, and political movements of the twentieth century that the New Deal represented. A general denigration of private property had been growing in Western political thought and was to be seen most clearly in the successes of socialism, a mild strain of which was clearly incorporated in New Deal ideology. Perhaps just as importantly, the assertion of property rights in the United States had come less and less from the small landholders, who were Jefferson's bulwark of liberty, and more and more from corporate enterprise. By a long-standing legal fiction corporations were persons. But that fiction could not disguise the disjunction that had in fact arisen between the interests asserted by individuals and those asserted by large economic organizations. It was that disjunction which seemed to endow the distinction between personal and property rights with what a Marxist would call objective reality.

THE NEW DEAL HISTORY OF THE SUPREME COURT

New Deal scholars also retrospectively shaped American constitutional history to support a distinction they found of such contemporary convenience. They argued that beginning in about 1890 the Supreme Court had increasingly abandoned its traditional role of constitutional interpretation to become the spokesman for a laissez-faire ideology and the champion of business enterprise. These commentators pointed particularly to two lines of doctrinal development. One they labeled dual federalism, the other substantive due process.

Under dual federalism, the Supreme Court was depicted as freeing business enterprise from government regulation through manipulation of the interstate commerce clause of the Constitution.[5] That clause gave to the federal government the power to regulate commerce "among the several states," while the power to regulate intrastate commerce–that is, commerce of essentially local nature within a single state–was retained by state governments. The New Deal story went that the Court would find that federal business regulations were unconstitutional because they infringed on local commerce whose regulation was reserved to the states. Then it would declare state business regulations unconstitutional because they impinged on interstate commerce that only the federal government was constitutionally empowered to regulate. Through this one-two punch the Court created a haven from all government regulation for big business enterprises.

Even more dreaded than dual federalism was that most terrible of all monsters of constitutional doctrine, "substantive economic due process."[6] The Fifth and Fourteenth Amendments provide that no person shall be deprived of his life, liberty, or property without "due process of law." One meaning of that phrase seems to be that if the government seeks to deprive someone of liberty or property, it must employ fair procedures such as trials, with adversary proceedings, or at least hearings in which both sides get a chance to argue and present evidence. This concept of due process is conventionally called "procedural due process" because it turns on whether the government used proper procedures in taking your property away from you, not on whether the government should have taken it. During the decade from about 1885 to 1895, the Supreme Court began to emphasize a second meaning of due process when passing on the constitutionality of statutes that authorized the government to interfere with private economic activity. It began to ask not only whether the procedures used by government to take property were fair but whether the government had a good reason to take the property at all. This was "substantive" due process in the sense that it concerned itself with whether the substance of the statute–the actual governmental policy it embodied–was sufficiently reasonable and beneficial to the society to justify governmental taking of private property.

It was "economic" substantive due process in the sense that the Court began to ask these questions about the reasonableness and social desirability of statutes that regulated economic activity such as the wages and hours of workers or the rates charged by railroads. Through economic substantive due process, or so the New Deal story went, the Supreme Court could strike down any or all government regulation of business. Any economic statute it didn't like the Court could hold to be an unreasonable interference with the sound operation of the free enterprise system under which economic decisions should be made by private entrepreneurs, not by the government.

Finally, the New Deal complaint read, in both dual federalism and substantive due process areas, the Court developed two opposite lines of precedent, one upholding governmental regulatory authority, the other declaring regulations unconstitutional. Thus, in any given case the justices could uphold or strike down a regulatory statute, depending upon whether they thought it economically wise or not. Whichever way they decided, they would have readily available a line of precedents to justify their decisions.

All these developments culminated in the dastardly attack of a laissez-faire, conservative, business-oriented Supreme Court on the glorious, democratic, and economically dynamic New Deal. In the early 1930s the Court struck down many of the major legislative efforts of the newly installed Roosevelt administration. But our New Deal story had a happy ending. After chastisement by President Roosevelt, the Supreme Court saw the truth. And the truth was that the Court should never, never interfere in the realm of economic policy making, which should be left to the president. Instead, it took on the approved New Deal task of protecting the constitutional rights of the underdog, and these rights were civil and personal, not economic. And so the Court lived happily ever after.[7]

NEW DEAL HISTORY REEXAMINED

There are a number of problems with this folk history of the Court. First of all, the Court of the 1880s and 1890s did not suddenly become the peculiar champion of property rights out of intoxication with the newly brewed ideology of laissez-faire. The turn-of-the-century Court was carrying on a constitutional tradition of concern with property rights that ran back to the political philosophy of the founding fathers and to the jurisprudence of John Marshall. Marshall had used both the commerce and contract clauses in seeking to achieve the same sorts of constitutional protections for property rights that the later Court was constructing from the commerce and due process clauses.[8] The rationale that an unreasonable law was not a valid law, which was at the heart of substantive due process, ran back far beyond Marshall to the quarry of medieval natural law out of which both the Constitution and the institution of judicial review had been hewn.[9] The notion that the government might not unreasonably and arbitrarily invade the property of an individual simply because it claimed to be doing so for the public good is so deeply imbedded in the original constitutional matrix that it need not have been, and indeed could not have been, invented by the justices of the 1890s.

Moreover, the Court was not the peculiar champion of laissez-faire. The belief that business ought to be left alone was widely shared by the personnel of all segments of government. State legislatures and Congress refused to pass thousands of proposed business regulation statutes for every one struck down by the Supreme Court. State and national executives vetoed hundreds of regulation bills for every one vetoed by the Supreme Court. To be sure, a Supreme Court veto of an economic regulation statute passed by one state might serve as a constitutional precedent discouraging passage of similar legislation by other states. So one Supreme Court "no" counts for a great deal more than one legislative or executive "no." Nevertheless, it would be quite false to view the historical scene as one in which the Supreme Court stood as the great nay sayer against state and federal efforts to bring the robber barons to heel. The greatest barrier to government economic regulation of business at the turn of the century was Congress and the state legislatures, which typically rejected regulatory proposals completely or passed them in emasculated form. More often than not the Supreme Court served not as an opponent of the legislature but as a coconspirator in the creation of a statutory scheme that would leave the regulated industry with a maximum of independence.[10]

As to the New Deal commentators' criticisms of the Court's doctrine of dual federalism, they tended to ignore what the New Deal itself so passionately wished to ignore, that the Constitution did contain a commerce clause. If the Court was to maintain any remnant of the constitutional distinction between interstate and intrastate commerce, it had to draw lines somewhere. As the American economy developed, interstate and local commerce ceased to be distinct entities. In reality, there was a continuum in which raw materials were harvested and mined locally, sent to other places, often in other states, for processing and manufacture, and then the finished products sent to still other places for local sale and consumption. An unbroken chain existed between activities as local as weeding a cotton field and other activities as local as buying a dress at the corner store. That chain passed through activities of manufacture and distribution that straddled the interstate flow of materials from their raw state to their final consumption. One could argue that weeding a cotton field was a purely local activity in which neither the worker nor the weeds ever saw a state line. Or one could argue that weeding was in interstate commerce because it was in aid of the growth of cotton that would eventually be shipped to another state where factories made the cotton into cloth. Either argument is equally logical and equally unrealistic. But the first has the virtue of preserving some distinction between interstate and intrastate commerce. The second abrogates the commerce clause. In effect, it rewrites the Constitution so that it reads "Congress shall have the power to regulate all commerce" rather than "Congress shall have the power to regulate commerce among the several states." Since the line to be drawn between interstate and intrastate commerce is necessarily artificial, we can quarrel endlessly about where it should have been drawn at any particular stage of American history. But there seems to be no reason to condemn the Court or suggest some special laissez-faire conspiracy between the justices and the capitalists simply because the Court chose to draw the line somewhere short of complete abrogation of the constitutional provision.

For instance, two of the favorite targets of New Deal attack were *Carter v. Carter Coal Company* (1936)[11] and *Schechter Poultry Corporation v. United States* (1935),[12] one of which held that coal mining and the other that retail sales of chickens were not in interstate commerce. Yet if men working at the very first link of the chain of commerce–the gathering of raw materials–and at the very last link–retail sale to the ultimate consumer–are engaged in interstate commerce, there is no such thing as local commerce. Indeed, the New Deal Court finally did abrogate the commerce clause entirely in decisions such as *Wickard v. Filburn* (1942),[13] holding that wheat harvested to feed animals on the same farm on which it had grown, which had traveled only the few hundred yards from the field to the trough, was in interstate commerce. As a matter of pure policy preference, one may prefer *Wickard* to *Carter* and *Schechter.* Given that the Court is pledged to uphold the Constitution, however, it is difficult to see why we should condemn the justices for issuing *Carter* and *Schechter* and praise them for *Wickard* rather than vice versa.

Similar problems arise for critics of the economic substantive due process decisions of the Court. The same critics who assail the Court for reading laissez-faire into the Constitution often praise it for its desegregation decision. Yet *Brown v. Board of Education* (1954)[14] is as much a reading of the best contemporary psychological and sociological theory into the Constitution as the old decisions were the reading in of the best economic theories of their day. If we look at the old cases, we find a Court bent on making sound public policy on the basis of what the best social theory of the day suggested would best serve the public interest. Those New Dealers who favored complete judicial self-restraint might condemn the old decisions along with such new ones as *Brown, Mapp,*[15] and *Miranda.*[16] However, those liberal commentators who applaud the activism of the Warren Court would do well to remember that the economic theories of the turn-of-the-century Court were as public interest-oriented, more clearly articulated, better scientifically grounded, and show greater survival value than the sociological, psychological, and criminological theories that shimmered just below the surface of much of what the Warren Court did.

As to the New Deal charge that the Court maintained two lines of precedent in both its commerce clause and its due process jurisprudence, it is difficult to see why that should have been offered as a criticism at all. The fact that the Court did uphold a substantial number of business regulation statutes when the businesses involved were clearly located within the stream of interstate commerce,[17] or when it appeared reasonable to interfere with the workings of the free market, indicates that the Court was not a blind, fanatic champion of laissez-faire but was attempting to engage in sound economic policy making. Its record is not necessarily one of caprice or inconsistency but of a mixture of allegiance to laissez-faire doctrines *and* pragmatic interventions where the free market seemed to be yielding poor results. This mixture was precisely the basis for policy making used by legislatures, executives, and political parties during the same period and was clearly the governing economic ideology of American political life. While the Court might disagree with a particular legislature at a particular time as to whether a particular governmental intervention in the economy was justified, the justices and the legislators shared the economic truth that free competition was to be the rule and intervention the exception. In almost every instance in which the Supreme Court struck down a state economic regulation statute, other state legislatures had considered and rejected similar statutes. There is no doubt that the Court was making economic policy, but it was doing so within the same parameters as its contemporaries in other segments of government.

In one area, however, the Court seemed to go considerably farther than other segments of government in the protection of free enterprise. In *United States v. E. C. Knight* (1895)[18] the Court ruled that manufacturing was not in interstate commerce and so could not be regulated by the federal government. The case involved the "Sugar Trust," a number of sugar refineries all of whose manufacturing operations were concentrated in one locality, Philadelphia, but which drew their supplies of raw sugar cane from Louisiana and the Caribbean, and shipped their finished product throughout the United States. To proclaim that the manufacturing facets of such an operation were a local matter, of concern only to Pennsylvania authorities, seemed to run against the grain of economic reality. And until 1937 the Court persisted in the view that manufacturing was local.[19] This doctrine did seem to present an inflexible barrier to federal regulation of the growing industrial giants.

However, a number of factors must be borne in mind in placing *Knight* in perspective. First of all, while it tended to exempt the manufacturing operations per se of the big corporations, it did not preclude federal intervention against their distribution and sales practices, as the successful antitrust prosecution of Standard Oil shows. Second, while the *Knight* decision itself may have been an inhibiting factor, Congress and the president did not show any terribly marked enthusiasm for interfering with the corporate giants in the period between 1890 and 1932. Indeed, neither did the New Deal itself except in building up the countervailing power of the industrial unions. Thus, the Court's exclusion of manufacturing from the scope of the federal commerce power was in harmony with the general disinclination of the federal government to regulate in that area. *Knight* involved the Sherman Antitrust Act, which was itself an interesting illustration of the tacit antiregulation coalition between the various segments of government. The Sherman Act was passed by a Republican Congress that self-consciously and deliberately drafted it in such a way that the courts would have extremely great discretion in determining its actual meaning. And the Congress delegated much of its lawmaking authority to the judges, knowing full well that the courts were likely to construe the statute in line with their laissez-faire perspectives.

Finally, a flat declaration that manufacturing was in interstate commerce would have rendered the distinction between inter- and intrastate commerce virtually meaningless because much American manufacture was essentially local. A Court that wished to preserve the limits of the commerce clause, and also realistically deal with the growth of national industries, would have had to rule that some large-scale manufacturing was in interstate commerce while other manufacturing was local. It would then have had to decide on a case-by-case basis which manufacturing firms were and which were not in interstate commerce. Endless borderline instances would have arisen to plague the justices. In short, an attempt to work out an economically realistic doctrine on manufacturing as commerce would have led to a legally unrealistic one. The eventual congressional solution to this problem, in writing federal minimum wage laws, was arbitrarily to exempt certain industries, and firms under a certain size, from federal control. But such an arbitrary solution, while available to a legislature in writing new statutes, is not available to a Court seeking a boundary line that can be rationally defended in terms of the language and history of the Constitution.

In *Knight* the Court did choose an economically unrealistic doctrine in order both to preserve a constitutional distinction and to avoid excessive judicial labor. If it had chosen an economically more realistic doctrine, it would have had to engage in even more of the kind of economic policy making for which it was criticized by New Dealers in the course of deciding which manufacturing operations were in and which were not in interstate commerce. It might have been better to choose the more judicially active alternative. This is particularly true since such a choice might have reduced the subsequent reaction of the Roosevelt Court, which, with equal and opposite unrealism, declared that everything was in interstate commerce. In any event, the choice the Court made was consonant with the constitutional distinction between interstate and intrastate, the prevailing economic policies of the rest of the central government, and the goal of holding judicial discretion within reasonable boundaries.

ST. ROOSEVELT AND THE DRAGON COURT

When we come to the New Deal commentators' hagiography of St. Roosevelt against the Dragon Court, there are far too many attacks along far too many dimensions to survey here. But it is important to make a few points directly related to the problem of economic rights. First of all, the early stages of the New Deal were marked by enormous rush and confusion. One of the most condemned of the Supreme Court's actions was its invalidation of the National Industrial Recovery Act.[20] Yet the NIRA was an ill-conceived bit of state capitalism which the Roosevelt administration never made the slightest attempt to revive after the Court had become more friendly. Indeed, the administration must have breathed a great sigh of relief that the Court had rid it of such an embarrassment. The second major New Deal program struck down by the Court was the Agricultural Adjustment Act.[21] This act was a curious mixture of fashionable radical ideology and pragmatic devices to raise farm income. After the first AAA was struck down by the Court, the New Deal put together a second AAA which stuck to farm income and abandoned invidious attacks on those property interests despised by the left. The Court upheld the second AAA, with Justice Roberts, who had written the first AAA opinion, writing the second as well.[22]

Second, it must be remembered that normal constitutional processes broke down in the early stages of the New Deal. The newly elected, overwhelmingly Democratic Congress of 1933 blindly rushed to do the President's bidding. It passed presidentially drafted bills that most congressmen had neither read nor understood—in some instances, bills that had not even been printed. Some of these new laws made sweeping delegations of congressional power to the President without standards, safeguards, or means of surveillance by Congress of presidential activity. One of these sweeping delegations, the Hot Oil Act, was rushed through so quickly that its criminal provisions were lost in the shuffle. They were not officially published as part of the act until after the first arrests were made for their violation.

The New Deal hagiography bitterly attacked the Court for striking down these hurried and sweeping delegations, including the Hot Oil Act.[23] New Deal commentators often conveniently forgot to point out that not only the conservatives but the liberals, Cardozo and Brandeis, opposed such delegations. The *Schechter* case,[24] which contains the major Supreme Court attack on delegation run rampant, has always been the central symbol of the Court's sins against the New Deal–sins so grievous that they could be redeemed only by total judicial abstention from further economic decisions. Yet a younger generation of political observers, for whom the romance of the New Deal is less compelling, have come to glorify *Schechter* as a call for congressional responsibility and a warning against the kinds of delegation that have enhanced the powers of the president and the federal bureaucracy without insuring that those powers are employed in the public interest.[25]

Third, it must be recalled that the New Deal economic program basically rested not on the kinds of statutory provisions the Court struck down but on what was, for those days, massive federal spending. The Court did little to interfere with that spending. The minor depression of 1937, which followed a cutback in the spending programs, showed clearly that the New Deal had not dealt with the fundamental causes of the depression, but only ameliorated its effects by pumping money into the economy. Only the even more massive spending associated with rearmament for World War II really ended the depression. It was in the area of New Deal tinkering with the structure of American capitalism that the Court and the New Deal came most into conflict. As it turned out, it was precisely in this area that the New Deal programs were largely irrelevant to economic recovery.

Upon closer examination, then, the Supreme Court's pre-1937 activities in the economic realm were not so unrelated to the specific provisions of the Constitution and the Marshallian tradition, nor so arbitrary, nor so out of line with other facets of American politics, nor so inimical to the alleviation of the Great Depression that the Court needed to absolve itself from its peculiar and egregious sins by abjuring the jurisprudence of economic rights. Nevertheless, that is the position that New Deal commentators and New Deal justices took. Indeed, as we have noted, most of them went further and demanded that the court surrender all its political authority to the President and a presidentially controlled Congress.

PREFERRED POSITION AS NEW DEAL IDEOLOGY

As we have also noted, the more subtle wing of the New Deal adopted a more finely honed strategy. First it blackened the Court's economic reputation, insisting that in the economic realm the Court had been simply enacting its own stupid policy preferences rather than enforcing true constitutional guarantees. The vehicle for this tactic was the historical myth we have just reviewed. Then it sought to show that while the Court should not make economic policy, it did have a very special constitutional responsibility to protect personal and civil rights. The vehicle for establishing this disjunction was the preferred position doctrine.

In 1937 and 1938 the Roosevelt administration gained control of the Supreme Court through the appointment of Justices Black and Reed. In one of the earliest of many decisions in which the Court promised to let the New Deal have its way, *United States v. Carolene Products Company* (1938), Justice Stone and his clerks composed the famous footnote 4, which suggested that while surrendering on economic rights, the Court might remain active (1) where specific prohibitions of the Constitution such as the first ten amendments were involved, (2) where the government sought to restrict "political processes," or (3) where statutes were directed at particular religious . . . or national . . . or racial minorities.[26] Rarely has a Supreme Court doctrinal pronouncement been more transparently political. The Court was forbidden to aid the business community, which was the New Deal's enemy. The Court was to protect the political process, a process that New Dealers were then convinced had become one of mass politics that would invariably favor them against the "monied interests." It was especially to protect the free speech so dear to the intellectuals who were overwhelmingly allied to the New Deal (the First Amendment is the most specific of the specific prohibitions of the first ten amendments). And it was especially to protect religious, national, and racial minorities—this uttered at a time when a major factor in the Democratic party's massive domination of the political process was its successful building of a coalition of ethnic and racial minorities. The preferred position doctrine has survived to bolster constitutional doctrines of freedom of speech that seek to protect all speakers, not simply friends of the New Deal. This fact, however, should not obscure how specifically footnote 4 sought to align the Supreme Court with precisely those political forces that seemed at the time to favor the indefinite triumph of the New Deal.

We cannot trace here the detailed subsequent history of the preferred position doctrine or its stablemate the doctrine of judicial self-restraint. One point, however, must be emphasized. The judicial proponents of these two doctrines were typically portrayed by Supreme Court commentators as opposed and contending wings of the Court.[27] Indeed, they were on some specific issues. But in a broader political context they represented two wings of a New Deal coalition that totally dominated the Court and the major law schools throughout the 1940s and 50s. During those two decades an almost unchallenged New Deal ideology pervaded both the Court and the political scientists and academic lawyers who wrote about the Court. That ideology held that the Supreme Court must either totally abdicate to the president and *his* Congress,[28] or, if it had any authority to act at all, it was only on behalf of personal and civil rights—that is, on behalf of those interests that carried the New Deal certificate.

CONTINUITY OF SUBSTANTIVE APPROACHES

That this orthodoxy was essentially an ideology masking basic continuities between the behavior of the pre- and post-1937 Supreme Courts can be readily seen by examining certain key aspects of the modern Court's work. The first of these is the notion of "*substantive* due process." In applying this label to the work of the turn-of-the-century Court, commentators seek to point out that the Court was not only requiring fair procedures, but insisting that certain substantive rights might not be invaded by the government except when it could convince the justices that it had particularly good reasons to do so—reasons that outweighed the normal preference for the free market. The post-1937 Court followed precisely this "substantive" approach in a number of areas, most notably freedom of speech. Without tracing the some thirty years of pulling and hauling over details, we can succinctly state the current Supreme Court doctrine on freedom of speech. Freedom of speech is the rule and government regulation of speech the exception. But regulation of speech may be constitutionally justified where the government can demonstrate to the justices' satisfaction that there are particularly compelling reasons of social policy that require narrowly limited invasions of the freedom.[29] Substitute the word "contract" for the word "speech," and you have precisely the substantive due process of 1900.

Beginning with a suggestion in footnote 4 itself, New Deal justices and commentators have often argued that the specificity of the First Amendment ("Congress shall make no law") justifies a substantive approach, where the vague wording of the due process clause does not. But again, beginning with footnote 4, they have coupled the specificity of the First Amendment with the vagueness of the Fourteenth to make prohibitions against limitation on speech applicable to state as well as federal governments.[30] If specificity justified a more substantive approach, then we would expect the Court to be more active in its enforcement of speech guarantees against the federal government than against the states. In reality, however, the Court has not distinguished between federal and state governments in its freedom of speech jurisprudence. Of all of the justices serving since 1937 only Justice Harlan has sought to do so with any degree of consistency, and he only in the special area of obscenity regulation.[31]

The substantive free speech cases run in a long series that begins before the New Deal victory of 1937 and continues after it without pause or interruption, thus clearly indicating that the New Dealers were not abandoning substantive approaches but only changing their beneficiaries. This point is illustrated even more clearly by *Skinner v. Oklahoma* (1942).[32] During the preceding five years the Roosevelt court had clamorously displayed as its hallmark the presumption of constitutionality of legislative acts, rather than independent judicial assessment of the reasonableness of legislative policy, and condemned the vicious meddling in legislative business of its predecessors. Yet in *Skinner* Mr. Justice Douglas wrote that where "the basic civil rights of man" are subject to "invidious . . . discrimination" then the presumption of constitutionality disappears and the Court must engage in its own "strict scrutiny" of the statutory policy.[33] Of course, *Skinner* involved not the taking of property from a businessman but the sterilization of a habitual criminal with a penchant for armed robbery. It was one of the earliest and clearest signs that certified underdogs were going to get the judicial benefits now denied to the New Deal's enemies.

While the Court's freedom of speech jurisprudence and *Skinner* show the continuity of substantive due process most clearly, it might also be traced easily in such areas as religion and rights of the accused, if space permitted. In the religion area the Court has repeatedly made policy-oriented adjustments to its alleged "wall of separation" between church and state. Among other things it has managed to uphold tax exemptions for religious institutions while striking down tax-funded subsidies for religious institutions and tax deductions for those who use them.[34] Economically these decisions make no sense at all since a tax exemption is in reality a subsidy. But they do make the same kind of rough political and public policy sense as many of the old substantive decisions did. The culmination of this substantive approach to religion was a set of decisions in which the Court managed to uphold the granting of government money for science laboratories at parochial colleges but not for science and other secular instruction at parochial elementary and secondary schools.[35] Here again the wall of separation is the rule, but the Court grants prudential exceptions where the policies involved appear to it to be desirable.

In the rights of the accused area, there is a sense in which the Court must employ substantive due process. The touchstone of the substantive approach was always judicial inquiry into whether the government's action was "reasonable." The specific wording of the Fourth Amendment debars "unreasonable" searches and seizures. So here the Court is specifically commanded to use a reasonableness standard. More generally, the Warren Court used the search and seizure, self-incrimination, and right to counsel clauses as bases for quite literally composing a national policy manual dictating uniform procedures for the conduct of searches and arrests and the subsequent handling of prisoners. It transposed the scattered specific negatives of the Constitution into a positive substantive program of reform of police patrol and station house behavior. That the Burger Court justices have been in partial disagreement with the Warren Court as to how the details of the new manual are to read should not obscure their basic agreement that the Court should actively concern itself with the substance of police policy.

The continuity of the substantive approach from the old Court to the new may perhaps best be observed in its new equal protection clause jurisprudence. Indeed, so striking is the continuity between the old substantive due process of the turn of the century and the Warren Court's handling of equal protection that a number of commentators have used the term "substantive equal protection" to describe the Warren Court approach. Fortunately, professors Mendelson and Gunther[36] have traced the new substantive equal protection with such elegance and detail that it is unnecessary to relate the full story here. In brief, they find that the Warren Court developed a two-stage test. Under that test the Court first asked whether a statute created a "suspect" classification, such as race, or impinged on a "fundamental right." If not, the Court entertained the "normal," that is the New Deal, presumption that the statute was constitutional. If the statute did employ a "suspect" classification, or impinged on a "fundamental right," the Court did not employ the normal presumption, but instead engaged in "rigid scrutiny" of the statute to determine whether the government could show a "compelling state interest" that could justify the classification. Of course, a suspect classification was one that the Court found generally unreasonable. And the "scrutiny" was really a wide-ranging social, economic, and political investigation of whether the policy embodied in the statute was sufficiently desirable to justify use of the otherwise unreasonable classification. In short, equal and identical treatment of all persons was the rule. Government action to classify some persons and treat them differently with respect to a "fundamental right" was the exception to be allowed when the Court found such action reasonable on policy grounds. All of this amounts to a curious translation of laissez-faire doctrines to the age of the positive state. The premise is no longer: that government is best which governs least. The premise is now: that government is best which governs equally. And exceptions to the new premise, like the old, are to be granted when the Court concludes that there are good policy reasons for deviating from the norm.

Professors Mendelson and Gunther are both charter members of the New Deal Club. While having described and decried with great acumen what they consider to be the reprehensible judicial activism of the Warren Court, both, I fear, engage in a bit of New Deal wishful thinking when they purport to find that the Burger Court has retreated from substantive equal protection. To be sure, the Burger Court has reduced the tendency to hang the label "suspect" on more and more legislative classifications.[37] And because some of its justices hold different policy views from their predecessors, the Burger Court will sometimes find classifications reasonable that the Warren Court would have found unreasonable. But there is as yet insufficient evidence to conclude that the Burger Court will cease to enforce its policy preferences through the equal protection clause.

Among the clearest illustrations of the continued substantive concerns of the Burger Court justices are such cases as *Eisenstadt v. Baird* (1972)[38] and *Weber v. Aetna Casualty Company* (1972).[39] In the first, the Court struck down a law prohibiting the sale of contraceptives to the unmarried on the ground that there was no rational basis for distinguishing between married and unmarried persons in granting access to contraceptives. This case shows a pure substantive approach, with the Court doing its own independent assessment of public policy. Surely there is *a* rational basis for distinguishing married from unmarried persons here in terms of seeking to provide disincentives to intercourse among the unmarried. It is simply not a rational basis that the Court finds persuasive.

The *Aetna* case involved a state statute that placed certain illegitimate children in a less favorable position than other offspring to inherit property from their parents. The state had sought to defend the statute as serving a number of proper policy goals, including the discouragement of illegitimacy. In ruling for the majority that the statute violated the equal protection clause, Justice Powell's language clearly reveals a Court bent on examining broad issues of social policy, choosing proper goals for state action, and judging whether the statutory schemes are reasonably likely to achieve an approved goal at a reasonable cost to individual property rights.[40] If we were to substitute the words "due process" or "equal protection" in this decision, it would be impossible to tell whether it had been written in the 1970s or in the early 1900s during the heyday of the Court's substantive due process defenses of economic rights. Moreover,

Justice Powell's approach clearly echoes the free-ranging standard of reasonableness adopted by Justice Douglas in the precedent case to *Aetna, Levy v. Louisiana* (1968).[41] In a perfect illustration of the 1900 style of judicial decision making he said: ". . . A State . . . may not draw a line which constitutes an invidious discrimination. Though the test has been variously stated, the end result is whether the line drawn is a rational one." And in both *Levy* and its companion, *Glona v. American Guarantee Liability Insurance Company* (1968),[42] Douglas makes it absolutely clear that it is the Court's conclusions as to reasonableness, not the legislature's, that govern the constitutional outcome.

Justice Powell's opinion in *Aetna Casualty* also nicely illustrates a more general point about substantive approaches. The single best clue, the ultimate symptom, of substantive approaches is the citation of legislative facts in judicial opinions. Typically, courts deal with facts immediately relevant to the dispute before them. Was X in fact the illegitimate child of Y? Did Y actually intend that he should not inherit? There are other facts that we label legislative because they are the kinds of broad facts about general social conditions on which legislatures typically base decisions on new legislation.[43] Many commentators argue that in reality all courts inevitably consider legislative facts even when they purport to be dealing only with the immediate facts of a case—in other words, that courts always take general social conditions into account in settling the case before them. Be that as it may, clearly when a court openly treats of legislative facts, it must be concerning itself with the substantive wisdom or reasonableness of the statute itself as well as its applicability to a given case. This is what Justice Powell did in the *Aetna* case.

We do not have a historical census of Supreme Court legislative fact finding. Perhaps it did fall off in the period of the Stone and Vinson Courts, although in the latter the justices certainly involved themselves in endless legislative-style analyses of the alleged facts of the international Communist conspiracy. (Perhaps the most bizarre example was the Supreme Court-approved opinion of Learned Hand in the *Dennis* case, which in part supported its conclusions on the constitutionality of the Smith act by a factual analysis of the fall of Czechoslovakia to the Reds.) There is certainly no dearth of legislative fact finding in either the Warren or Burger Court. (The prize of the Burger Court is surely the *Abortion* cases,[44] which range over a truly amazing variety of medical, psychological, and sociological data in order to construct a social policy that is totally the Court's own invention and rests totally on considerations of social and political prudence that cannot possibly be subsumed under any constitutional principle.) So long as the Supreme Court continues to address itself openly to issues of legislative fact, we can be sure that the substantive approach is alive and well. By arbitrarily interchanging "substantive" and "economic," commentators leave the impression that the Court changed its basic role when in reality all it did was change the set of interests it was willing to aid by substantive intervention in policy making.

CONTINUITY OF ECONOMIC CONCERNS

It is possible to allege that, while there was a continuity in substantive approaches, the post-1937 Court had at the very minimum abandoned *economic* substantive due process. But in reality there is hardly the briefest hiatus in the Court's constitutional intervention on matters of economic policy.

Until at least 1942 the justices remained involved in economic questions as they dismantled the earlier Court's constitutional limitations on federal control of industrial and agricultural management.[45] And by the early 1940s the new Court was already involved in a series of "free-speech picketing" cases which plunged it into the very center of labor-management relations. The justices openly admitted to particular problems with these cases because even the most New Deal and libertarian of them had to concede that labor union picketing was not simply free speech protected by the First Amendment but "speech plus," that is, speech plus economic activity. Thus, the cases played havoc with the preferred position strategy. Nevertheless, the Court dealt with these cases through a mixture of free speech and economic policy arguments and in doing so again picked up its economic burdens within historical moments after allegedly laying them down.[46]

Beginning in the early 1950s, the Court began to hear a massive series of government employment cases.[47] Involved was the most fundamental of all economic rights, the right to a job, and by the 1950s government was one of the largest employers in the United States. But these cases arose under various state and federal anticommunist, loyalty-security programs and so have generally been treated as involving First Amendment and procedural due process issues—that is, as "personal" or "civil liberties" cases. Yet what is most striking about them is that they see the Court evolving from its early position that public employment is a privilege[48] to a final position that such employment, once obtained, involves a constitutionally protected expectation of continued employment—in short, a property right.[49] By 1974 the employment right cases had totally escaped their earlier connection with freedom of speech to become pure substantive economic due process cases. In *Cleveland Board of Education v. La Fleur* (1974)[50] the Court struck down a set of pregnancy leave rules of a local school board. Its substantive economic due process approach, with its total confidence that it was in command of the technology and working conditions of the industry involved, the medical and public health aspects of the problem, and the techniques of personnel management, is strikingly similar to the old *Lochner v. New York* (1905),[51] *Bunting v. Oregon* (1917),[52] *Adkins v. Children's Hospital* (1923)[53] style. By the early 1970s the Court was explicitly saying that under many circumstances public employment was "property" within the meaning of the due process clause.[54] Along with the picketing and government employment cases that maintained the continuity of the Court's economic concerns in the 1940s and 1950s, the justices handled cases involving intersections between racial discrimination and property ownership and management.[55]

The 1950s also witnessed the first of a long line of cases involving economic rights in education, cases which begin in a Jim Crow setting that would make them appear to be not about economic rights but about personal freedom from government action separating blacks from whites. Indeed, the school desegregation cases themselves contain a personal or civil rights dimension that is noneconomic. But from the very beginning these cases have also had strong economic overtones. One of the very first, *Sweatt v. Painter* (1950),[56] which involved a law school, heavily stressed the vocational aspects of education and the handicaps that racial discrimination in legal education would place on blacks seeking success in the legal professions. Indeed, the whole line of cases from *Brown v. Board of Education* (1954)[57] onward must thus be seen as judicial intervention not only in race relations but in the fundamentally economic policy area of the delivery of government services and the impact of that delivery on the economic status of the recipients.

By the 1970s the Court was dealing with such purely economic aspects of public education as tuition fees[58] and the collection and distribution of school tax monies.[59] By 1975, totally outside the context of racial discrimination, the Court was saying that "the state is constrained to recognize a student's legitimate entitlement to a public education as a property interest which is protected by the Due Process Clause. . . ."[60]

We saw earlier that even the religion clauses had a substantive aspect. That they also have had an economic aspect can be seen in a number of cases. The *Sunday Closing Law* cases (1961)[61] dealt with statutes requiring businesses to close on Sunday, thus imposing economic burdens on Sabbatarians for whom Saturday was the prescribed day of rest. In *Sherbert v. Verner* (1963)[62] the Court dealt with the eligibility for employment benefits of a Sabbatarian unavailable for work on a normal working day. In 1970 the Court dealt with tax exemptions for religious institutions.[63]

In both the race and religion areas the provision of educational services is a central economic issue precisely because access to government services and revenues is a key to economic survival for many people. This point is made even more clearly in the welfare area. What right could be more purely and fundamentally economic than the basic subsistence provided by welfare benefits? Yet the Court's first entry into this area, *Shapiro v. Thompson* (1969),[64] comes wrapped in, of all things, an alleged civil liberty, the right to travel. For a time it appeared that the Warren Court was in the process of creating a "fundamental right" to subsistence or at least denoting poverty a "suspect classification" under its two-stage substantive equal protection approach.[65] The Burger Court entered the welfare field through the typical route of requiring procedural due process.[66] Also quite typically, procedural soon turned into substantive due process as the Court heard a series of cases calling upon it to judge the policy justifications for various substantive welfare and disability policies.[67]

The Burger Court has not continued down the path of the Warren Court to hold that welfare was a fundamental right or poverty a suspect category per se. On the other hand, it certainly has not left this field, nor has it been particularly hesitant about making independent judicial assessments of the reasonableness of welfare policies. Its opinions have contained a strange melange of Warren Court substantive equal protection approaches, ritualistic recitals of New Deal deference to the judgment of the legislature, and ambiguous combinations of the two. All this indicates that the Court will do its own judging on the reasonableness of welfare policies but will not be as sympathetic toward the welfare recipient as was the Warren Court.[68]

There are ambiguities in the Court's position that Professor Gunther dresses in more professionally suitable language when he characterizes the Burger Court as engaging in "balancing" rather than the two-stage equal protection approach of the Warren Court or the strict presumption of constitutionality of New Deal days.[69] Certainly, anyone reading the bold survey of legislative facts and the self-confident judicial policy making of *Department of Agriculture v. Moreno* (1973)[70] is more reminded of the "balancing" of property rights versus government interest to be found in *Fletcher v. Peck* (1810),[71] *Allgeyer v. Louisiana* (1897),[72] and *Village of Euclid v. Ambler Realty Company* (1962)[73] than of the balancing of *Dennis v. United States* (1951).[74]

While the Burger Court sporadically continues to proclaim it is following the Warren Court's two-stage approach, in reality it is showing varying degrees of deference to the legislature and varying degrees of reliance on its own policy judgments from case to case in the economic sphere, depending upon how much the justices approve or disapprove of what the legislature is doing.

Along with the provision of educational and welfare economic benefits, the Court has become involved with other government-supplied economic benefits as well. *James v. Valtierra* (1971)[75] involves low rent public housing. The Court's insistence on government-supplied legal services for the indigent began on the criminal law side in conjunction with the Sixth Amendment right to counsel. More recently, however, the justices seem to have guaranteed the indigent access to divorce courts.[76] Once a right to government-provided free legal services moves from the criminal to the civil side, we have clearly entered the realm of economic interests.

In addition to these "new" economic interests in the flow of government services, the Warren and Burger Courts have also become deeply involved in a number of matters that clearly involve economic and property rights even by the most conventional definitions. The Court has rendered a series of decisions extending constitutional supervision over wage garnishments for debt, eviction for nonpayment of rent, and repossession of property for debt.[77] We have already noted the cases concerning the economic interests of illegitimate children. Of course, throughout the period of its supposed economic quiescence the Court has continued to handle economic cases in the traditional areas of state taxation and regulation of businesses involved in interstate commerce.[78]

In this survey of the continuity of the economic concerns of the Supreme Court, we have saved the sexual discrimination cases for nearly the end because they finally and completely must obliterate any notion that the Court has more recently abstained from the kind of economic judgments it made in an earlier period. For the women's cases bring up precisely those issues of wages, hours, conditions of employment, freedom of contract, practice of professions, and regulation of business that were at the heart of the "old" economic due process.

In a series of sex discrimination cases, the Court has dealt with preferences for men over women as administrators of estates,[79] preferences for women over men in property tax exemptions,[80] mandatory pregnancy leaves,[81] differential treatment of pregnancy in disability insurance programs,[82] preferences for women over men in mandatory discharges from the armed services,[83] preferences for men over women in Social Security survivors' benefits,[84] and preference for boys over girls in child support.[85] There is no pattern in these cases. Sexual distinctions are sometimes upheld and sometimes knocked down. The Court applies some kind of reasonableness standard, considers a wide range of legislative facts, and engages in sweeping economic and social conclusions. The justices have not agreed on what reasonableness standard they are using, as the leading case, *Frontiero v. Richardson* (1973),[86] makes clear. But whatever test it is, it is certainly not total deference to legislative and administrative judgment. There is every sign that this line of cases is going to continue, with women's overtime pay laws and more pregnancy cases clearly bound for the Court. The overtime pay cases bring up precisely the same issues of freedom of contract and the ability, or lack of ability, of the "weaker sex" to take care of itself that were central to the old cases that have always been considered at the heart of traditional substantive economic due process, such as *Lochner v. New York* (1905),[87] *Muller v. Oregon* (1908),[88] *Bunting v. Oregon* (1917),[89] and *Adkins v. Children's Hospital* (1923).[90]

Closely tied to these cases are the racial job discrimination cases. The Court has shown itself quite willing to become involved in the most detailed examination of the operation of industrial plants in order to arrive at totally independent judicial conclusions on whether their personnel policies are discriminatory.[91] It has already heard its first affirmative action, or reverse discrimination, cases.[92] There is no question that on questions of racial as well as sexual job discrimination the Court is going to play a role.

Finally, in this economic survey we ought to note that just as some of the earliest post-1937 economic cases, those involving government employment of alleged subversives, presented combinations of First Amendment and property issues, so do some of the most recent. The Court has been busy striking some sort of "reasonable" balance between private property rights and free speech rights in cases where picketers have appeared on the grounds of privately owned shopping malls.[93]

In a fragmented, internally contradictory set of opinions, which is not defensible in terms of any logic to be derived either from constitutional law or political science, and is liberally sprinkled with legislative fact finding, the Court has recently rewritten the Campaign Financing Act. Whatever its decision means, it certainly makes clear that the Court was quite willing to intervene in the economic aspects of political campaigning and to employ a totally substantive approach in doing so.

What must be emphasized at the conclusion of this survey is that the rights or interests involved in all these areas are clearly and in the most fundamental sense economic: the right to rent or buy real property, to get or retain a job, to receive welfare or other government economic assistance, to inherit or act as the trustee for property, to receive educational benefits where education is viewed as essentially a tool for economic betterment. These are all either property rights in the older sense or expectations of government economic assistance, which are a principal form of property right in the age of the positive, welfare state. But with a very few exceptions they are not the economic rights of management or capital. Instead, they are the economic rights of wage earners, government employees, the poor, and minorities–in short, the economic rights of the clients of the New Deal. No matter how tightly these economic rights are wrapped in the mantles of freedom of speech, free exercise or no establishment of religion, procedural due process, racial and sexual equal protection, and right to travel, they remain economic. Judicial interventions in their behalf remain economic policy making. Thus, the Court was not knocked out of the economy by the New Deal but simply became part of the New Deal economic policy-making coalition.

CONCLUSION

We have seen that (1) the Court continued its substantive approach after 1937, both in the sense of defending individual rights and applying standards of reasonableness; (2) the Court continued its concern for property rights and economic policy; and (3) it continued to combine (1) and (2). In short, a truly Bicentennial, as opposed to New Deal, view of the Supreme Court shows that, with the usual peaks and valleys, the Supreme Court always has intervened, and continues to intervene, in the economic policy-making process guided by its own assessments of what constitutes reasonable economic and social policy.

We may react to that continuity in a number of different ways. Learned Hand once noted that Justice Stone and company had never really explained why property rights were not a species of personal rights.[94] He did so in the context of rejecting the preferred position doctrine and opting for the less clever and less flexible New Deal policy of total judicial self-restraint under which the Court would stop helping the New Deal's enemies but also stop helping its friends. One could conclude from the survey just presented that, because Supreme Court activism always leads to Supreme Court substantive policy making in the economic realm, the Supreme Court should not be active at all.

Second, we might react simply by condemning the continuity and insisting that, even if it did not do so when we thought it did, the Court ought now to get out of the economic field and reserve its energies for the protection of a few favored constitutional rights.[95] The preferred position doctrine need not be based on a false and purely verbal distinction between economic and personal rights. As I have shown elsewhere,[96] it may be defended on the basis of political analysis. It can be argued that, in our society, interests in speech are substantial but so diffuse that they are not easily represented by interest groups, parties, legislatures, or executives. On the other, property interests may be sufficiently concentrated to facilitate their representation by these political instruments. It would follow that the Supreme Court might choose to take on special responsibilities for representing speech and certain other diffuse interests in order to improve the representative quality of the political system taken as a whole. This is not to argue that there is something essentially wrong with the Court's defending economic interests, but that, as a matter of political prudence and the economizing of its scarce political resources, the Court ought to choose to defend those social interests that are not adequately defended elsewhere in the political process.

Third, one may take a more sanguine view of the Court's resources and a less sanguine view of the capacities of property interests to achieve success in the legislative and executive processes. The Court itself has recently attacked the distinction between property and personal rights in the context of extending greater judicial protection to property in its decision in *Lynch v. Household Finance Corp.* (1974).[97] And in a recent concurrence Justice Powell has been so bold as to suggest that there might even be extreme circumstances under which the Court would be justified in constitutionally intervening to save business property from uncompensated expropriation resulting from government taxing and public ownership policies.[98] Given that Justice Stewart wrote the opinion in *Lynch,* that Justice Rehnquist can be expected to be sympathetic to traditional property interests, and that Justice Powell certainly is, the recent appointment of Justice Stevens appears to be one of the endless series of ironies and misperceptions of presidential appointment politics. For here the Republican President Ford appoints a new justice to the bench precisely because he is a strong proponent of the extreme New Deal strategy of judicial self-restraint, and this at least temporarily inhibits the formation of a powerful new bloc of justices who might move the Court toward greater activity in defense of private property interests. Nevertheless, given the continuity of its concerns and the philosophies of its current personnel, it is certainly not entirely visionary to suggest that the Court may play a substantial role in protecting economic interests.[99]

Nor can even the New Dealers be so sure as they once were that this would be a bad thing. Liberals, radicals, and conservatives all display increasing suspicion of the Washington bureaucracy. The implication of the IRS, along with the FBI and the CIA, in the alphabet of government harassment of "the enemies" has begun to remind us again, as the Communist cases of the 1950s reminded us, that depriving a person of his income may be a vital element in government suppression of dissent. It may be precisely because laissez-faire is fading that economic rights, both old style and new, must again be elevated in the constitutional pantheon. For as all Americans, from capitalists to welfare recipients, become more and more economically dependent upon government, economic repression becomes more and more significant as a weapon of government against the people. The conservative enemies of the New Deal have been saying this from its inception. The liberal descendants of the New Deal may now be coming to accept this old view, and with it a newer vision of what a Court dedicated to freedom ought to be doing. In any event, it is now fruitless to debate about whether the Court can or cannot involve, or has or has not involved, itself in constitutional economic policy making since the New Deal. It can. It has. It does. And there is no sign it is going to stop.

6 *C. HERMANN PRITCHETT*

JUDICIAL SUPREMACY FROM MARSHALL TO BURGER

The Supreme Court of the United States is a group of nine more or less elderly lawyers, none of whom at the present time has ever faced the voters in an election for any public office, most of whom lack any substantial pre-judicial experience in public life, four of whom were appointed by a president who subsequently had to resign his office to avoid impeachment and one by a president who was not elected by the voters as executive. Yet these nine justices make, and their predecessors for the past century and three-quarters have been making, some of the most important political decisions in the operation of the American republic. They exercise this dominant influence on national policy by reason of their authority to interpret the Constitution, and because of this authority our system has been widely referred to as one of judicial supremacy.

Exercising the prerogatives of judicial supremacy, the Court in January 1973, in the cases of *Roe v. Wade* and *Doe v. Bolton,* declared most state criminal abortion laws unconstitutional in a melange of medical findings and ethical judgments. Exercising the prerogatives of judicial supremacy, the Court in July 1974, in the case of *United States v. Nixon,* held that a presidential claim of executive privilege had to yield to a subpoena for the production of evidence needed in an ongoing criminal prosecution, and thereby caused the first resignation of a president in American history. Exercising the prerogatives of judicial supremacy, the Court in January 1976, in the case of *Buckley v. Valeo,* ruled that key features in the Federal Election Campaign Act of 1974 were unconstitutional, thus seriously limiting the principal congressional effort to prevent a repetition of the 1972 presidential election scandals. State legislatures, Congress, even the president, bow before judicial supremacy.

The American doctrine of judicial supremacy is generally regarded as founded in John Marshall's decision in the case of *Marbury v. Madison* (1803), where he seized upon a minor dispute about Secretary of State James Madison's failure to deliver a commission of appointment as justice of the peace to one William Marbury, to declare the power of his Court to hold an act of Congress unconstitutional. Though the late Julius Goebel, Jr., contended that the early Court demonstrated professional acumen and moral courage,[1] the general view has been that the pre-Marshall Court was in a very weak position. During its first decade the Court had three chief justices and little business. One of its decisions was so unpopular that it was almost immediately overridden by the Eleventh Amendment. The justices were all Federalists, whose party was defeated in the election of 1800 by Thomas Jefferson, an inveterate foe of a strong federal judiciary. But as one of his last acts President John Adams appointed John Marshall as chief justice, and for the ensuing thirty-five years, through the administration of five Democratic presidents, Marshall was largely successful in establishing and maintaining Federalist doctrines of a strong federal system and a powerful Supreme Court.

The Court did not declare a second act of Congress unconstitutional until the *Dred Scott* case in 1857, but in the meantime the power of the Court to rule on the legality of presidential action had been asserted as early as 1804 in the case of *Little v. Barreme,* where the Court struck down an executive order on the ground that it contravened specific legislation by Congress. The Court's authority to pass on the constitutionality of state legislation had been recognized by Congress in section 25 of the Judiciary Act of 1789. Early exploitation of this power occurred in *Ware v. Hylton* (1797), where the Court held unconstitutional a Virginia statute violating the terms of the 1783 peace treaty with Britain, and, more importantly, in *Fletcher v. Peck* (1810), which ruled that a Georgia statute impaired the obligation of contracts. Resistance by state supreme courts to review of their decisions by the U. S. Supreme Court was firmly put down by the Marshall Court in *Martin v. Hunter's Lessee* (1816) and *Cohens v. Virginia* (1821).

Marshall's case for judicial supremacy was grounded on his contention that the Court was, by necessity, the ultimate interpreter of the Constitution. His argument was primarily an exercise in logic, based on the recognition of "certain principles, supposed to have been long and well established. . . ." The major principle was that the Constitution is the supreme law of the land. The Supreme Court has taken an oath to uphold the Constitution. The conclusion logically follows that when an act of Congress (or of the president, or of a state) conflicts with the superior law, the Supreme Court cannot enforce it but must declare it null and void.

This position has been so long accepted that the logic supporting it may seem unassailable. Yet is it not equally logical to argue that, since the Constitution is the supreme law of the land, and since the president has taken an oath to support the Constitution, he cannot enforce a decision of the Supreme Court that conflicts with the Constitution, but must act as though it were null and void?

The problem is simply not one to which logic can guarantee a correct answer. The fallacy of the logical form may be made clearer by stating a part of Marshall's argument as a syllogism.

Major premise: A law repugnant to the Constitution is void.
Minor premise: This law is repugnant to the Constitution.
Conclusion: This law is void.

Assuming the validity of the major premise, the soundness of the conclusion depends upon whether a particular law *is* repugnant to the Constitution. That is a matter of informed opinion and judgment, on which persons equally learned in constitutional law and history may disagree. Marshall blandly assumed that judges had superior legal knowledge and that a judicial finding of repugnance between a statute and the Constitution was, as Thomas Reed Powell put it, "equivalent to an objective contradiction in the order of nature and not a mere difference of opinion between two different guessers."[2]

The case for judicial supremacy has rested, however, not only on alleged judicial infallibility and expertise, but also on contentions concerning the intentions of the framers. There is no specific language in the Constitution from which Supreme Court control over the constitutional interpretations of the president or Congress can be deduced. Consequently, the intention of the framers has been sought by recourse to the convention proceedings, which are known to us primarily through the notes recorded by James Madison. Unfortunately, the record on this issue is not entirely clear, for the surprising fact is that the convention never squarely declared itself on judicial review.

There was, it is true, a group in the convention, led by James Wilson and Madison, which wanted to give a veto power over congressional legislation to a council of revision, on which both the executive and Supreme Court judges would sit. There was also a suggestion that the Supreme Court as a whole have power to revise legislation. But both ideas were rejected. This of course does not prove that the framers opposed the John Marshall type of judicial review. In fact, Charles A. Beard's 1912 study of Madison's notes convinced him that seventeen of the twenty-five men most influential in the convention declared directly or indirectly for judicial control.[3] But in 1953 W. W. Crosskey concluded after a review of the same evidence that the Constitution had not intended to authorize general judicial review of acts of Congress,[4] and in 1958 Learned Hand took the equivocal position that judicial review was "not a logical deduction from the structure of the Court but only a practical condition upon its successful operation."[5]

The legitimacy of judicial supremacy has thus been a subject of perennial controversy, and the argument has not been simply academic. As Alan Westin has said, we have had a Supreme Court fight almost every generation.[6] Jefferson's open animosity toward Marshall was highlighted by their confrontation in the course of the Aaron Burr treason trial.[7] Marshall was still on the Court a generation later when President Andrew Jackson issued his famous (and probably apocryphal) challenge: "John Marshall has made his decision; now let him enforce it."

In his first inaugural address Lincoln justified his opposition to the *Dred Scott* decision by saying:

> If the policy of the government, upon vital questions, affecting the whole people, is to be irrevocably fixed by decisions of the Supreme Court, the instant they are made, in ordinary litigation between parties, in personal actions, the people will have ceased to be their own rulers, having to that extent, practically resigned their government into the hands of that eminent tribunal.

Shortly thereafter Chief Justice Roger Taney counterattacked by reading Lincoln an indignant, but futile, lecture for his dictatorial action in suspending the writ of habeas corpus.[8]

Theodore Roosevelt was quite unhappy about the refusal of the Court, and particularly his new appointee Justice Oliver Wendell Holmes, to support his trust-busting policy. Franklin Roosevelt's frustration at the torpedoing of his New Deal by the Nine Old Men is one of the classic stories of American politics and needs no elaboration here. President Dwight Eisenhower was notably unenthusiastic about the decision in *Brown v. Board of Education,* and regarded his appointment of Chief Justice Earl Warren as "the biggest damn fool mistake I ever made." Richard Nixon used the Court, particularly its alleged failure to promote law and order by its criminal justice decisions, as a campaign issue in 1968 and vowed to replace its members as soon as possible with "strict constructionists."

Congressional assaults on the Court have sometimes synchronized with executive displeasure, but on other occasions have had independent origins. Stuart Nagel has identified seven periods of intense Court-curbing legislative activity up to 1965.[9] In every period the flurry of legislative proposals was stimulated by judicial invalidation of congressional or state legislation.

In the first period, 1802-4, anti-Court animus stemmed from Jeffersonian states rights convictions, and in the second period, 1823-31, the Democratic Congress was still reacting to Marshall's federalism. The third period was 1858 to 1869; this was the post-*Dred Scott*, Civil War, and Reconstruction era when the Court got on the wrong side of history and plunged to its nadir.

Nagel's next two periods were 1893-97 and 1922-24. In spite of the time span, the two scenarios were similar. A conservative, business-oriented Court which generally mirrored dominant national opinion was subjected to ineffectual harrassment from congressional spokesmen for agriculture and labor. Successful in meeting these challenges from the left, the Court continued to stonewall remedial social and economic legislation into the depression of the 1930s and laid itself open to the congressional attacks of the sixth period, dating from 1935 to 1937. Finally, the period from 1955 to 1959 saw the novelty of a Court under assault because it was more liberal than its detractors in Congress.[10] It should be noted that of the 165 Court-curbing bills identified by Nagel, over half (90) came in these last two periods. Bringing Nagel's study up to date, one could identify an eighth period from 1965 to 1968 featuring congressional resistance to the Court's criminal justice and "one person, one vote" decisions, and a ninth period of controversy fueled by the 1972 capital punishment and the 1973 abortion decisions.

Considering the entire historical record, one can only conclude that congressional opposition to the Court has been generally ineffective. Nagel found that only nine of the 165 Court-curbing measures had been adopted by Congress. During the nineteenth century Congress did succeed several times in changing the size of the Court for political reasons, and more favorable retirement conditions were enacted after the Court-packing fight in 1937 as a way of encouraging over-age justices to retire.

The most significant congressional successes have come with the passage of three constitutional amendments revising Supreme Court rulings. These were the Eleventh Amendment, already mentioned, which forbade suits against states by citizens of other states; the Sixteenth, reversing the 1895 ruling against a federal income tax; and the Twenty-sixth, which guaranteed the right of eighteen-year-olds to vote in state elections after the Court had held a statute to that effect unconstitutional.

However, proposed constitutional amendments to reverse the Court's Bible-reading in public schools, one-person one-vote, and abortion decisions have (so far) failed of adoption. Repeated efforts to require more than a bare majority vote to declare acts of Congress unconstitutional have uniformly failed, as have attempts to limit the appellate jurisdiction of the Supreme Court.[11] The Jeffersonian impeachment proceedings against the Federalist Justice Samuel Chase in 1804 were unsuccessful, and the only other attempt to impeach a Supreme Court justice, that led by Gerald Ford against William O. Douglas in 1970, never got out of committee.[12]

The president is in a much better position than Congress to influence the Court, primarily through his power to appoint its members. This is by all odds the most significant external influence on the Court.[13] Given a sufficient number of vacancies, a president can change the entire constitutional philosophy of the Court, as Roosevelt did between 1937 and 1942, when he chose a chief justice and made eight other appointments. Nixon transformed the Warren Court into the Burger Court with four appointments between 1969 and 1971. Few other presidential decisions have such potential long-range effects. For example, Franklin Roosevelt had a representative, William O. Douglas, on the Court for thirty years after his death.

Apart from the appointing power, presidents have been scarcely more effective in opposing the Court than Congress. It was Marshall rather than Jefferson who put his imprint upon the Constitution. Lincoln had the military might to defy Taney's writ of habeas corpus, but after the war was over Lincoln's reading of presidential power was reversed in *Ex parte Milligan* (1866). The classic instance of presidential defeat, of course, was that experienced by Roosevelt in his proposal to pack the anti-New Deal Court by adding six new justices.

So the Court has not only survived in competition with the two political branches, but has won almost universal acceptance for its major role as a partner with the president and Congress in the making of American public policy. Judicial review has come to be regarded as a distinctive American contribution to the art of government, and since World War II supreme courts more or less on the American model have been established in several democratic countries, particularly West Germany, Italy, and Japan. It is scarcely necessary to recall the many major constitutional interpretations that have come from the Court in the past decade or two—on racial segregation, legislative representation, voting rights, freedom to associate and to demonstrate, equal rights for women, new definitions of obscenity, protection of the poor, abortion, freedom of religion and limitations on public aid for religious schools, capital punishment, and a considerable number of protective rulings on procedures in criminal prosecutions.

On the Court itself there has been division of opinion concerning the legitimacy of such active participation in policy making. In oversimplified terms, the controversy has been between judicial activists and those who counsel judicial self-restraint. The activist judge tends to be goal-oriented;

that is, he has a stronger concern for achieving the right result in controversies that come before him than for the process by which the Court arrives at that result. He feels a personal responsibility for the court's conclusions, an obligation to make use of the power he has as a judge to achieve the right result. He knows what the right result is because he has strong commitments to a value system that tells him what is right.

The self-restrained judge, on the other hand, is more sensitive to countervailing pressures which limit his freedom to judge, and has other goals that may divert his attention from the immediate result to be achieved. It may be said that he is role-oriented; that is, he accepts as his major obligation the skillful manipulation of judicial techniques. He is primarily concerned with determining what it is proper for him as a judge to do. To the extent that he submerges himself in the judicial mystique and thinks of himself as dominated by a role with prescribed limitations and expectations, to that degree he loses his freedom to pursue his policy goals and feels a lesser personal responsibility for the results achieved. The most eloquent exponent of judicial self-restraint on the recent Court was Justice Frankfurter, who wrote in the second *Flag Salute* case:[14]

> As a member of this Court I am not justified in writing my private notions of policy into the Constitution, no matter how deeply I may cherish them or how mischievous I may deem their disregard. The duty of a judge . . . is not that of an ordinary person. It can never be emphasized too much that one's own opinion about the wisdom or evil of a law should be excluded altogether when one is doing one's duty on the bench. The only opinion of our own even looking in that direction that is material is our opinion whether legislators could in reason have enacted such a law.

Goal orientation and role orientation are of course tendencies, not hard and fast dichotomies. Moreover, these contrasting conceptions of the judicial role cannot be related to general political attitudes. The goals of an activist judge may be either conservative or liberal. In fact, until the New Deal the Supreme Court had historically been dominated by conservative activists. While John Marshall was the prototype of conservative activism in his general commitment to the values of a commercial republic, he had many successors, all the way from Stephen J. Field to Pierce Butler. It was the activist Court of the 1890s that declared the income tax unconstitutional and put Eugene V. Debs in jail.[15] It was the activist property-oriented Court that earned the praise of conservatives as "the sheet anchor of the Republic." When this long control of the Court by conservative ideology was finally broken by the Roosevelt and Warren Courts, there was a sense of betrayal, if not outrage, in conservative circles.

A Court that did not protect the status quo was seen as faithless to its historic stabilizing and conserving function.

It is generally assumed that, after this relatively brief experience with an activist liberal Court, Nixon's four "strict constructionists" on the Burger Court have returned the Court to its traditional stance. But this is not a stance of self-restraint. The Burger Court has by no means yielded up its right to second-guess legislatures or to develop new constitutional doctrine. Its surprising capital punishment decision was, it is true, opposed by the four Nixon appointees and may soon be reversed or limited.[16] But the equally controversial action invalidating state antiabortion laws came by a 7 to 2 vote.[17] In a two-hundred-page opinion the Burger Court as already noted second-guessed the Election Campaign Act of 1974, accepting some provisions and throwing out others.[18] And in perhaps its most creative role the recent Court has been actively extending the rule of equal protection into a number of new fields.[19] No matter what the political coloration of its members, the Supreme Court has demonstrated that it does not propose to yield its supremacy, that is, its activist right to judge.

What are the strengths of the Court that have enabled it successfully to assert and maintain its activist role? In no. 78 of *The Federalist* Alexander Hamilton forecast that the judiciary would be the weakest of the three branches of government. Congress had the power of the purse, and the executive controlled the sword. The courts had merely the power of judgment. Obviously, by most tests the judiciary is the weakest branch–in numbers, resources, appropriations–yet in conflict with the other branches, just reviewed, it has been generally successful. To take only the most recent example, the Warren Court lined up a formidable panel of enemies by its stand against racial segregation, its restrictions on Communist hunting by congressional committees, its development of new procedural rights for criminal defendants, its attack on malrepresentation in state legislatures and the U. S. House of Representatives, its tolerance of obscenity, and its refusal to approve Bible reading in the public schools. Yet the congressional Court-curbing drive of 1955 to 1959 produced only one minor piece of anti-Court legislation.

We may begin to analyze the sources of judicial power and prestige in a rather unlikely place, namely, Freudian psychology. Freud posited the interplay of three elements in the human personality–the id, ego, and superego. It is perhaps not entirely fanciful to analogize these concepts with the three branches of government. The subconscious, irrational, uncontrolled subterranean drives of the personality bear some resemblance to the conflicts and strivings of the legislative arena. The ego, which rationalizes and directs these primal drives toward perceived goals, is comparable to the executive, which undertakes to give practical effect to legislative urges. The role of the superego is to assess the appropriateness of goals and the correctness of means. People want not only to achieve their purposes; they need to believe that their purposes are proper and their methods legitimate.

The Supreme Court is the superego of the political system. Its function is to legitimate id-drives and ego-operations or, conversely, to condemn them as bad, unacceptable, unconstitutional. In fact, approbation is much more common than condemnation. From 1803 to 1970 only 88 federal statutes or sections of statutes were declared unconstitutional by the Court, or about 1 every two years. State statutes or municipal ordinances fail to withstand Court scrutiny much more often; the statistic is 737, but this still averages out to only 4 holdings of unconstitutionality per term. The rest of the time the Court's review in constitutional cases approves and legitimates executive or legislative action, providing valued assurance that the rules of the political system have been observed, that the father figure approves, that ancestral norms have been honored. The Court cannot provide such assurance unless the validity of its status is recognized. Its approval is worthless unless its right to declare the higher law is conceded.

A related factor in the Court's success story is its proprietary relationship to the Constitution. Marshall's brash assertion of judicial monopolism over constitutional interpretation has been ratified by time. The Court's role as official interpreter of the Constitution means that some of the respect, even reverence, felt for the document inevitably rubs off on the Court. Even when there is disagreement with the reading which the Court gives to constitutional provisions, it is credited with being the one branch of the government that really takes the Constitution seriously. The other branches can evade or ignore constitutional issues. Once when Franklin Roosevelt was proposing a novel legislative measure, he advised congressmen that they should pass it and leave the constitutional question to the Court.

Of course, the Court can avoid constitutional issues also. It does not go out looking for problems. It decides constitutional questions only because they are presented in lawsuits with which it must deal. And there are ways to avoid dealing with them. The Court can deny certiorari, it can fail to find a substantial federal question, it can limit the issues considered on appeal, it can interpret statutes narrowly. But if litigants persist, eventually the Court must bite the bullet. Perhaps the best illustration is the Court's more than half-century evasion of the racial segregation issue, which finally came to an end when the Court could no longer in good conscience avoid the plain mandate of the equal protection clause.

Again, the Court's supremacy is fortified by the mystique of the judicial process. It is true that lawyers have not been universally held in high esteem. Plato was wary of the divisive force that lawyers exert in a society, and they have felt the biting sting of the satire of Dean Swift and Charles Dickens. In act 4 of Shakespeare's *King Henry the Sixth*, part 2, Dick the Butcher proposes to Jack Cade, "The first thing we do, let's kill all the lawyers." In 1939 Fred Rodell of the Yale Law School castigated the legal profession as a "high class racket." "In tribal times," he wrote, "there were the medicine men. In the Middle Ages, there were the priests. Today there are the lawyers." In spite of such ambivalence, however, the law is an honored profession and today is enjoying unprecedented popularity as a career choice for college graduates.

While the operation of the courts is a perennial subject for complaint, perhaps never more so than today, and while individual judges may be condemned as too liberal or too conservative, coddlers of criminals, short-tempered autocrats, and occasionally even corrupt, no system of public decision making enjoys greater public confidence than that of the courts. Basically this is because decisions of courts are arrived at openly, with the participation of those affected, and under adversary procedures which offer a substantial guarantee that the relevant facts will be brought out and that the decision will be based on those facts. This is to some extent an idealized version of what goes on in courtrooms, but compared with the administrative bureaucracy or the legislative maelstrom, the judicial world offers structured and responsible procedures that are summed up in the basic concept of due process of law.

Another reason why the Supreme Court's supremacy has been accepted, if not welcomed, is that the Court has generally told the country what it wanted to hear, and provided a constitutional case for what the dominant interests in the nation wanted to do. In a well-known 1958 article Robert A. Dahl contended that, apart from short-lived transitional periods, "the Supreme Court is inevitably a part of the dominant national alliance . . . [and] of course supports the major policies of the alliance."[20]

This result is assured by the process of Supreme Court appointment which confines the presidential choice to persons who have been socialized by law training and practice, who with rare exceptions have won distinction and acceptance by working within the system, and who are representative of major social groups or political tendencies. John Schmidhauser, after an intensive study of the social and political backgrounds of appointees to the Court, concluded that if the Supreme Court is the keeper of the American conscience, "it is essentially the conscience of the American upper middle class sharpened by the imperative of individual social responsibility and political activism, and conditioned by the conservative impact of legal training. . . ."[21]

There have of course been the exceptional situations. Marshall was able to resist the Jeffersonian national alliance in part because of his superb tactical skill and in part because his vision of the federal union was a more accurate prediction of national development than Jefferson's. When there is no national consensus, as in the 1850s on the slavery issue, the Court's attempt to make national policy on its own in the *Dred Scott* case led it into disaster. As for the Court that tried to declare the New Deal unconstitutional, it was speaking for a national alliance whose viability had been destroyed by the depression. The liberal activist Warren Court had by 1968 become vulnerable to a national mood rather disenchanted with New Deals, Fair Deals, Great Societies, and war on poverty which never seemed to achieve their goals.

But in the more normal situation where the Court is in tune with the country, it can provide invaluable support for the power structure by transforming ideology into constitutional doctrine. Thus, John Marshall took the contract clause and, by employing a far broader conception of contract than the framers had intended, and by combining this conception with the principles of eighteenth-century natural law, was able to make of the clause a powerful instrument for protection of the vested rights of private property—even, as in the case of *Fletcher v. Peck*, when those rights had been secured by bribing legislators.

Even more impressive was the legerdemain that the Court employed to transform the due process clause of the Fourteenth Amendment from a protector of procedural rights such as notice and fair hearing, into a guarantee of property rights against social welfare legislation. The doctrine of "substantive due process," as it came to be called, was the most audacious of the Court's inventions during its first century. On the basis of the theory that due process authorized judges to second-guess legislative actions impinging on property rights or business practices, the Court struck down laws regulating wages, hours, prices, working conditions—even the size of loaves of bread and the price of theater tickets. Substantive due process provided the classic decision in *Lochner v. New York* (1905) when Justice Peckham held that a ten-hour law amounted to "meddlesome" interference with the right of bakers to work as long as they pleased.

Dahl's dominant national alliance explanation of the acceptability of judicial power has its limitations, however. It does not take account of an important difference between access to the courts and access to the political branches of the government. The national alliance does dominate access to the executive and the legislature. They respond to pressures which, to be effective, usually come from mass constituencies. While the president, the Senate, and the House all have separate constituencies, they are in each case mass constituencies. Only large interests and effective pressure groups have the chips to get into the game of politics today.

The courts, however, are accessible to any individual or group with a valid case or controversy. Minorities that are too small to be effective in the political arena may find the courts are the only public agencies willing to listen to them. That the courts have in fact an obligation to give special regard to the plight of interests unable to secure representation through the political process was a thesis first specifically propounded by Justice Harlan F. Stone in what is probably one of the two most famous footnotes in Supreme Court history.[22] In the case of *United States v. Carolene Products Co.,* 323 U. S. 18 (1944), (1938), Stone had occasion to restate the familiar case for judicial restraint in dealing with congressional statutes, the assumption being that legislatures are bodies of reasonable men who must be assumed to have some good reason for passing legislative acts. But, he added, the Court might be justified in a "more searching judicial inquiry" in situations where "prejudice against discrete and insular minorities . . . tend seriously to curtail the operation of those political processes ordinarily to be relied upon to protect minorities. . . ."

So it was that America's largest racial minority, even after it had begun to organize through groups such as the NAACP, lacked the political power to secure an effective hearing from a series of presidents and Congresses. It was only in the courts that its constitutional claims to equal protection could be registered. Without either the purse or the sword, the weakest of the three branches of government proved to be the only one with the conscience, the capacity, and the will to challenge the long-established scandal of racial discrimination.

Similarly the channels of the legislative process were closed to those who were protesting inequality in legislative districts. Clearly, the beneficiaries of the rotten boroughs were not going to abolish the system that sustained them. So again it was the courts, where the weight of a constitutional argument does not depend upon the number of battalions supporting it, that subjected the naked struggle for electoral power to the rule of law.

There are other factors in the Court's success. It has known how to shift its ground on occasion, how to retreat from positions that have become untenable. Mr. Dooley didn't know whether the Constitution followed the flag, but he did know that the Supreme Court followed the election returns. Moreover, the Court has various methods for avoiding issues that threaten to be too hot to handle. There is even a doctrine of "political questions" which the Court has principally used to escape getting mired down in foreign policy problems, such as the constitutionality of the Vietnam War.[23]

Admittedly, however, the trend has been toward greater judicial policy involvement. This is true even of the Burger Court, which was supposed to correct the activism of the Warren Court. In the recent Federal Election Campaign Act the Court rushed in with distinctly undeliberate speed and produced what was almost an advisory opinion about an untried statute which it condemned in a muddled two-hundred-page opinion.

Because the courts are readily accessible, and because they take the Constitution seriously, there is a considerable risk that they will suffer from overuse. It has become almost automatic for losers in the political process, or those who find it unresponsive, to take their claims to the judiciary. Judges are now managing the agonizing school desegregation process. They are taking over the supervision of prisons. They are deciding how equal women are to men. They are deciding whether suburbs can shut out central city minorities by exclusionary zoning. They are balancing environmental protection claims against economic costs. They are drawing the boundary lines for legislative districts. They are reading dirty books and looking at X-rated movies to decide how explicit depiction of sexual activity has to be to make it legally obscene. They are deciding whether lawyers can fix minimum fees, and whether professional athletes should be freed from bondage to the club owners. The list could be extended almost endlessly.

There are problems, then, with judicial supremacy, and judges need to be reminded occasionally, as Justice Stone did in *United States v. Butler* (1936), that "courts are not the only agency of government that must be assumed to have capacity to govern." But my conclusion is that, on balance, judicial supremacy has been a success. There are protections against a Court that allows success to go to its head. It is not true to say that the Court has the "last word" on constitutional issues. Its word is the last word for a time. Justice Robert H. Jackson remarked that the Court was not final because it was right, but it was right because it was final. However, it is final only so long as the other branches of government and the political process permit its last word to stand. In essence, all that the Court can do with its great power is to enforce a waiting period during which its doctrines are subject to popular consideration. If the judicial reasoning fails to convince the court of public opinion, it will be overridden by Congress or abandoned by the Court itself as new appointees come onto the bench or as the present members bow to the pressure of the times.

The Supreme Court's great merit is its unique qualification for determining and enforcing the basic principles of a democratic system, within which majority power and private rights must be balanced if democratic goals are to be achieved under the pressure of big government and mass society. It is not that judges are necessarily wiser and more sensitive than others to these needs. But they are placed in a situation where they are forced to think about them, and they operate in a context which gives them considerable help in that task. Legislators and executives see people in the mass. Judges see them as individual plaintiffs and defendants. The consequences of a judicial decision one way or the other can be clearly visualized, and reasoning can be checked by an assessment of its probable results. Although increasingly crowded, the judicial agenda provides more time to take thought, and the end product is a reasoned opinion that must make sense in the here and now, but also be reconcilable with the lines of doctrine reaching back to the earliest interpretations of the constitutional provisions in question.

As with any wielder of power, the Supreme Court may abuse its position of supremacy. If so, there are ways of disciplining it. If the Court makes mistakes–it has done so in the past and can be counted on to do so in the future–there are effective ways of correcting them. The Court's decisions are opinions offering themselves for belief. There is, in the long run, nothing to support them but the strength of their reasoning and their faithfulness to American ideals.

7 LOUIS HENKIN

THE CONSTITUTION AND FOREIGN AFFAIRS

Our Bicentennial celebrates independence and the political truths and human values which we associate with 1776, and with which we identify today. The Constitution of the United States will not be two hundred years old for yet another thirteen years, but some of the ideas it reflects—the sovereignty of the people, limited government, separation of powers, an independent judiciary, free elections, individual rights and liberties—may properly be celebrated now, for they are rooted in the Declaration of Independence and in the Virginia Declaration of Rights, both vintage 1776.

Our nationhood, and our ways as a nation with other nations, also began that year, and embassies, alliances, and treaties were crucial during the war for independence and in the following years before the Constitution was conceived. But whether our foreign relations are seen as two hundred years old or a decade or so younger, the prevailing spirit of national celebration and self-appraisal (perhaps self-congratulation) suggests that we ponder also our unique system for making foreign policy and conducting foreign relations, a way authentically our own, shaped less by English antecedents than by political compromises among our political ancestors, by the world into which we were born as a new nation and by our early experiences in it.[1]

During its near-two hundred years the Constitution has been the focus of periodic political controversies, and a few of these approached constitutional crisis. But few of the constitutional controversies involved the conduct of foreign relations, and perhaps the first near-crisis implicating foreign affairs came with Vietnam, on the eve of our Bicentennial. The Constitution has also been in issue in thousands of judicial cases, and a substantial number of them are famous in American constitutional law and are part of our common national culture. But foreign affairs have not often come to court, and even students of constitutional law could not recite a list of foreign affairs cases.[2]

Lack of controversy about foreign affairs might suggest that they were not of serious concern either to those who made the Constitution or to the generations that followed them. We know, however, that unhappiness with how foreign relations had been conducted under the Articles of Confederation was one of the principal forces that brought the constitutional fathers to Philadelphia, and "the draftsmen could not often assemble the words of a sentence without some reference to the foreign affairs of the little republic to be."[3] Foreign affairs also agitated political life during the early years of the republic and periodically thereafter. Lack of controversy could not be a consequence of the clarity and explicitness of the Constitution in regard to foreign affairs, settling old questions and putting even new ones beyond doubt and dispute; in fact, the Constitution says only a little about foreign relations, leaving more unsaid, and when constitutional issues arise, lawyers and courts and students of the Constitution find remarkably little to guide them.[4] Nor is it a fact that in our history the conduct of foreign relations and formulation of foreign policy left little to be desired, and no one unhappy enough to criticize or dispute it; to the contrary, from George Washington's day to ours, presidents and Congresses and their political or academic champions have disputed and recriminated, and publicists and scholars and citizens have condemned or defended what officials and legislators did and how they did them.

Why foreign relations have enjoyed extraordinary invulnerability to scrutiny, controversy, or litigation, must find other explanation. I think the reasons lie in the character, and in the means and ways, of foreign relations as they have interacted with our presidential system of representative democracy. The same international facts and factors, and the same institutional and political forces in our government, in their contemporary manifestations, may help explain the near-crisis that finally came in the wake of Vietnam, the difficulty of resolving it, and the context and conditions of any constitutional adjustments that might result.

Vietnam opened wide, once again, the principal issue: Is the control of our foreign affairs properly allocated and distributed between president and Congress? In our traditional way, we seek the answer to that question in ancestral wisdom and authority, if only because an answer cannot be easily reached on other principles or in other reasons. But our ancestors did not tell us everything, and, in any event, we would do well to ask also why experience during the intervening centuries divided authority between the president and Congress as it did, whether that division is desirable now, and, if it is not, if there is any escape from it.

Our accepted American recourse, the courts, will afford us only a little guidance through these constitutional uncertainties. Jurisdictional and other "technical" obstacles have kept many foreign affairs issues out of court, and judges have seemed determined to avoid deciding other issues, from prudence or other kinds of wisdom. But the courts may yet acquire at least an interstitial voice in foreign affairs, for now that the immunity of foreign affairs to political controversy is waning, their invulnerability to judicial scrutiny under the bill of rights may also be further eroded.

I inquire first into what our fathers intended.

The constitutional distribution of authority in foreign affairs is easy to describe. Congress is given authority to regulate commerce with foreign nations; to define and punish piracies and felonies committed on the high seas, and offenses against the law of nations; and to declare war, grant letters of marque and reprisal, and make rules about captures. The president is to make treaties and appoint ambassadors, with the advice and consent of the Senate; he shall also receive ambassadors. The states are expressly denied the power to make war or treaties, and lesser contacts are permitted to them only with the consent of Congress.[5]

Contrary to common misimpression, that division between legislature and executive has prevailed throughout our history, and prevails today. It has not been seriously challenged, and has not been, and is not now, the ground of controversy. The area of uncertainty and conflict, and the root of crisis, are in what the Constitution left unsaid or undefined.

To me the Constitution has long seemed to be strangely incomplete. One might have expected that the transformation from a league of states under the Articles of Confederation into a nation with a central government under the Constitution would be explicitly remarked and celebrated. The united states, a plural, common noun with an exaggerating adjective, would be declared to be henceforth The United States, a composite proper noun, capitalized and singular. We would be proclaimed a nation among nations, and the fathers would expressly vest all relations with other nations in the new government of the United States and would deny any role to the states. The Constitution might then proceed to allocate the authority of the United States in foreign affairs among the branches of the new central government, in gross or in detail.

The Constitution, we know, does little of that. It says nothing of nationhood, and almost nothing of a government of the United States.[6] It does not say expressly that the United States will maintain relations with other countries or that it is the federal government that will maintain them. It allocates some foreign affairs powers to Congress, and some to the president (largely together with the Senate), but there is no general grant to either and no explicit principle of distribution between them; nor is any such principle obviously reflected or implied. And the particular powers which are expressly allocated do not begin to add up to the totality of the powers of the United States in foreign affairs.

These lacunae have moved me to speculate whether the fathers had a limited conception of foreign affairs; or, even, whether they had a conception of the Constitution different from the one we have come to have–selective rather than complete, immediate rather than eternal, a suggestive guide for reasonable men in their time rather than a tight legal document to be parsed and argued by lawyers and judges for centuries. Justice Sutherland, however, offered a less heretical solution to the mystery. Writing in 1936, in *United States v. Curtiss-Wright Export Corp.*,[7] Sutherland suggested that the powers to conduct foreign relations are not fully expressed in the Constitution because they do not derive from it; they antedate the Constitution. They are inherent in our nationhood and sovereignty, which began in 1776, and were vested in the "collective," in "the United States," from that time. The Constitution therefore took for granted both nationhood and the plenary powers of the nation in foreign affairs. The federal government, then, would have had complete and exclusive authority even if the Constitution said nothing about it. But unhappy experiences since independence impressed the framers with the need to reemphasize the supremacy of the United States in foreign affairs and the exclusion of the states. For the rest, the purpose of various foreign affairs clauses in the Constitution was to allocate national power between the political branches of the new central government so as to define their respective authority.

Sutherland's theory has been criticized and defended[8] but, valid or not, it does not speak to the issues which concern us. Accepting it to explain the lack of an explicit grant of foreign affairs powers to "the United States" or to "the federal government," and as confirmation of the plenary and exclusive power of the federal government in foreign affairs, it does not explain why many powers of the federal government are not distributed and allocated, and it does not help us to supply those omissions. It does not tell us by which agency the federal government is to make foreign policy or conduct foreign relations generally, or do particular acts other than those expressly provided.[9] Is it Congress or the president, or perhaps the president jointly with one or both houses of Congress, that has authority to determine current and recurrent issues of national policy? How many immigrants shall be admitted to the United States, and from which countries? Shall the United States deploy armed forces abroad other than for engagement in international war—to support a friend in civil war (Angola, 1975), prevent a Communist takeover (Dominican Republic, 1965), or restore order and protect lives (Lebanon, 1975, or pre-World War China)? Shall the United States recognize the People's Republic of China, or resume relations with Castro's Cuba? Conclude a bases agreement with post-Franco Spain, or make other international agreements that are not treaties? Denounce or otherwise terminate treaties or other international agreements? Commit the faith and credit of the United States to give aid of arms or money? Make and settle claims against other countries or receive and settle their claims against the United States? Assert or forgo national jurisdiction to air or sea space? Declare a Monroe Doctrine, or an Open-door Policy in nineteenth-century China, or an Eisenhower Doctrine, or some new Pacific Doctrine?

Lawyers—and members of Congress and of the executive branch—have tried their hand at answering these questions by the traditional methods of constitutional construction and interpretation, by extrapolation and interpolation from and between the lines of the Constitution.[10] The power of Congress to regulate commerce with foreign nations was once held to include authority to control immigration.[11] Congress's power to declare war, it has been asserted, implies power to grant or deny the president authority to deploy the armed forces or to use force even in situations that do not amount to war, if only because they might lead to war. From the president's power to appoint ambassadors (albeit with the advice and consent of the Senate) and his responsibility to receive foreign ambassadors, it has been concluded that the president has authority to recognize governments and determine whether to maintain relations with them. The president's power to make treaties has suggested that he has authority to unmake them, whether by denouncing a treaty pursuant to its terms, or when the international law of treaties permits it, or even in violation of international law.

This process of interpretation, however, has not brought ready or unanimous answers to all issues, for some unlisted powers cannot persuasively be inferred from any provision in the text, while some can be derived from powers allocated to one branch as plausibly as from those vested in the other. For example, shall we infer a presidential authority to break treaties from his power to make them (and require perhaps the advice and consent of the Senate for the former as for the latter)? Or, since breach of treaty might lead to war, does the authority perhaps belong to Congress?[12] Does the power to deploy troops other than to engage in war belong to Congress as an extension of its powers to declare war, raise and support armies, and provide for calling forth the militia, or is it within the president's authority as commander in chief?

Inference from particular clauses, moreover, leaves unanswered larger issues in the separation of powers. Does the Constitution insist that all powers are exclusive with one branch or the other, or were some left for either Congress or the president to exercise?[13] If any power is concurrent, does the first branch to act or the second prevail, or does the Constitution provide some other principle for resolving conflict between them?[14] Does Congress perhaps have final authority to "make policy" on all matters relating to foreign affairs as it has in domestic affairs, with the president committed to see to it that congressional policies, like legislative acts of Congress, are faithfully executed?

Long ago Alexander Hamilton offered us a ready solution to these questions.[15] For him the Constitution was not laconic or delphic; it spoke clearly, in the language of the eighteenth century. There are no missing powers, and there is no mystery as to their distribution between Congress and the president. When the Constitution provided that "the executive Power shall be vested in the President," it gave him, of course, what we ordinarily think of as executive power, the authority and the responsibility to see to it that the laws of Congress are faithfully executed. But it gave him, Hamilton insisted, something else and very different in addition: it vested in the president all that power which was "executive" in the conception of government inherited by the framers from Locke and Montesquieu, including, notably, authority over foreign relations. The framers, then, said Hamilton, intended that the president shall control foreign relations, subject only to particular derogations and modifications which they deemed desirable. Thus, as the executive, the president would have had sole power to make treaties, but the framers imposed the requirement of advice and consent of the Senate. The executive power would have included even authority to declare war, but the framers explicitly gave that to Congress instead. In a word, the control of foreign relations is "executive altogether"[16] except insofar as the Constitution expressly denies or limits the president's power or directs him to share it.

There is, however, a case for a different "power map," as James Madison argued.[17] Our constitutional system began in representative self-government (albeit, in most states, only for freeholders), and it was essentially legislative in character.[18] When the states confederated for common purposes, including the conduct of foreign relations, the "collective" also developed institutions that were legislative in character, indeed without any "executive." Under the Articles of Confederation, drafted early in independence (in 1776-77), it was Congress—"the united states in congress assembled"—that "made foreign policy"; the Congress also appointed ambassadors, gave them their instructions, received their reports, followed their negotiations, approved or rejected their product.

The constitutional framers came to Philadelphia largely agreed that the conduct of international affairs by the quasi-legislature of a confederation of states had not worked well, and the transformation from league of states to nation, and the creation of an executive, responded largely to the needs of foreign relations. But although the fathers were unhappy with diplomacy by Congress, and wanted an executive, there is little evidence that they intended to abandon representative government in foreign relations, and to give plenary independent power to the selected (not elected) president.[19] What evidence there is, it is argued, is rather the other way. Nothing in the Constitution suggests any difference between domestic and foreign affairs. In the Constitution, Congress comes first, for all purposes. The important substantive powers, indeed, the principal substantive powers in foreign affairs—the power to regulate commerce with foreign nations, and to decide for war or peace—were given to Congress. It is arguable, indeed, that the power given to Congress to regulate commerce with foreign nations meant the power to regulate all intercourse with them.[20] Letters of marque and reprisal permitting retaliation for offenses against American nations or vessels—an act of force short of war—could also be issued only under the authority of Congress. It is significant, too, that authority to consent to agreements or compacts and other limited contacts by the states with foreign governments was lodged in Congress, not in the president.[21]

The only substantive power given the president was the power to make treaties. Even that power, taken from Congress (where it had been under the Articles of Confederation) to permit centralized control of negotiations, was to be shared with Congress. The president was required to have the advice and consent of the Senate, which, it seems likely, was not only to approve or disapprove a particular treaty, but was to advise as to whether to make or not to make treaties, with which countries, on what subjects, in which terms—in sum, to have a full participation in determining the important issues of foreign relations.

It is plausible, then, that the fathers intended to move as little as could be from a system of government in which Congress, the representative branch, was all; that in principle, and except as was otherwise expressly provided, Congress was to "legislate," make law or other policy, in foreign as in domestic affairs, and the president was to be the executing agent of congressional policy; the only exception was treaty making, where the president was to be governed by the Senate only, but with an unusual two-thirds majority instead of a majority of the two houses.[22]

Under this view, the Constitution made limited exceptions to congressional power in favor of the president, not—as for Hamilton—specific grants to Congress as exceptions to plenary presidential power. Authority to determine the foreign policy of the United States, then, belongs to Congress except as otherwise provided, and even the conduct of foreign relations is subject to congressional control. Perhaps a president might properly assume congressional consent or acquiescence if he makes minor decisions arising out of the conduct of foreign relations; but surely Congress may direct, regulate, or overrule him.

These two different conceptions of the constitutional blueprint have divided students of the Constitution ever since Hamilton and Madison debated. The differences have been replayed repeatedly in our history, again in the wake of Vietnam, when Senator Fulbright, for example, insisted that Congress makes foreign policy and the president only conducts foreign relations pursuant to that policy.[23]

I do not presume to decide that controversy. The courts–the only authoritative arbiter–have never squarely addressed Hamilton's thesis,[24] and even presidents, increasingly more distant from the pervasive and authoritative influence of Locke and Montesquieu, have alluded to it only gingerly.[25] Hamilton's thesis finds some support in the constitutional text, in that while Congress is given "all legislative Powers herein granted," the president is given "the executive Power"; the framers, then, may well have intended to give the president general, unenumerated "executive powers" including foreign affairs powers.[26] It is not obvious, however, that they intended thereby to include all the authority in foreign affairs that Hamilton's theory might claim, or that they intended the president's authority to be exclusive and final, not subject to direction or control by Congress.[27]

What the Constitution says and what it does not say, in the light of what we know of what our ancestors thought and experienced, suggests that the framers intended a "mixed" system in foreign affairs rather than starkly separated powers,[28] but their exact recipe for the mixture, if indeed, they had one, is impossible to recover.

We do not really know how the fathers thought our foreign relations would be governed. But if the framers did not intend all that Hamilton claimed for the president in foreign affairs, the experience of government has largely given it to him. The growth of presidential authority did not result from any determination by presidents to act on Hamilton's conception, or otherwise to aggrandize their office and its powers. Early presidents, indeed, seemed cautious, and reluctant to claim large authority for themselves or to deny it to Congress. The famous early instance, Washington's Neutrality Proclamation, did not claim presidential authority to the exclusion of Congress, but only the president's right to act pending and subject to congressional action;[29] indeed, it was argued that Washington had to act in order to preserve the situation so as not to prejudice the power of Congress to decide whether or not to go to war. Adams, and surely Jefferson, acted as though they had limited authority, and even that authority was held subject to congressional control.[30] Neither Madison nor Monroe nor their immediate successors claimed any great powers in foreign affairs to the exclusion of Congress.

Presidential power accreted, almost inevitably, from the character of foreign affairs and the president's situation in relation to them. Even in our earliest days, when our international relations and diplomatic missions were few and our diplomacy toddling, the conduct of foreign relations was a continuing process and it threw up issues for decision every day. These came to the president, the "sole organ of communication" with foreign governments, through the ambassadors he had appointed and his secretary of state. Someone had to decide these questions for the United States. The power to decide was not explicitly assigned to Congress, and many of the decisions were ad hoc, not general policy for which formal act or resolution by Congress might suggest itself. Deliberation and action often required secrecy, which might have been beyond even the small Congress of the early years. Sometimes decision was urgent, and much of the time Congress was not in session, could not be quickly called into session, or even readily consulted as to whether it should be called into session. With questions arising daily, moreover, to call Congress into session lightly or frequently would convert Congress into a continuous rather than a sessional body to be convened specially only "on extraordinary occasions."[31] The president, on the other hand, was always in session. He had all the information and could maintain necessary secrecy. He could act quickly. He could improvise and act ad hoc, informally, without exalting every action to the level of an act of state.

Almost against their will, scrupulous, nonself-aggrandizing, nonimperial presidents, began to take actions on behalf of the United States, effectively asserting constitutional authority to do so. At first some members of Congress resented and resisted presidential independence. But the growth of parties and partisan politics soon overwhelmed principle, converting constitutional issues between president and Congress to partisan issues between Federalists and Republicans and their respective successors. Congressmen of the president's party were not likely to condemn but were quick to defend him. Objections from the opposition appeared, or were made to appear, partisan rather than principled. Later the practice of informal consultations with congressional leaders disarmed Congressmen who might have been disposed to constitutional battle, and helped confirm presidential authority to act without formal congressional participation.

Congress contributed to the continuing growth of presidential power, although, perhaps, it could not have prevented it. Congress early recognized and confirmed the president's control of daily foreign intercourse,[32] and the executive monopoly of information which resulted, supported by the accepted diplomatic mores of confidentiality, promoted the president's claims of expertise and Congress's sense of inadequacy. Congress did not organize and inform itself, or acquire expertise, to establish for itself the dominant authority in foreign relations, or even a continuous, informed participation in them. It did not, and was not equipped to, even follow closely what the president was doing. It did not often bestir itself to disown or to dissociate itself from what the president had done, to condemn him for having done it, even to question his authority to do it. Increasingly, indeed, Congress delegated huge parts of its own admitted authority to him. Increasingly Congress turned to domestic matters, leaving foreign affairs to the president, even resisting participation and refusing responsibility.[33] In time the issue became not whether the president had authority to act, but what were the limits on his authority; not whether the president could act when Congress was silent, but, even, whether he could act contrary to the expressed wishes of Congress; whether Congress could direct, control, or supersede his decisions; whether Congress was constitutionally free *not* to implement *his* policies by appropriations or legislation.

Congress, of course, retained its formal constitutional role, and its expressed powers, and the president could not do without it. Congress passed tariffs and other trade laws, declared our few formal wars[34] and authorized other military excursions, appropriated funds, adopted occasional necessary and proper legislation. But the initiative usually came from the president, except, periodically, in international trade, when local interests inspired Congress to impose protective tariffs. The Senate consented to some treaties and appointments and refused consent to or "shelved" others, but the policies were those of the president and his secretary of state. Even when Congress (or the Senate) was constitutionally indispensable, it usually paid summary attention; only infrequently did it participate actively, scrutinize closely, exercise tight control.

Formal acts apart, the president often went his way. Monroe made his declaration, later presidents opened Japan, traded in China, maneuvered and intervened in Latin America, built the imperial presidency. Presidents recognized and refused to recognize governments, sent agents (without Senate participation) instead of ambassadors, concluded executive agreements (without consent of Congress or the Senate), sent troops abroad without congressional authorization, even to fight (as recently as in Korea, 1950), expanded intelligence and "covert activities," acted on the world arena for the United States, making its policies, committing its honor and credit. Presidents, moreover, made policy not only in identifiable, discrete acts, but in the manner in which they conducted foreign relations and in the attitudes they reflected every day in an increasing number of foreign capitals and to a growing number of embassies in Washington. Congress generally confirmed, sometimes nibbled at, infrequently frustrated presidential authority in foreign affairs. Since Congress gave the president almost full rein, the courts followed, accepting presidential "plenary" authority, treating his secrecy and his discretion as sacred, his agreements and declarations as law.[35]

That was the road to Vietnam. Presidents involved the United States in Indo-China originally by small steps, with hardly a glimmer of fear that they might lead into terrible war, and with little congressional participation, interest, or awareness. In time the president invited Congress, and Congress, dependent, without adequate information or deep understanding, gave the president the authorization, the troops, the weapons, and the money he requested. Only when repeated assurances of success repeatedly failed, when allies abandoned and world opinion condemned us, when domestic public opinion became disaffected as never before, did Congress begin to seek a halt, and even then without commanding authority or determination.[36]

The failure of presidential foreign policy in Vietnam, and the embarrassment of the presidency following Watergate, produced proposals for modifying or clarifying the distribution of authority between president and Congress. The remedies proposed were addressed, of course, to what their authors perceived the problem to be. Many saw it as presidential usurpation and nonaccountability, considering periodic elections too infrequent and the threat of impeachment too uncertain to serve as an effective check. Some saw our system as essentially unworkable, surely for the United States of today in the world of today, in that we fragment authority to make foreign policy among president, president-and-Senate, and Congress; leave much foreign policy to the president but authority to go to war to Congress; and separate the making of important policy from control over its execution. Some looked for radical constitutional change; some spoke even of moving to parliamentary government.

Proposals for constitutional amendment have not flourished. Our system for conducting foreign affairs is intricately and inextricably part of our total system of government and could not be modified without transforming the rest. There is no agreement, moreover, on the changes that are needed,[37] and without wide agreement radical change could not be achieved and efforts to bring it about would be deeply divisive. If there were essential agreement, many of the changes could probably be put into effect without formal amendment.

Within Congress the mood has not been for constitutional surgery or tinkering. But, encouraged by the disarray of the presidency (following Watergate, near-impeachment, Nixon's resignation, and the inauguration of a minor political figure who had not been elected to the office and could not wield any popular mandate), Congress began to challenge the special character of foreign affairs and the president's claims to special authority in regard to them; to reassert what many members believed to have been the intention of the fathers, and to recoup powers which Congress had let slip from its fingers. The War Powers Resolution purported to define the constitutional authority of the president to deploy forces for hostilities, and to regulate such deployments even for hostilities short of war.[38] Congress asserted authority over the national budget, and effectively ended presidential claims of authority to impound or divert funds which Congress had directed the president to spend for given purposes.[39] The Case Act demanded that Congress be informed of all executive agreements made by the president on his own authority;[40] and congressional committees have considered legislation to regulate and limit the president's authority to make such agreements. Congress has increased its demands to be informed about foreign affairs, and its challenges to assertions of executive privilege as a basis for denying information to Congress. Congress also reclaimed authority which was indisputably its own but which it had given away. It ended some grants of emergency power and other huge delegations to the president. It turned attention to intelligence and other covert activities abroad, which, though notorious, had been uncontrolled and unattended for decades. It scrutinized and resisted presidential requests for weapons, and for foreign aid in arms and money. It prevented deep United States involvement in Angola. It insisted on a voice in concluding new bases agreements with Spain and Turkey.

I cannot say with confidence—*pace* Alexander Hamilton—that in recent years Congress has claimed more than the fathers gave it and has arrogated to itself authority intended for the president; much of what Congress has done, surely, is constitutional, desirable, even necessary. It is not obvious, however, that what Congress has resolved and legislated reflects the principal lessons of our two hundred years, or provides the machinery for governing foreign affairs which the United States will need for her third century. The uncertainties of distribution of authority will not be resolved by congressional resolutions, in which maximum claims by the president are confronted by maximum claims for Congress. What

Congress has done will help prevent, curtail, discourage, or delay action by the United States; but the interests of the United States do not always lie in not doing. The occasional need for prompt, adequate, and effective action by the United States will not be met if Congress denies the president authority he needs, requires him to sacrifice dispatch, secrecy, flexibility and refinement of policy, to seek formal congressional approval in advance in all cases, engenders presidential hesitation and indecision, and encourages other governments to doubt our purposes, commitments, determination.

Above all, while Congress has acted to enlarge its say in the foreign policy process, it has done little to assure that its part will be independent and effective. Congress cannot conduct foreign relations, or make foreign policy in the small important ways in which it is made from day to day by those who conduct foreign relations; to date, it has not shown itself capable of initiating, planning, and resolving the broad and long outlines of national foreign policy. Congress does have the responsibility and the capacity to legislate and to spend, to consider whether the United States should undertake major hostilities, to participate in concluding major agreements; it can also subject what the president does to attentive oversight. But Congress cannot do what it must itself do, or survey effectively what the president does, as long as the governance of our foreign affairs supports presidential monopoly and congressional exclusion; as long as Congress remains distant from foreign policy planning in place and in time; as long as foreign affairs come to Congress for action only too late, and for oversight only with hindsight, after policies have been developed, initiatives launched, commitments made.

Neither Vietnam nor Watergate has changed the character of foreign affairs, the president's control of them, or Congress's handicaps in participating in them. They have confirmed how important it is that the part which Congress must play—legislation, regulation of trade, authorizing hostilities or approving important agreements, spending for defense, foreign aid, and other general welfare, appropriation, investigation, and oversight—should be meaningful, intelligent, and responsible. That can only be, I believe, if Congress brings itself closer to day-to-day foreign relations, develops adequate sources of information and independent expert advice, organizes itself and makes arrangements for participation in the foreign policy process on a continuing basis—including, perhaps, institutionalized, regular, high-level meetings of representative legislators with the executive branch.

Congress has also to learn and maintain discipline. Even if Congress develops its own sources of information, it will have to depend on information and advice from the executive. Congress is, I believe, constitutionally entitled to obtain from the executive branch such information, in such detail, as it must have to carry out its constitutional powers intelligently. On the other hand, the president has a constitutional privilege to protect the confidentiality and integrity of the executive branch, and a constitutional duty to maintain the confidentiality of military or diplomatic information when the national interest requires it. I do not believe that we are compelled to choose between Congress's constitutional right (or duty) to know and the president's duty (or right) to withhold. Congress has to be seen as part of the foreign policy process, with the same right and need to know as major executive officials. But the need of Congress to know does not necessarily mean that 535 members of Congress must know, when only some authorized committee or subcommittee really needs to know. The need to know some things does not necessarily mean a need to know everything. The need to know substantive matters does not necessarily mean a need to know delicate or titillating details that may jeopardize confidentiality within the executive branch or in diplomatic relations. And, as the constitutional fathers, and Congresses, and the American people have understood ever since we became a nation, the need to know does not necessarily mean the need to make public, when public knowledge is not in the public interest. If Congress organizes itself and disciplines itself to be content with what it needs to know and to maintain necessary confidentiality about it, the claims of executive privilege to withhold from Congress will not prevail.

The constitutional fathers, I believe, intended Congress to have an active part in foreign affairs. It may be that foreign policy cannot be made or foreign relations conducted in our kind of government with true, cooperative participation by president and Congress. We do not know, because it has never been tried. It is worth trying.

The courts have established their role as final arbiter of what our Constitution means and requires. Constitutional uncertainties and controversies about allocation of federal powers between Congress and the president also come into their ken, and powerful presidents and Congresses have bowed to the judicial mandate.[41] To date, however, the courts have not resolved any of the major issues of our foreign policy process.

In part, the reasons are technical. Courts do not advise president or Congress on request. They decide constitutional issues only in actual cases or controversies initiated by parties with authentic personal interests. President and Congress have themselves not been deemed to be proper parties to bring their controversies into court,[42] and in the past, at least, foreign affairs threw up few cases involving private interests. Even cases between parties with standing to raise constitutional issues, and ripe and otherwise appropriate for a court's attention, are sometimes avoided if the constitutional issue is a "political question," as the courts have defined it, and many issues of foreign affairs have been seen as political altogether[43]: the foreign relations of the United States have been seen as exalted, delicate, involving the highest stakes, overriding mere private interests, and requiring secrecy, expertise, discretion, and judgment beyond the capacity of courts to review. The Supreme Court in particular, which can readily avoid most cases because its jurisdiction is very largely discretionary, has refused to hear even "important" foreign affairs cases, recently those arising out of Vietnam.[44]

Judicial deference and abstention in relation to foreign affairs may be beginning to wane somewhat. Courts have established their competence and confidence to resolve delicate political issues generally, including conflict between Congress and the president.[45] The era, beginning in the New Deal, when government could do no wrong and the courts would not hamper its pursuit of the national interest as the political branches saw it, has largely passed. The growing complexity of foreign affairs, and the increasing scope and intensity of transnational relations, have brought foreign policy home to millions of individuals, affecting their interests in ways that readily afford them standing to come to court and encourage courts to hear their complaints. Included in foreign policy now are many attitudes and acts of government that clearly do not partake of those qualities of high national interest, top secrecy, and delicate discretion that led courts to consider them "political" and not justiciable. The willingness of Congress to challenge presidential claims in foreign affairs has doubtless been inviting to the courts also, even to arbitrate political controversies.

The principal occasion for judicial intervention in foreign affairs will probably be provided by the growing willingness of judges to examine the impact of foreign affairs on individual rights. Even during recent decades, when individual rights have flourished and courts have protected them against domestic policies and procedures, the conduct of foreign relations remained largely invulnerable to their claims.[46] When claimants have surmounted obstacles of standing and "political question," the courts have balanced private right against public good, and foreign affairs, with their real or hypothetical relevance to war or peace, to national survival and welfare, have weighed heavily in that balance. Of course, individual lives and fortunes, their autonomy, dignity, and privacy, have bowed in time of war; but even in less stringent and dramatic circumstances, the claims of individual rights have not been heeded because, in the contemporary constitutional idiom, the foreign affairs needs of the nation were a compelling public interest overriding even "fundamental" rights after the strictest scrutiny.[47]

The claims of the individual have been growing and spreading, however, and the constitutional business of the courts is concerned increasingly, almost exclusively, with individual rights.[48] In domestic affairs the courts have been uncovering undreamed-of rights in our "Open Constitution" and giving them unsuspected invulnerability, and they have given to old rights also new protections. Slowly the courts are becoming willing also to look behind claims of national need in foreign relations. Not all foreign policy issues, we now know, raise "political questions" which the courts may not scrutinize. The assumption in the traditional rhetoric that all aspects of foreign affairs are ultimately related to war is surely unreal. Freedom of thought and speech, the right to travel abroad, the indefeasibility of citizenship, the freedom of the press from prior restraint, the right of a civilian to a jury trial, have recently survived limitations rooted in foreign policy considerations.[49] A lower court upheld a claim of Americans to exchange ideas with a foreign subject who had been denied admission under our immigration laws.[50] Some lower courts and some Supreme Court justices were prepared to consider even private complaints that the president was unconstitutionally engaged in war in Vietnam.[51] Will the courts begin to give strict scrutiny and require compelling public interests to justify inhumane deportation laws, and irrational immigration laws generally? to persistent denials of equality to aliens or discrimination among aliens of different nationality? to the taking of property, e.g., the settling of private claims of citizens, by international agreement in the national interest, without just compensation?[52] And if the courts lose their reluctance to scrutinize foreign policy and the conduct of foreign relations for alleged violations of individual rights, might they also feel free to decide the long-troubling issues of separation of powers in foreign affairs?

Foreign affairs have been and will doubtless remain constitutionally "special." But the line between them and domestic affairs has become increasingly uncertain, and the reasons for that line increasingly questionable, as more and more events here as well as abroad acquire transnational character and impact. The blurring of foreign-domestic lines blurs lines of authority between Congress and president that developed in reflection of once-sharp differences in conception, process, and responsibility. It casts doubt too on the special invulnerability and undue weight accorded to "foreign affairs"—rhetorical, undifferentiated—in the balance against individual rights. Whether in regard to the allocation and separation of powers in the federal government, or the balance between private right and public good, many of the traditional implications of special quality attributed to the Constitution and foreign affairs may not long survive.

8 *WALTER F. MURPHY*

THE ART OF CONSTITUTIONAL INTERPRETATION
A Preliminary Showing

For people who grind their daily bread from the flowering of law and politics, the implications of constitutional interpretation are both obvious and immense. A constitution embodies certain fundamental decisions about a society's political goals, processes, and institutions. At minimum, it traces general orbits of authority among public officials and usually also sketches borders beyond which no public official is allowed to travel.

Determining the exact character of such goals, processes, institutions, and boundaries is hardly an easy task, in part because in critical places a constitution is likely to admit of several quite different meanings. The problem, as James Madison noted, is not unique to politics: "When the Almighty himself condescends to address mankind in their own language, his meaning, luminous as it must be, is rendered dim and doubtful by the cloudy medium through which it is communicated."[1] For secular affairs, at least, Madison identified three sources of difficulty: the complexity of the relations to be regulated, the imperfections of human concepts about politics, and the inadequacy of words to convey ideas with precision and accuracy. He might have added two other sources: the frequent necessity for framers of a constitution to compromise competing ideals, values, and interests, and a failure among those framers to think through political problems and carefully rank the objectives and values that they seek to foster.

Because infusing constitutional clauses with definite meaning plays a significant part in shaping the fundamental nature of the polity itself as well as in setting a host of specific public policies, how to interpret a constitution poses crucial political problems. And, because there are many possible avenues to constitutional interpretation, choice is inevitable as well as politically important.

As its title indicates, this paper attempts to analyze the process—the art—of interpreting a constitution. Five general questions are critical here. First, what are the scope and meaning of "the Constitution"? Second, what is the Constitution's relationship, if any, to some higher law? Third, what is the ranking of various values that the Constitution seeks to promote? Fourth, what general approaches to interpretation are legitimate? Should the Constitution be broadly or narrowly interpreted? Which, if any, of its components have a fixed meaning? Which are flexible? Fifth, to what extent is it valid to use such interpretive techniques as intent of the framers, literal application of words, or reliance on previous judicial decisions? I shall concentrate on the first three of these inquiries, without, of course, implying that the others are unimportant.

Several other restrictions need to be clearly stated. First, I focus only on judicial interpretations[2] and also only on the work of the Supreme Court of the United States. Second, I pass over the technical means by which the justices can avoid interpreting the Constitution and start at the point where they have decided to confront constitutional issues. Third, I exclude matters of strategy from analysis, using as an excuse that I have discussed them at length in an earlier work.[3]

This paper also rests on an assumption that, while simple, should be explicitly stated: If a judge wants to persuade others, he or she should write intellectually convincing opinions. To do so, he or she must display not only literary elegance but also internally consistent reasoning that can be explained and justified not only for the decision in a particular case but also in terms of general principles of jurisprudence. This assumption touches on the debate that Herbert Wechsler sired two decades ago by his plea for judicial decisions grounded on neutral principles.[4] To avoid raising those ghosts, I prefer to treat the simple proposition just stated as an assumption and defend it in another work.

Here I would note only a few points. First, giving fair warning of the general principles that guide decisions seems a minimal judicial duty in a polity that claims to follow the rule of law. Such a proposition need not rest on a belief that a judge's jurisprudence should be static. Nor does such an assumption imply a quest for a philosopher's stone that, if rubbed against particular factual matrices, will yield the proper results—or even the same results over time. Finally, any conceivable set of rules or general principles will confer advantages on some interests and disadvantages on others. The question is not whether rules can be neutral,[5] for that is an impossibility; rather, the real questions are who or what will benefit and how. Like the rest of us, judges know that legal arguments, even those based on high and supposedly sacred principles, often are designed only to legitimate appeals to protect the material interests of particular individuals or groups. It is precisely because general principles cannot operate in a neutral fashion that it is important for each judge to work out—or accept—a constitutional jurisprudence and both be aware of and be able to justify its consequences.

THE MEANING AND SCOPE OF "THE CONSTITUTION"

What is the Constitution? The first question facing a judge is: What is it that I must interpret? This question breaks down into several subsidiary queries. Is the Constitution a multilateral contract among sovereign communities or among private citizens? Alternatively, is the Constitution merely an extraordinary statute? Or, again alternatively, is a constitution a charter for government, functioning as a symbol of national unity stating societal goals, restricting and distributing power, establishing procedures to set more specific goals, and creating institutions and processes to determine and enforce duties and rights, costs and benefits, and settle disputes?

Asking subquestions in such a way predetermines the answer in a modern American context. One could make a contract or a statutory theory much more attractive by attaching the same sorts of subqueries.[6]

A charter for government? Responses to these questions—as to most others posed in this paper—could be placed on a continuum ranging from an extreme view of a constitution as an analogue to a contract among private citizens and subject to the relatively narrow rules proper to interpreting such a document, to the somewhat broader notion of special statute,[7] and finally to that of a set of general principles to govern all political—and many social and economic—relations within a polity. Given the popularity of John Marshall's dictum that "we must never forget, that it is a *constitution* we are expounding,"[8] it is a reasonable assumption that in the United States the overwhelming majority of judges would opt for positions on the continuum near that of "a charter for government." But proving the validity of such an assumption would not end analysis. Leaving aside empirical questions about precisely where different judges would place themselves on such a scale, we face a problem of ranking functions. Previous discussion listed several of the many tasks that the notion of "charter for government" implies for a constitution. Questions will inevitably arise about priorities (or "lexical order") among these or similar items. When two or more such functions conflict, which takes precedence? Or to restate this question in a more sophisticated if less clear way, which aspects of each function take precedence over other aspects of that and other functions? Or, are all such functions of equal rank and importance? Section 3 of this paper returns to the general issue of ranking, but it raises its horns in every aspect of constitutional interpretation.

Whatever they have done in the privacy of their own minds, offices, and conferences, in their published opinions[9] the justices have seldom confronted the basic question of the nature of a constitution or tried to establish priorities among its functions. At a lower level of abstraction judges have occasionally, albeit unsystematically, tried to formulate theories regarding the priority of certain rights, such as those of freedom of speech and press,[10] over others. Although those efforts point toward rather than reach the heart of the matter, one can catch glimpses of judges acting on intuitions if not analyses of this basic question. For instance, some judges have translated broader philosophical concepts such as pragmatism into constitutional law and have viewed the U.S. Constitution as a charter for government whose primary task is to establish certain processes to resolve disputes.

Felix Frankfurter, of course, was a classic model of what C. Herman Pritchett has termed the "functionally oriented judge."[11] In one case Frankfurter chided the majority for reaching out to decide an issue which, though substantively important, he did not believe was before the Court: "After all, this is the Nation's ultimate judicial tribunal, not a super-legal-aid bureau."[12] Or again: "This is a court of review, not a tribunal unbounded by rules. We do not sit like a kadi under a tree dispensing justice according to considerations of individual expediency."[13] In these instances, as in those involving constitutionality of compulsory flag salutes,[14] capital punishment,[15] or the Smith Act's ban on promulgating Communist doctrine,[16] the critical questions for Frankfurter were not what he or other judges would have decided had the choice been theirs, but whether popularly elected public officials had followed constitutionally prescribed procedures to arrive at decisions that were not patently unreasonable. More positively, Frankfurter reminded his brethren in 1945 that "the history of American freedom is, in no small measure, the history of procedure."[17]

At the opposite end of the spectrum from Frankfurter, Frank Murphy believed that substantive constitutional rights took precedence over procedures. "The law," he wrote, "knows no finer hour than when it cuts through formal concepts and transitory emotions to protect unpopular citizens against discrimination and persecution."[18]

Constitutionalism and democracy. Any dispute over the priority of constitutional functions inevitably bottoms on the fact that the American constitutional system tries to combine two very different sets of political ideas: *constitutionalism,* with its central values of individual liberty and thus also limited government; and what has grown over the years from restricted popular participation to *democracy*, with its core values of popular (or majority) rule. The tensions here are both obvious and enormous.[19] By definition, limited government means that there are some things that political institutions, even those accurately reflecting deeply felt wishes of a majority of the people, cannot do.

There has been long and heated debate within the Supreme Court over such concepts as "judicial self-restraint" and the peculiar status in a supposed democracy of constitutional review by appointive officials over decisions of elected officials. This debate has been fascinating, but it has largely missed the fundamental problem. At the root have been the tensions between constitutionalism and democracy. These tensions exist because of the success of the framers' bold efforts to establish a hybrid polity. The men at Philadelphia, Madison proudly asserted, had "reared the fabrics of governments which have no model on the face of the globe."[20] What they constructed and what has continued to evolve is not a democracy, but what Alpheus Mason, in the tradition of the generation of the framers, calls "free government."[21]

To label the American polity a democracy may be useful as propaganda in foreign relations or electoral campaigns, but to do so when interpreting the Constitution only intensifies problems. Even as astute an observer as Alexander Bickel fell into this ideological trap when he claimed that "judicial review is a deviant institution in the American democracy."[22] In a democracy judicial review would indeed be deviant. In a constitutional democracy it is a normal—although not a necessary—institution. As a restriction on power it fits in well with federalism's divisions of authority between states and nation, with a Senate in which each state has two votes regardless of population, with staggered elections that make it difficult for a popular majority to gain at one swoop control of the executive branch and both houses of the legislature, with an electoral college that overrepresents the less populous states and interposes itself between presidential candidates and the popular will, and with a backup apparatus of choosing the president by the House of Representatives, with each state, again regardless of population, having one vote. Neither does judicial review appear deviant if one takes seriously Madison's boasting in *The Federalist* that the framers had created an institutional web that could—as surely it often has—effectively thwart the popular will.[23]

My point is not that judges should be incautious about using their power or treat with disrespect decisions of state or other federal officials. Rather, my point is that it does not help and probably hurts whatever progress can be made in the art of constitutional interpretation for judges—or scholars—to pretend that the Constitution is something very different from what it is. Judicial attention should concentrate on the difficulties of preserving a strange and delicate union whose partners disagree on certain fundamentals. In short, judges are more likely to preserve the partnership if they recognize that the tensions are both inevitable and systemic, than if they pretend that the marriage itself does not exist.

What is included in a constitution? Equally basic and closely related to these questions are: Exactly what is the constitution that must be interpreted? Is it, in the widest Aristotelian sense, a way of political life?[24] Or is it merely a specific document or set of documents with various amendments? Or is it a set of documents plus some ideals, understandings, and practices not specifically listed? The U.S. Supreme Court has rarely tried to answer these questions. There are several pieces of dicta in opinions for the Court written by William O. Douglas[25] and Earl Warren[26] that seem to include at least part of the second paragraph of the Declaration of Independence. I believe, however, that Hugo Black's statement that "our Constitution is written in a single document" more accurately reflects the attitude implicit in much of the Court's work.[27]

Yet American practice is hardly consistent with the notion of "the Constitution" as a self-contained unit. The justices have often spoken of such concepts as state police power, "the rule of law," and the presumption of innocence as if they were equal in authority to the specific terms of the document itself. As Justice George Sutherland noted for the Court in 1936: "The powers to declare and wage war, to conclude peace, to make treaties, to maintain diplomatic relations with other sovereignties, if they had never been mentioned in the Constitution, would have vested in the Federal government as necessary concomitants of nationality."[28] Judges have also baptized into the constitutional communion certain practices, judicial review itself being the most glorious example. The *Watergate Tapes* case presented many ironies, not least of which was that Chief Justice Warren E. Burger, nominated by Nixon as a "strict constructionist," invoked judicial review, a doctrine not explicitly in the Constitution, to limit executive privilege, also absent from the Constitution's language.[29] Thus, an alleged strict constructionist decided, as he had to, a great case in constitutional law largely outside the confines of the constitutional document.

A careful reading of the formal basic law of any constitutional democracy leads to the conclusion that only the most crabbed judicial mind could honestly restrict "the constitution" to a single document. In this respect, Black was being unfair to himself. He did explicitly accept the legitimacy of judicial review, and I doubt if any judge would have rejected more angrily than he an argument that the Constitution did not include the rule of law or a presumption of innocence. Thus, like most, if not all, American judges, he accepted certain concepts and practices as part of the Constitution. What Black did not do, just as no other American judge has done, is to explain systematically which practices and concepts he read into the Constitution and to justify those choices.

The spirit v. the flesh. Occasionally judges have tried to define the reach of the U.S. Constitution by divining its spirit. In *Chisholm v. Georgia* (1793), for instance, Justice James Wilson spoke of "the *general texture* of the Constitution" as a secondary justification for national supremacy.[30]

Fiery old Samuel Chase leaped at the opportunity presented by *Calder v. Bull* (1798) to define the spirit and fundamental principles of the Constitution:

> I cannot subscribe to the *omnipotence* of a State Legislature, or that it is absolute and without controul; although its authority should not be expressly restrained by the Constitution, or fundamental laws of the State. The people of the United States erected their Constitution . . . to establish justice, to promote the general welfare, to secure the blessings of liberty; and to protect their persons and property from violence. . . . There are acts which the Federal, or State, Legislature cannot do. . . . It is against all reason and justice to entrust a Legislature with SUCH [despotic] powers; and therefore, it cannot be presumed that they have done it. The genius, the nature, and the spirit of our State Governments, amount to a prohibition of such [unlimited] acts of legislation; and the general principles of law and reason forbid them.[31]

Twenty-three years later, in *Cohens v. Virginia,* John Marshall asked rhetorically whether "the spirit of the constitution" would justify Virginia's exempting itself from Federal jurisdiction.[32] In *McCulloch v. Maryland,* when the chief justice laid down his great test for the legitimacy of congressional action under the "sweeping clause" of Article I, section 8, he said: "Let the end be legitimate, let it be within the scope of the constitution, and all means which are appropriate, which are plainly adapted to that end, which are not prohibited, but consistent with the letter and *spirit* of the constitution, are constitutional"[33] (italics supplied).

At times the spirit did not move Marshall. In *Sturges v. Crowninshield* the defendant had argued that, despite the constitutional clause forbidding a state to impair the obligation of contracts, the spirit of the Constitution allowed a state to pass an insolvency statute affecting debts contracted before the statute was enacted. Speaking for an apparently unanimous Court, the chief justice[34] conceded that "the spirit of an instrument, especially a constitution, is to be respected not less than its letter," but added that "the spirit is to be collected chiefly from its words." And in this particular case Marshall thought that the words of the contract clause specifically prohibited the sort of state statute under review.

In the *First Legal Tender* case Chief Justice Salmon Chase's opinion for the Court devoted three pages to the spirit of the Constitution and concluded that Congress's requiring paper money to be accepted as legal tender in payment of private debts contracted before enactment of the statute violated both the spirit of the Fifth Amendment and the ban in Article I on impairing obligations of contracts. Chase freely conceded that the latter clause specifically bound only the states. But, he added:

> We think it clear that those who framed and those who adopted the Constitution, intended that the spirit of this prohibition should pervade the entire body of legislation. . . . We cannot doubt that a law not made in pursuance of an express power, which necessarily and in its direct operation impairs the obligation of contracts, is inconsistent with the spirit of the constitution.[35]

Justice Strong's opinion for the Court in the *Second Legal Tender* cases[36] took up, point by point, the chief justice's assertions regarding the implications of the spirit of the Constitution, and after four pages of reasoning rejected them all. Strong did not, however, question the propriety of appealing to the Constitution's spirit.

Perhaps the most striking–although silent–American appeal to the Constitution's spirit of limited government came in the cases that culminated in *Ex parte Young* (1908).[37] There the justices performed a monumental act of prestidigitation to hold that, despite the Eleventh Amendment's apparent removal of federal jurisdiction to hear suits by private citizens against state governments, federal courts could enjoin state officers from enforcing a statute. Instead of reasoning directly that the Fourteenth Amendment had modified the Eleventh, the justices circled their logic around the problem. On the one hand, they held that in such suits federal courts could obtain jurisdiction under congressional statutes carrying out the Fourteenth Amendment's prohibition against certain kinds of state action. On the other hand, the justices said that such suits were not directed against a state in the Eleventh Amendment's sense because a state lacked authority to confer immunity on an official to violate the federal Constitution.

Like the Lord, the justices had both given and taken away the mantle of state action. The most that bewildered state officials could obtain was passage, two years later, of a congressional statute requiring a special district court of three judges to hear a suit to enjoin enforcement of a state statute. "Logic," Justice Douglas later explained, "cannot justify the rule of *Ex parte Young*. . . . *Ex parte Young* and its offspring do, however, reflect perhaps an even higher policy: the belief that courts must be allowed in the interests of justice to police unruly, lawless government officials who seek to impose oppressive laws on the citizen."[38]

In each of these cases except *Sturges,* the justices begged the question whether it was proper to look at the spirit of the Constitution and ignored the problem of how to discover that spirit. In more recent decisions the justices have tended to deny requests to seek constitutional shades,[39] but as section 2 will show, the quest continues. Nevertheless, American constitutional law still lacks any penetrating judicial analysis of the legitimacy or even the problems of finding, using, or not using the spirit of the Constitution.

THE CONSTITUTION AND THE HIGHER LAW

An issue closely connected to the nature of a constitution involves the relationship, if any, of a constitution to higher law—either international law[40] or one or another of those clusters of precepts that exist under such rubrics as natural law and natural rights. For lack of space, I limit discussion here to the second category.

A constitution, such as that of Eire,[41] may explicitly say a great deal about its relations to transcendent moral standards, but the plain words of the American Constitution contain only enough to tickle the imagination. On the one hand, the Constitution proclaims itself "the supreme law of the land." On the other hand, references in the preamble to terms such as "liberty" and more especially "justice" were not likely to have been meaningless to educated people during the Enlightenment, when natural law and natural rights were commonplace concepts.

Yet the possibility that the Constitution might be permeated with notions of natural law and right often comes as a surprise to contemporary judges and even scholars. Perhaps the positivistic biases of early sociological jurisprudence and even more so of legal realism are to blame. Despite the ridicule that they heaped on most aspects of John Austin's jurisprudence, the realists seldom attacked the basic propositions that underlay legal positivism's rejection of natural law and rights. While scorning such concepts as sovereignty, they generally accepted the thesis that law was what judges and other public officials actually enforced. The realists seldom made creative efforts to weave judges'—or their own—ideas about right and justice into theories about law.[42]

Part of the reason for this lack of interest probably lay in most realists' acceptance of the fact-value dichotomy that has beset modern social science. There may have also been more personal causes. Oliver Wendell Holmes, who functioned as the spiritual godfather–and waspish don–of both realism and sociological jurisprudence, was passionate in his hatred of the word "justice."[43] While that emotion was to some degree a reaction against careless legal argument, it was also a product of a skepticism that bordered on cynicism. Like a good Austinian, Holmes could advocate the "bad man" theory of law and declare that "the prophecies of what the courts will do in fact, and nothing more pretentious, are what I mean by the law."[44]

Positivism, however, has not been the invariable rule of American law, either past or present. Coke's jurisprudence had been studded with references to natural law, "which God at the time of creating the nature of man infused into his heart," as an essential part of all law.[45] His famous dictum in *Bonham's* case stated that "when an act of parliament is against common right and reason, or repugnant, or impossible to be performed, the common law will controul it and adjudge such an act to be void."[46] He strengthened this assertion insofar as natural law was concerned when he wrote in *Calvin's* case "that the law of nature was before any judicial or municipal law in the world . . . is immutable, and cannot be changed."[47]

Whether or not Coke actually gave the reported judgment in *Bonham's* case is less important than that his claim was widely accepted in America. Indeed, Coke's teachings were generally as influential in the colonies as in England, if not more so. Jefferson said that "Coke's Lyttleton was the universal lawbook of students. . . ."[48]

Later Blackstone's *Commentaries* rivaled Coke's popularity, to the extent that the *Commentaries* could be called the "handbook of the American revolutionary."[49] And Blackstone, too, espoused a doctrine of natural law, although close examination shows that either he did not fully understand or he did not believe what he was saying, since at places he asserted that positive law is the ultimate criterion of legal right and wrong. Still, he could piously proclaim that natural law was "coeval with mankind," authored by the Almighty, "superior in obligation to any other . . . no human laws are of any validity if contrary to this, and such of them as are valid derive their force and all their authority, mediately or immediately, from this origin."[50] As Benjamin F. Wright noted, "Americans simply took over those passages and ideas that suited their needs and ignored the remainder."[51]

Thus, through Coke and Blackstone most American lawyers in the eighteenth century–when formal legal training was often confined to reading one or both authors–were fully exposed to the idea that standards of natural law formed an integral part of the actual legal system. Better educated members of the bar were also aware of similar, more philosophic arguments by Grotius, Vattel, Pufendorf, and the now wisely forgotten Burlamaqui. A few attorneys may even have been acquainted with Catholic writers like Suarez and Vitoria. And in New England a number of publicists developed natural law theories from Protestant theology.[52]

Probably the single most important influence, other than that of Coke and Blackstone, was John Locke. While the natural law doctrines of the medieval schoolmen and later Coke had concentrated on concepts such as justice and obligation, Locke stressed rights of individuals. This difference of focus has a number of important consequences for politics and ethics,[53] but as far as the notion of limited government is concerned, the two strands reinforce each other. Under Locke's doctrine men in the state of nature had enjoyed certain inherent rights; and it was to protect these that they formed society and later accepted government. When they entered civil society, men did not surrender their rights, only the authority to enforce them. Obviously, government could not legitimately violate that which it had been established to foster and protect.

Concepts of universal law and rights justified by natural reason reinforced the rationalistic faith that the publicists of the American Revolution and later the framers of the Constitution shared with their European colleagues during the Enlightenment. The Declaration of Independence, John Adams claimed, and Jefferson conceded, contained nothing that "had not been hackneyed in Congress for two years before."[54] There was consensus among the Revolution's leaders that certain rights were not only "unalienable" but also existed before government. It was not the function of government to *confer* such rights but to *secure* them. As Jefferson repeated in 1816:

> Our legislators are not sufficiently apprised of the rightful limits of their power; that their true office is to declare and enforce only our natural rights and duties, and to take none of them from us. . . . When the laws have declared and enforced all this, they have fulfilled their functions; and the idea is quite unfounded that on entering into society we give up any natural right.[55]

The framers of the Constitution may have become less egalitarian than Jefferson or than they themselves had been a decade or so earlier,[56] but they remained children of the Enlightenment with faith in reason,[57] nature, and the universal sanctity of certain rights. Indeed, the Bill of
viewed as an attempt to protect some "natural" rights
n historic rights under the common law. This sort of
oth the preamble's reference to justice and the Ninth
eep more understandable.
eral acceptance of natural law and rights, it would be

expected that many early judges would use these notions. And the treatises of Kent[58] and Story[59] show some such influences. So, too, did many official opinions of Supreme Court justices. Charles G. Haines went so far as to contend that, without application of restrictions on government that flowed from doctrines of natural law, judicial review "would have had relatively slight influence on American government and politics. . . ."[60] What happened was a judicial reading of natural rights into "the spirit" of the Constitution. For example, in 1795 Justice Paterson, on circuit, could assert that "the right of acquiring and possessing property, and having it protected, is one of the natural, inherent, and unalienable rights of man."[61] For a state to take property without compensation was "inconsistent with the principles of reason, justice, and moral rectitude. . . ." Section 1 quoted at length from Samuel Chase's opinion in *Calder v. Bull* regarding the "general principles and reason" that the spirit of the Constitution imposed on the states.

Although in his official opinions John Marshall made few references to natural law and rights, he both believed in the validity of those ideas and was willing to apply them in constitutional adjudication. His reasoning in *Fletcher v. Peck,* for instance, is only partially grounded in the contract clause of the Constitution. There, after Georgia revoked a huge land grant that speculators had fraudulently obtained from an earlier legislature, people who had bought land from the speculators brought suit. Marshall opened the opinion of the Court with a discussion of "certain great principles of justice, whose authority is universally acknowledged" to restrict legislative power. After examining these principles, the chief justice wrote that "the validity of the rescinding act, then, might well be doubted, were Georgia a single sovereign power."[62] Only after three pages of discussion of "these great principles of justice" did Marshall analyze the contract clause of the Constitution. Near the close of his reasoning he returned to the "great principles of justice" and made it clear that the Court's decision rested on alternative grounds: "The state of Georgia was restrained, either by general principles which are common to our free institutions, or by the particular provisions of the constitution of the United States, from passing a law whereby the estate of the plaintiff . . . could be constitutionally and legally impaired and rendered null and void."[63]

In a separate opinion Justice William Johnson based his conclusion on one argument: "I do not hesitate to declare that a state does not possess the power of revoking its own grants. But I do it on a general principle, on the reason and nature of things: a principle which will impose laws even on the deity."[64]

Seventeen years later Marshall again coupled natural rights with a positivistic argument. Protesting the Court's sustaining a state statute that he thought impaired the obligation of contracts, the chief justice said: "Individuals do not derive from government their right to contract, but bring that right with them into society.... This results from the right which every man retains to acquire property, to dispose of that property according to his own judgment, and to pledge himself for a future act. These rights are not given by society; but are brought into it."[65]

Slavery and natural rights. Slavery challenged and until 1865 defeated the jurisprudence of natural law and rights. Before the Civil War most American judges, even such strong-willed opponents of slavery as John MacClean, Joseph Story, and Lemuel Shaw, enforced fugitive slave laws.[66] Other judges, such as those in Wisconsin, refused.[67] Many jurists who went along agreed that slavery violated natural law and natural rights, but they chose to follow the Constitution's compromise, what the abolitionists called "a covenant with death, and agreement with hell." These judges did so even though the Constitution itself imposed no specific obligation on the federal government to assist in recapturing fugitives.[68]

In the *Antelope* case (1825) Marshall faced the problem of resolving his own acceptance of natural rights with the claims of Spanish and Portuguese slave traders. Their slaves had first been taken from them by privateers, who themselves were later captured by an American naval vessel. At that point the original "owners" sued to regain their "property." Speaking of the slave trade, the chief justice said:

> That it is contrary to the law of nature will scarcely be denied. That every man has a natural right to the fruits of his own labor, is generally admitted; and [that] no other person can rightfully deprive him of those fruits, and appropriate them against his will, seems to be the necessary result of this admission....
>
> Whatever might be the answer of a moralist to this question, a jurist must search for its legal solution, in those principles of action which are sanctioned by the usages, the national acts, and the general assent, of that portion of the world of which he considers himself as a part, and to whose law the appeal is made. If we resort to this standard as the test of international law, the question . . . is decided in favor of the legality of the [slave] trade.[69]

Marshall's final solution, however, was to place the burden of proving ownership on the claimants and to order the return of only some of the slaves.

The chief justice's sense of what was politically good for national unity obviously took precedence over other values. No one who has read many of his other opinions could doubt that, had he deemed it expedient, he would have quickly disposed of the slavers' claims—as, in fact, Joseph Story had done in a similar case[70] and, more generally, as Salmon P. Chase later did.[71]

The new dispensation. Both before and after the slave cases American judges frequently applied a jurisprudence of natural rights. Later the framers of the Thirteenth Amendment made it clear that their objective was to return to blacks "the sacred rights of human nature," "natural and God-given rights," by applying "that self-evident truth 'that all men . . . are endowed by their Creator with certain unalienable rights.'"[72] The framers of the amendment, tenBroek[73] says, "combined and recombined" two major ideas: "first, the Lockean presuppositions about natural rights and the protective function of government; second, slavery's denial of these rights and this protection not only to blacks, bond and free, but to whites as well." After the war Chase, now chief justice, could proclaim the "fundamental principles of morality and justice which no legislature is at liberty to disregard,"[74] while Justices Joseph Bradley, Stephen Field,[75] and even on occasion Samuel Miller[76] grandiloquently incorporated traditional Lockean language about natural rights into the Constitution.

In 1910 Justice John Marshall Harlan I candidly conceded that "courts have rarely, if ever, felt themselves so restrained by technical rules that they could not find some remedy, consistent with the law, for acts, whether done by government or by individual persons, that violated natural justice or were hostile to the fundamental principles devised for the protection of the essential rights of property."[77] Nevertheless, by the end of the nineteenth century "due process of law" had pretty much taken over the functions that natural law and rights had performed in protecting property for earlier generations. As Wright put it in 1931, near the apogee of laissez-faire: "The ancient concept of a supreme law of nature lives on in the constitutional theory of American courts." He agreed that contemporary judges were carrying protection of property to extreme lengths, but added that there could be no doubt that those judges "are holding steadfastly to the tradition of the founding fathers, and are adhering to the theories expounded by Wilson, Paterson, Chase, Marshall, Story, Kent, Cooley, and other makers of American constitutional law. . . . Due process today means very much what earlier jurists understood by the various phrases used to express the concept of natural law."[78]

It is only fair to add, however, that social Darwinism was fundamentally at war with the concepts of human dignity, mutual obligation, and social justice that formed the nucleus of traditional doctrines of natural law.[79] Furthermore, exclusive judicial concern with the natural right to property perverted the notion of a wide range of natural rights.

While the problem of the proper role of natural law and rights in constitutional interpretation lives on, judicial debate has not greatly helped clarify the issues. On several occasions Hugo Black accused Felix Frankfurter of trying to read natural law into the Constitution, most notably in *Adamson v. California.*[80] Black's fundamental purposes were to foster individual liberty in the political sphere and to allow legislators to set economic policies. The history of the old Court had led him to believe that accomplishment of these ends required curbing judicial discretion and literally applying the Constitution's commands. These concerns may have led him to mislabel Frankfurter's heresy.

In *Adamson* and elsewhere[81] Frankfurter defended himself by claiming that reliance on "civilized standards" did not free judges to write their personal notions of justice into constitutional law. Moreover, he never advocated using natural law or rights to interpret the Constitution. As a venerator of Holmes, Frankfurter may have been as emotionally opposed to these concepts as was Black. And, insofar as "civilized standards" refer to positive rules applied by judges and/or legislators in various jurisdictions, they hardly fit the classic mold of transcendental standards. Nevertheless, one of Frankfurter's closest analysts[82] concluded that he "cannot be dissociated from a variant natural law position in that he thinks due process of law approximates the enduring values of human existence, or, at least, human existence in the Anglo-American world."

In any event, neither Black nor Frankfurter faced up to the question whether, in light of the "plain words" of the preamble and the Ninth Amendment and the frequently expressed beliefs of the Constitution's framers, such considerations were legitimate. This omission is especially strange in Black's case, since in Adamson he quoted with approval from an opinion by Justice Miller: "It is never to be forgotten that in the construction of the language of the Constitution . . . we are to place ourselves as nearly as possible in the condition of the men who framed that instrument."[83] And two years earlier, Black had thought it appropriate to seek the First Amendment's meaning by reviewing "the background and environment of the period in which that constitutional language was fashioned and adopted."[84]

Other opportunities for analysis and debate suffered a similar fate. In 1946 Justice Frank Murphy reacted angrily to what he saw as basically unfair trials of accused Japanese war criminals:

> The immutable rights of the individual . . . belong not alone to the members of those nations that excel on the battlefield or that subscribe to the democratic ideology. They belong to every person in the world, victor or vanquished, whatever may be his race, color or beliefs. They rise above any status of belligerency or outlawry. They survive any popular passion or frenzy of the moment. No court or legislature or executive, not even the mightiest army in the world, can ever destroy them.[85]

But like a shrewd lawyer who finds himself in a positivistic environment, Murphy also anchored the "immutable rights of the individual" in the due process clause of the Fifth Amendment, not alone in general principles of natural law and right.[86] Unhappily, the majority simply ignored him, and he himself did not explore the jurisprudential implications of his eloquent libertarianism.

Murphy, however, was not yet done. Black's fears in *Adamson* of a rejuvenation of natural law had been triggered by the Court's reaffirming that the Fourteenth Amendment incorporated and so made binding on the states only those "more fundamental" freedoms listed in the Bill of Rights, those that Cardozo had earlier described as "implicit in the concept of ordered liberty." Consistent with his goal of protecting individual liberty by restricting judicial discretion, Black argued that the Fourteenth Amendment incorporated each of the first eight amendments. While conceding that Black came nearer the true meaning than did the majority, Murphy wanted to go further: "I agree that the specific guarantees of the Bill of Rights should be carried over into the first section of the Fourteenth Amendment. But I am not prepared to say that the latter is entirely and necessarily limited by the Bill of Rights."[87]

Wiley Rutledge joined in Murphy's dissent, and in private Murphy and Black discussed their differences[88]—which Black, apparently missing the opening for natural law and rights that Murphy had created, insisted were minimal. Publicly, however, there was no debate about the implications of Murphy's argument.

William O. Douglas joined Black's rather than Murphy's dissent. Earlier, in 1942, Douglas had written the opinion of the Court invalidating Oklahoma's criminal sterilization act. "We are dealing here," he had said, "with legislation which involves one of the basic civil rights of man."[89] On the other hand, his joining with Black in *Adamson* and elsewhere[90] seemed to place him firmly among the positivists. In 1954, however, he noted in *An Almanac of Liberty:* "In our scheme of things, the rights of man are unalienable. They come from the Creator, not from a president, a legislator, or a court."[91] "Man," he reiterated in 1958, "is a child of God entitled to dignified treatment."[92] In 1963 he repeated and strengthened these statements: "Men do not acquire rights from the government; one man does not give another certain rights. Man gets his rights from the Creator. They come to him because of the divine spark in every human being."[93]

In 1961, amid these assertions of traditional natural right, Douglas dissented from the Court's refusal to decide the constitutionality of Connecticut's anti-birth-control legislation. There he publicly acknowledged his agreement with Murphy in *Adamson:* "Though I believe that 'due process' as used in the Fourteenth Amendment includes all of the first eight amendments, I do not think it is restricted and confined to them."[94] In a later footnote Douglas quoted approvingly from a lecture by Justice Owen Roberts that the due process clause "guarantees basic rights, not because they have become petrified as of any one time, but because due process follows the advancing standards of a free society as to what is deemed reasonable and right."[95]

Four years later, in the *Griswold* case,[96] all the justices finally faced up to the constitutional problem of Connecticut's anti-birth-control law. It was then that Douglas, now speaking for the Court, found a broad right to privacy in penumbras of various clauses of the Bill of Rights—the First Amendment's protection of a right to associate, the Third's ban against quartering troops in civilian homes in time of peace, the Fourth's prohibition of "unreasonable searches and seizures," the Fifth's bulwark against self-incrimination, and the Ninth Amendment's catch-all language.

Black, of course, thundered against this revival of "natural law due process philosophy." Quoting at length from his dissent in *Adamson,* he claimed that "adoption of such a loose, flexible, uncontrolled standard . . . will amount to a great unconstitutional shift of power to the courts which I believe and am constrained to say will be bad for the courts and worse for the country."[97]

Although Black was more concerned about the defection of his usual allies, Harlan's concurring opinion was even more pregnant than Douglas's with arguments from natural law and rights:

> In my view, the proper constitutional inquiry in this case is whether this Connecticut statute infringes the Due Process Clause of the Fourteenth Amendment because the enactment violates basic values "implicit in the concept of ordered liberty." . . . While the relevant inquiry may be aided by resort to one or more of the Bill of Rights, it is not dependent on them or on any of their radiations.[98]

Several times Harlan reiterated the views he had expressed in his dissent in *Poe v. Ullman.* There he had relied in part on Justice Bushrod Washington's opinion in *Corfield v. Coryell*[99] (1823) regarding those rights "which are . . . fundamental; which . . . belong . . . to the citizens of all free governments," and on the Lockean opinion of Samuel Chase in *Calder v. Bull* (quoted above) regarding those rights for "the purpose [of securing] which men enter into society."[100]

One can also trace the spoor of natural law and rights to opinions by Earl Warren,[101] William J. Brennan,[102] and Potter Stewart.[103] The point of this discussion, however, is not to track the lion of natural law to his lair, but to note that he still on occasion roars and that judges need to acknowledge his existence. They need not, of course, accept his claim to rule; but they cannot, if they hope to create an intellectually defensible jurisprudence, deny his potential importance. Section 4 returns to these doctrines of universal justice and immutable rights.

ORDERING VALUES

Probably the most difficult intellectual and practical task a judge faces in interpreting a constitution is ranking the importance of its functions and the values that it tries to protect. Section 1 mentioned some of the difficulties in assigning priorities to a constitution's functions. This section will focus on ordering the values that a constitution is supposed to safeguard.

The problem. At the root of the problem is that the American Constitution–like all such charters–tries to foster not one or two but a whole cluster of values. If we take seriously, as the modern Supreme Court has not, the Constitution's own listing, these include: a more perfect union, justice, domestic tranquility, the common defense, general welfare, and liberty. These are difficult enough to attain singly; mutual achievement, or even accommodation, poses a Herculean task. Liberty, for instance, must include the right to advocate change and so to jeopardize stability if not tranquility. The Nisei can testify from bitter experience that what clamoring officials call the common defense can rape justice as brutally as it can liberty.[104] Certainly, the Cold War hysterics of Joseph McCarthy and the colder, more systematic thuggery of Richard Nixon, J. Edgar Hoover, and their minions[105] prove Justice Jackson's claim that "security is like liberty, in that many are the crimes committed in its name."[106]

In the real world, where justice and the general welfare lie depends in large part on decision makers' objectives. Those who see "true" liberty as dependent on the existing social order are likely to be tolerant of governmental restrictions on individual rights. On the other hand, those who view government's primary obligation as protecting liberty are more likely to be suspicious of restrictions. Those who believe the real function of the polity is to establish virtue[107] rather than freedom or order—the good society rather than either the free or the tranquil society—are likely to pursue an eclectic course, although more probably coming down on the side of restrictions on individual liberty when people display their well-known penchant for sinning. Each of these approaches threatens the viability of constitutional democracy. "It is a melancholy reflection," Madison lamented to Jefferson, "that liberty should be equally exposed to danger whether the Government have too much or too little power and that the line that divides these extremes should be so inaccurately defined by experience."[108]

Judges must arrange constitutional values in hierarchical order because the cases that they receive typically involve, as Frankfurter put it, "the clash of rights, not the clash of wrongs."[109] Only rarely does a case present clear-cut choices between constitutional virtue and unconstitutional vice. Rather, the usual constitutional case involves a clash between the authority of state and federal officials, between overlapping or vague grants of power to the presidency and Congress, the right of a private citizen to argue that the system should be overthrown against the authority of government to protect domestic tranquility, or the right of one citizen to speak his mind against the right of another to a decent reputation.

Equality of values. A simple solution to this sort of problem would be to treat all constitutional clauses as equal. What has just been said in this section, however, creates a strong temptation to label such a solution as simple-minded. But at times intellects as powerful as those of Felix Frankfurter and Robert H. Jackson have suggested equality of constitutional provisions. "We cannot give some constitutional rights a preferred position without relegating others to a deferred position," Jackson wrote in 1949: "we can establish no first without thereby establishing seconds."[110] Although early in his judicial career Frankfurter said in private that he accepted Stone's distinctions among constitutional values,[111] he later wrote for the Court: "As no constitutional guarantee enjoys preference, so none should suffer subordination or deletion."[112] And on another occasion he referred to the theory of preferred freedoms as "a mischievous phrase."[113]

A judge could intelligently rank two constitutional values as so nearly equal in importance as to preclude choice, as Chief Justice Burger did in the *Nebraska Press* case, when he claimed to refuse to choose between free press and fair trial.[114] But there is great intuitive difficulty in according equal dignity and importance to all constitutional guarantees, for example, on the one hand, the Seventh Amendment's protection of a right to a jury trial in all civil cases where the amount in dispute exceeds twenty dollars and, on the other hand, the First Amendment's guarantee of free exercise of religion. Moreover, equal ranking of constitutional values flies directly in the face of Cardozo's doctrine—which Frankfurter continually defended as his own—that only some portions of the Bill of Rights were "so rooted in the traditions and consciousness of our people as to be ranked as fundamental" and to form "the matrix, the indispensable condition of nearly every other freedom."[115] If only some rights are fundamental, then, logically, other rights must be less than fundamental.

What saves the Frankfurter-Jackson solution from being simple-minded is Frankfurter's, and later Jackson's, insistence that judges were not the primary resolvers of political conflict. Although Frankfurter could not resist intervening when he saw a threat to a value that he especially cherished, such as academic freedom,[116] he persistently preached that the judicial function in interpreting the Constitution was largely complete when the judge found that the legislative choice among competing values had not been unreasonable. The Court should always sustain a legislative decision unless it had been "outside the pale of fair judgment."[117] To support this sort of judicial deference or self-restraint, one can add the old rule that courts will presume a statute constitutional. The challenger must carry the burden of proof of legislative irrationality.

I would argue that a judge cannot intelligently accept the notion that all constitutional clauses are of equal importance without both accepting the propriety of Frankfurter's limited scope for judicial review and at the same time believing that judges can consistently practice such restraint. Given Frankfurter's patterns of behavior off as well as on the bench,[118] the second condition may erect greater barriers than the first. At any rate, accepting equal importance and an austere function disposes of none of the problems of constitutional interpretation; such an acceptance merely pushes the burdens off on other officials.

Plain words. Black's alternative to ranking constitutional values was to use the plain words of the Constitution as the prime if not sole criterion for judgment.[119] Thus, judges should give preference to those rights phrased in absolute terms over those phrased in qualified terms. The shortcomings of such an approach are as serious as they are evident. Some, indeed most, constitutional grants of authority to government are as unqualified as those of many constitutional prohibitions. Congress's power to regulate commerce is no less absolute than the First Amendment's protection of speech, press, or religion. Intuitively, it is hard to accept an argument that congressional control over commerce should override protection against invasions of private homes because the authority of Congress is unqualified and the protection against searches and seizures is limited by the word "unreasonable."

Accepting the argument that all grants of power are limited by the Bill of Rights removes only some difficulties, for the simple reason that application of certain provisions of the Bill of Rights may, on occasion, conflict with other provisions of the first ten amendments. To illustrate the point, one need only refer to the potential clash between free press and fair trial by "an impartial jury" that looms whenever a newspaper prints lurid information regarding a criminally accused person. Chief Justice Burger's refusal to rank the two values[120] does not lessen their potential conflict.

Reliance on the Constitution's plain words also raises grave linguistic difficulties. Language changes over time, and those changes may have significant consequences for American constitutional interpretation since that document was drafted almost two centuries ago, when rules of grammar and syntax as well as meanings of specific words were quite different from today's. W. W. Crosskey spelled out in great detail what many terms in the Constitution meant in eighteenth century usage,[121] and his conclusions, such as those regarding the meaning of "among" in the commerce clause, contradict much of our modern understanding of the polity. Thus, to allow the plain words of the Constitution to settle a controversy, judges must either become linguistic historians or adopt some version of the doctrine that the Constitution's meaning changes over time. While the latter alternative may be appealing, its acceptance vitiates any claim that the plain words of the Constitution, rather than judges' translations of those words, govern.

In sum, the exact wording of the Constitution provides the obvious starting point for constitutional interpretation. Even mechanical resort to language can reduce some of the competition among values enshrined in various clauses. But the plain words themselves cannot eliminate a large share of that competition for the simple reason that those words are the proximate causes of many of those problems.

Unamendable constitutional provisions. As a step toward deducing a hierarchy of constitutionally protected values, a judge might look at those provisions that are exempt from amendment. The Basic Law of West Germany, for instance, stipulates that a number of provisions regarding federalism, popular sovereignty, "the dignity of man," and the ultimate right of revolution shall not be altered.[122] These prohibitions have far-reaching consequences and form one source of the Federal Constitutional

Court's claim of authority to declare constitutional clauses unconstitutional.[123] In contrast, only one section of the American Constitution is explicitly unamendable, that establishing equal representation for states in the Senate. And even that provision could conceivably be changed because its own terms allow alteration by unanimous consent of the states.

One might argue, however, that American constitutional development has also made the First Amendment unamendable, at least to the extent of restricting its guarantees. The reasoning would proceed along the following lines:

1. Incorporation of the First Amendment into the Fourteenth means that the operative constitutional provision effectively reads: "Neither Congress nor the states, singly or together, can make a law abridging" freedom of speech, press, assembly, or religion.
2. Constitutional amendments are law;
3. Therefore it is outside the scope of state and federal legislative power to amend the Constitution to restrict the First Amendment's protections.

Such an argument is hardly fanciful. The Supreme Court of India used almost precisely this reasoning to strike down a duly approved constitutional amendment to that country's bill of rights.[124]

In any event, while federalism and the freedoms explicitly included in the First Amendment are certainly among the fundamental principles of the American constitutional system–and as such, it can be cogently argued, deserve special judicial protection–they do not exhaust that category. Thus, however useful in West Germany or in India before Mrs. Gandhi's coup, dependence on unamendable clauses only starts the search for a hierarchy of values in the American system.

Preferred freedoms. The most notable effort in recent decades to rank constitutional values was the doctrine of so-called preferred freedoms. First enunciated by Harlan Fiske Stone in a footnote to his *Carolene Products* opinion,[125] and developed–although never systematically–in a series of decisions during the 1940s, the doctrine allowed legislators a relatively free hand to regulate economic affairs but required rather tight judicial protection in certain other areas, such as speech, press, voting, criminal justice, and discrimination. The rationale ran along these lines:

1. Because the Constitution does not embody an economic theory, economic forces should be left to battle in the legislative processes. Judges should presume the outcome constitutional as long as it can be reasonably related to a valid legislative purpose.
2. If economic forces are to be free to persuade legislators to adopt a

wide range of public policies, judges carry a heavy obligation to keep channels of political communication open. In cases properly before them judges must accord special protection to rights to vote, speak, write, petition, assemble, and associate so that all contending points of view have a fair chance of winning support. Here there is no necessity to presume restrictive legislation constitutional. Rights pertaining to political expression should be "preferred" over other constitutional values.

3. There is also a special obligation to examine with "more searching judicial scrutiny" regulations directed at "discrete and insular minorities," who either have little hope of affecting public policy or whose interests are being curtailed by government. Here, too, judges should relax the usual presumption of constitutionality.

4. Because criminal trials fall specifically within the judicial orbit of responsibility, judges owe no special deference to other public officials. The judicial guidelines should be the Bill of Rights and other relevant constitutional provisions.

The doctrine of preferred freedoms was useful in justifying the Court's shifting its attention from general economic matters to civil rights. But it still presented many difficulties as a set of general rules of constitutional jurisprudence. The justices, for example, never offered specific criteria to define a "small and insular minority," nor did even the more fervent apostles of preferred freedoms apply its terms with consistency. Stone and Black, for instance, initially agreed with Frankfurter in *Colegrove v. Green*[126] that gerrymandering was not a proper judicial concern. Indeed, at conference only Douglas maintained that gerrymandering was a violation of the right to vote that judges should try to remedy. More important, libertarian justices did not–or could not–account for additions to the ranks of fundamental rights, such as freedom to marry[127] and procreate,[128] travel,[129] retain one's national citizenship,[130] enjoy privacy,[131] and receive a minimum education.[132] That not a single one of these fundamental rights is listed in the Constitution is less important than that the doctrine itself could not explain how they fitted in with its rationale.

Preferred freedoms was not, however, a total failure. It was, at very least, an improvement over the "guess what we're going to do next" approach that has often characterized American judicial decision making. Furthermore, in emphasizing the significance of freedom of communication and the special judicial role in its protection, the justices were helping to reconcile some of the tensions between constitutionalism and democracy. And the justices' failure to explain satisfactorily particular choices among values or to establish operative criteria to determine which issues fell under what aspect of the doctrine's rationale are not irreparable shortcomings. Preferred freedoms was essentially an incomplete theory, just as is its recent reincarnation in truncated form under the title "strict scrutiny."[133] But, at minimum, preferred freedoms provides a building block for a more complete constitutional jurisprudence.

Balancing. Balancing or weighing conflicting interests or values against each other forms an alternative way of resolving specific suits. It is well suited to the common law's spirit of incrementalism and also conforms to the raw brand of pragmatism that permeates the American legal system. Much of balancing's popularity can be traced to Roscoe Pound. Frankly accepting a wide role for judges as "social engineers," Pound categorized interests as falling into three categories:[134]

1. demands or desires involved in or regarded from the standpoint of the individual life immediately as such (*individual interests*);
2. demands or desires involved in or looked at from the standpoint of life in a politically organized society, asserted in title of political life (*public interests*); or
3. those wider demands or desires involved in or looked at from the standpoint of social life in civilized society and asserted in title of social life (*social interests*).

Unfortunately, balancing does not, per se, offer much help in ranking values. In fact, it may obstruct that process. Deciding that some values are individual, others are public, and still others are social, and then balancing them against each other, misses much of Pound's point. One of his purposes was to show that there are several dimensions to almost every interest that competes for judicial protection. Thus, he explicitly warned: "When it comes to weighing or valuing claims or demands with respect to other claims or demands, we must be careful to compare then on the same plane. If we put one as an individual interest and the other as a social interest, we may decide the question in advance by our way of putting it."[135] Justice Harlan's use of balancing in *Barenblatt v. United States* (1959)[136] committed precisely the sin against which Pound had warned. Speaking for the Court, Harlan claimed to balance Barenblatt's private interest in a right to silence against a public interest in Congress's exercising its authority to learn about Communist activities and so protect the nation against subversion. As one would expect, the public interest triumphed. In dissent, Black pointed out that Harlan had begged the question. Black would not have used balancing at all; but, if it were a legitimate approach, he continued, Harlan had placed at least one wrong weight on the scale. The public interest in security should have not been weighed against Barenblatt's individual interest in silence but against "the interest of the people as a whole in being able to join organizations, advocate causes and make political 'mistakes' without later being subjected to governmental penalties for having dared to think for themselves."[137]

A more fundamental failing, perhaps, is that no advocate of balancing has yet explained what weights the Constitution requires to be put on each right, value, or interest; nor has anyone explained how to calibrate the "scales" on which competing interests should be weighed. An effort to balance interests may help a judge identify the issues underlying a case; but, without such a set of numbers–ordinal if not cardinal–balancing remains about as useful in deciding specific cases or establishing general principles of jurisprudence as the albegraic proposition $A = B < C > D$, when A, B, C, and D are all unknown quantities. "Plainly," as Archibald Cox said about a spate of cases in which the Court tried to balance interests, "the decisions reached reflect the Justices' view of wise policy rather than anything to be found in the Constitution."[138] My objection goes less to judicial policy making than to the tendency, in the absence of linkage to a set of constitutionally grounded priorities, for balancing to conceal from judges as well as the outside world the importance or even existence of any general jurisprudential principles.

On the other hand, after a judge has completed at least a preliminary ranking of values, balancing can be of considerable help in settling concrete disputes. If, for example, ranking produces a general decision that two values are approximately equal in importance, "weighing"–a euphemism for "speculating about"–the effects of a ruling one way or another in the peculiar circumstances of a case may provide a sensible way of deciding which takes precedence in that instance. Under extraordinary circumstances a judge might even intelligently rule that those special conditions make it more consistent with the function or purpose of the particular values to reverse their normal priority. In each type of situation, and more particularly in the latter, a judge has a heavy obligation to explain with great care and clarity the way in which he ranks competing values and why he allows special circumstances to affect that ordering.

Justice, natural law, and natural rights. Section 2 discussed at some length the implications of these concepts, and section 4 returns to them. Here it is sufficient to recall only a few points. Historically, theories of natural law and right deeply affected the thinking both of the framers and of early judges. More recently explicit references in judicial opinions have been far less frequent, but the latter pages of section 2 showed that individual judges have continued to rely on such concepts. The preamble and the Ninth Amendment provide ready vehicles to transport them into contemporary society. Thus, these doctrines could be legitimately used to differentiate between rights, such as those to fair and equal treatment, that are natural (i.e., more fundamental) and those, such as indictment by grand jury, that are merely conventional (i.e., less fundamental).[139] The basic difficulty, of course, lies in the vagueness of guidelines to silhouette justice and distinguish more fundamental from less fundamental obligations and rights.

TOWARD A NEW CONSTITUTIONAL JURISPRUDENCE

One who spends much of his time setting difficult tasks for judges, analyzing their failings, and on occasion snidely criticizing them for being less than perfect has a moral obligation to lay his own head on the block of logic-chopping and explain how the problems of constitutional interpretation should properly be solved. I acknowledge, albeit reluctantly, that obligation and shall sketch the outlines of a tentative solution, prudently leaving to a larger work a firmer, more detailed schema and justifications.

First of all, the American Constitution is a flexible, developing charter for government that must be viewed as an organic whole. To interpret it, a judge must, as Jerome Frank would say, play its music as well as recite its words.[140] The American Constitution may not be as metaphysical as the British "constitution," but it stretches more widely than the document the framers wrote and the twenty-six amendments added since the Philadelphia convention, more widely even than its kiting tail of judicial emendations. The American Constitution includes the spirit of "free government," a mixture of constitutionalism—with its stress on individual liberty along with limited government—and democracy, with its emphasis on majority rule. Along with liberty, equality has been reinforced through gradual triumph of the ideas of the second paragraph of the Declaration of Independence. Liberty has received additional strength through implantation into the Constitution of such notions as the rule of law, the existence of rights that government protects rather than confers, and the coexistence of certain obligations that people owe to each other and to society as a whole. Ideals more limited in scope, such as "one person, one vote," and particular governmental practices such as judicial review, senatorial courtesy, and executive privilege (although more restricted than Richard Nixon's majestic claims), have also become part of the Constitution.

I also believe that the Constitution contains a hierarchy of values. First, substantive goals take precedence over process. Indeed, a strict positivist might note that the preamble lists only substantive not procedural goals; and an historian might point out that, antedating William James and John Dewey by most of a century, the framers were not yet blessed with the insight that process takes priority over substance. In politics, of course, substantive goals and procedures normally are intimately related; and, in the American context, I would stress the general compatibility of, rather than tensions between, substantive goals and political processes. Without a doubt, however, serious conflicts do occur, and they can force important choices. Resolving those clashes is seldom easy, but the task can be less difficult if one keeps in mind that process is the handmaiden, not the mistress, of substantive rights.

Second, among the Constitution's substantive values, I believe the most fundamental has become human dignity. One can respond that the framers did not see it that way. Although as individuals most of them may have opposed slavery, when faced with a choice between slavery and national unity they chose the latter, sacrificing black people's dignity. Confronting much the same problem, Thomas Jefferson, John Marshall, and, for a time, Abraham Lincoln each made the same choice. One could counter that the options, as the framers saw them, were not so stark. They believed that the black man's dignity was lost no matter what they did. The only choices that they saw were one nation with slavery, or two nations, one with, the other without, slavery.[141]

Because I agree that the framers–and Jefferson, and Marshall, and Lincoln–put national unity ahead of the dignity of blacks (at least), I do not rest my case on original intent,[142] but on the internal logic of the polity as the framers built it and as it and its values have developed since 1787. The preamble's goals of liberty and justice were not mere rhetorical flourishes, but meaningful articles of hope–even faith, as William O. Douglas wrote[143]–that have, albeit with painful reverses, become more and more real over ensuing generations. Article I's restrictions on suspending the writ of habeas corpus, its ban on state and federal bills of attainder and ex post facto laws, Article III's narrow definition of treason and its requirement of jury trials for federal crimes, are all concrete illustrations of this hopeful faith.

Additional acknowledgment of such rights as freedom of conscience, communication, and privacy points in the same direction. The Constitution's commands for intricate procedures for criminal prosecution, the Warren Court said in 1966, force government "to respect the inviolability of the human personality."[144] "The basic concept," a plurality of the Burger Court repeated a decade later, underlying the prohibition against cruel and unusual punishments, is "the dignity of man."[145] Affirmation of human dignity bursts out of the Thirteenth Amendment and the abolitionists' long agitation and stern preachments about natural law, natural rights, and the wrath of God. The Fourteenth Amendment's four great clauses bestowing citizenship, privileges and immunities, due process, and equal protection speak the same language, though in more measured tones. The Fifteenth and Nineteenth Amendments' proscription of discrimination against the rights of blacks and women to vote reaffirms their equal share in humanity.

Together, these provisions, with the language of the Declaration of Independence, the sweeping words of the Ninth Amendment, and, most important in Madison's mind, the mutual checks of ambition pitted against ambition, create a network of restraints on governmental power, to protect the individual. What Earl Warren once wrote about the Fifth Amendment applies a fortiori to the Constitution as a whole: "All these policies point to one overriding thought: the constitutional foundation underlying the privilege is the respect that government–state or federal–must accord to the dignity and integrity of citizens."[146]

The linkages with doctrines of natural law and right are obvious. The "unassailable dignity of the individual"[147] has been at the heart of natural law and right since the early Sophists debated Socrates. These ideas deeply influenced the leaders of the Revolution, the framers of the Constitution, as well as John Marshall and his contemporaries; their philosophy continues to shape American law. "In the Declaration," Carl Becker noted, "the foundation of the United States is indissolubly associated with a theory of politics, a philosophy of human rights which is valid, if at all, not for Americans only, but for all men."[148]

Justice Potter Stewart, hardly a judicial libertarian, put it much the same way: The "basic concept of the essential dignity and worth of every human being . . . [is] at the root of any decent system of ordered liberty."[149] That its protection is primarily left to the states, he continued, "does not mean that the right is entitled to less recognition by this Court as a basic of our constitutional system." My argument, of course, goes further: human dignity is not merely one of the fundamental values of the American constitutional system, it is *the* fundamental value.

That concept shares the shortcoming that Madison described as afflicting all political discourse. It is broad, even vague, often functioning as an easy compendium for whatever users of the phrase deem noble. In essence, however, it means that the individual, as a person, is the basic unit of legal–and moral–accounting; that government must respect all persons, in Kant's terms, as ends rather than treat them as means; and that each person has equal claim to that respect, not because government so deigns but because we share a common humanity. Along with Thomas Jefferson and William O. Douglas,[150] religious writers would chorus that that dignity must be respected because it has been given by

God. It is sufficient for a nontheologian to note that to degrade a fellow human, to strip him of dignity or honor, is to degrade oneself.

The American Constitution does not affirm this belief as explicitly as Does Eire's Constitution or West Germany's Basic Law, nor does the American value rest as firmly as does the Irish on a systematically (and theologically) articulated doctrine of natural law and rights. Yet human dignity is at the center of the American polity's constitutional values, forming what, in Kelsen's terms,[151] is the basic norm to which all other norms of the political and legal system are subordinate. As Eugene V. Rostow phrased it, "the highest aim of our Constitution is that it seeks to protect the freedom and dignity of man by imposing severe and enforceable limitations upon the freedom of the state."[152]

To adopt this thesis, of course, does not solve all problems of constitutional interpretation. There is no magic formula in law or politics. Acceptance of human dignity as the basic norm neither solves the problem of ranking other constitutional values nor does it make the term itself more specific. But acceptance of human dignity as the nucleic value does, I believe, two things. It makes more understandable, although only in a general fashion, much of what the Constitution is all about; and by doing so it marks a beginning toward discovering a more complete hierarchy. In performing either function, it makes constitutional interpretation a less capricious art. That is not a trivial accomplishment.

Blessing judicial use of such concepts as the "spirit of the Constitution," "penumbras" of specific provisions, or natural law and rights to adjust the meaning of a fluid, flexible basic law to changing conditions may be downright perilous. Liberals should be as wary of what judges like Warren Burger and William Rehnquist will not read into the Constitution[153] as conservatives were fearful of what Earl Warren and William O. Douglas would find there. Thus, one can understand and admire as heroic Hugo Black's efforts to restrict judges to a literal interpretation of a specific document whose words are forever fixed in meaning. But Black's efforts would have been more properly addressed to constitutional draftsmen than to judges. For, as we have seen, a consistently literal interpretation even of the written American Constitution would be self-defeating.

One can take some, though not great, consolation in the fact that, despite Harlan Stone's eloquence,[154] there are many other restrictions on courts than judicial self-restraint.[155] And as prudent men of considerable experience in practical politics, judges have been aware of these limitations, sometimes painfully aware. One might take further, though even slimmer, consolation in the hope that judges will exercise their power with humility, as they contemplate the delicate blending of constitutionalism and democracy in the American polity. But there is no way in a political system like that of the United States that judges can always avoid choice and no way that the nation can always escape the consequences—sometimes beneficial, sometimes harmful—of those choices. Allowing judges to interpret a constitution is inherently risky, but so is an effort to maintain a polity based on both constitutionalism and democracy. The risks involved become attractive only when one considers the alternatives.

NOTES

INTRODUCTION

1. Martin Diamond, "The Declaration and the Constitution: Liberty, Democracy and the Founders," *The Public Interest* 41 (fall 1975): 39-55.
2. *Schneider v. Smith,* 390 U.S. 17, 25 (1968).

1. Alpheus T. Mason: AMERICA'S POLITICAL HERITAGE

1. There are remarkable parallels between 1776 and the constitutional crisis of 1974, striking similarities between the charges Jefferson leveled against King George III in the Declaration of Independence and the articles of impeachment the House Judiciary Committee voted against President Nixon. Both were charged with obstructing "the administration of justice." Jefferson portrayed King George as the rebel. On 28 March 1975 Federal District Court Judge Noel Fox, labeling President Nixon a "putative rebel leader," observed: "an insurrection and rebellion against constitutional government itself . . . an insurrection and rebellion which might have succeeded but for timely intervention by a courageous free press, an enlightened Congress, and a diligent Judiciary dedicated to preserving the rule of law" (*Murphy v. Ford,* 390 F. Supp., 1372-73 [1975]).
2. *Federalist,* Benjamin F. Wright, ed. (Cambridge: Harvard University Press, 1961), no. 14, pp. 154-55. Quotations are from this edition.
3. See Julian P. Boyd, *The Declaration of Independence: The Evolution of the Text as Shown in Facsimiles of Various Drafts by Its Author, Thomas Jefferson* (Princeton: Princeton University Press, 1945); W. S. Howell, "The Declaration of Independence and Eighteenth Century Logic," *William and Mary Quarterly* 18, no. 4 (October 1961): 463-84; Carl Becker, *The Declaration of Independence: A Study in the History of Political Ideas* (New York: Alfred A. Knopf, 1940).
4. Maryland constitution, article 6. Fifteen states have, at one time or another, specifically endorsed the right of the people to "alter, reform or abolish" the existing form of government. For a listing see Justice Douglas, dissenting in *Scales v. United States,* 367 U.S. 203 (1961), 278.

5. Roy P. Basler, ed., *The Collected Works of Abraham Lincoln* (New Brunswick: Rutgers University Press, 1953), I, 138–39.
6. Arthur M. Schlesinger, Sr., "Our Ten Contributions to Civilization," *Atlantic,* March 1959, pp. 65–69. Other contributions include: Federalism, Consent of the Governed, Status of Women, Melting Pot, Freedom of Worship, Public School, Voluntary Giving, Technology, and Evolutionary Progress.
7. Gaillard Hunt, ed., *The Writings of James Madison* (New York: G. P. Putnam's Sons, 1906), p. 164.
8. *Federalist,* no. 28.
9. John Locke, *Two Treatises of Government,* Peter Laslett, ed. (New York: Cambridge University Press, 1966). This and subsequent excerpts are from the Laslett edition.

At certain points Locke uses "rebellion" and "revolution" interchangeably; at others, these terms seem distinguishable.

The interpretation of Locke presented here owes much to N. C. Phillips, "Political Philosophy and Political Fact: The Evidence of John Locke," in *Liberty and Learning: Essays in Honor of Sir James Hight* (Christchurch, N. Z.: Whitcombe and Tombs, 1950).
10. "To avoid this State of War [due to want of a common power over all] is the great *reason of Mens putting themselves into society,* and quitting the State of Nature."
11. John Adams to Hezekiah Niles, 13 February 1818. Quoted in Richard J. Hooker, ed., *The American Revolution: The Search for Meaning* (New York: John Wiley & Sons, 1970), p. 9.
12. James Otis, *The Rights of the British Colonies* (1764). Quoted in A. T. Mason, *Free Government in the Making* (New York: Oxford University Press, 1965), p. 98.
13. Quoted in Carl Becker, p. 133.
14. Carl N. Degler, "The American Past: An Unexpected Obstacle in Foreign Affairs," *American Scholar,* spring 1963, p. 193.
15. Ibid.

"England, alone, had by violence effected it: America had contended ten years long, not against England, but against the revolution: America sought not a revolution; she yielded to it, compelled by necessity, not because she wished to extort a better condition than she had before enjoyed, but because she wished to avert a worse one prepared for her." Frederick Gentz, *The French and American Revolutions Compared,* trans. John Quincy Adams (Chicago: Henry Regnery Co., 1955), p. 56.
16. Edmund Burke, *Reflections on the French Revolution* (Maynard's English Classic Series), p. 18.
17. Daniel Boorstin, *The Genius of American Politics* (Chicago: University of Chicago Press, 1953), p. 68. For various interpretations of the American Revolution and the massive scholarship relating to it, see George Athan Billias, ed., *The American Revolution: How Revolutionary Was It?* (New York: Holt, Rinehart and Winston, 1965); Jack Greene, *The Reappraisal of the American Revolution in Recent Historical Literature* (Washington, D. C.: Service Center for Teachers of History, 1967).
18. Alexis de Tocqueville, *Democracy in America,* 1873, F. Bowen ed. (New York: Alfred A. Knopf, 1945), II, 123.
19. *Thoughts on Government* (1776), C. F. Adams, ed., *The Works of John Adams* (Boston: Little, Brown and Company, 1851), IV, 193–200. Reprinted in Mason, p. 144.
20. *Federalist,* no. 39.
21. Jefferson to R. C. Weightman, 16 June 1826. Quoted in Mason, p. 371.
22. Max Farrand, ed., *The Records of the Federal Convention of 1787* (New Haven, Conn.: Yale University Press, 1911), II, 278.
23. "The United States was born of rebellion and grew to greatness through

revolution. No other nation has had a revolutionary history so long or so comprehensive, and perhaps no other has a record that was, in the eyes of the world, so deeply subversive as ours." Henry Steele Commager, *U.S. Congress, Senate Hearings before the Committee on Foreign Relations,* 90th Cong., 1st Sess., 20 February 1967, p. 11.

Justice Holmes, recognizing free government's potentially subversive aspect, declared: "If in the long run the beliefs expressed in proletarian dictatorship are destined to be accepted by the dominant forces of the community, the only meaning of free speech is that they should be given their chance and have their way." Dissenting in *Gitlow v. New York,* 268 U.S. 652, 673 (1929).

24. In a remarkable letter to Karl Marx, two years before the *Communist Manifesto* was published, the French socialist P. J. Proudhon pleaded unsuccessfully with Marx to make the proletarian revolution self-consistent.

> Dear Mr. Marx:
> Let us seek together, if you wish, the laws of society, the manner in which these laws are realized, the process by which we shall succeed in discovering them; but, for God's sake, after having demolished all the *a priori* dogmatisms do not let us in our turn dream of indoctrinating the people; let us not fall into the same contradiction as your countryman, Martin Luther, who after having overthrown Catholic Theology, began at once with the help of excommunications and anathemas, to found a Protestant Theology. . . . I applaud with all my heart your thought of bringing to light all opinions; let us carry on a good and loyal polemic; let us give the world the example of a learned and far-sighted tolerance but let us not, because we are at the head of a movement, make ourselves the leaders of a new intolerance, let us not pose as the Apostles of a new religion, even if it is the religion of logic and reason. Let us gather together and encourage all protests, let us condemn all exclusiveness. . . . let us never regard a question as exhausted. On this condition, I will gladly enter into your association: Otherwise, No! (*Correspondance de P. J. Proudhon* [Paris: A. Lacroix and Co., 1875], II, 198–202).

25. To W. S. Smith, 15 November 1787. Julian Boyd, ed., *The Papers of Thomas Jefferson* (Princeton, N.J.: Princeton University Press, 1955), XII, 356.

26. See B. F. Wright, *Consensus and Continuity, 1776–1787* (paperback ed., New York: W. W. Norton & Company, 1958).

27. P. L. Ford, ed., *The Works of Thomas Jefferson* (New York and London, 1904–5), X, 269.

28. *Federalist,* no. 45.

29. Daniel Leonard, *Massachusettensis,* Letters Addressed to the Inhabitants of the Province of Massachusetts Bay, 1775. Quoted in Mason, p. 119.

30. Quoted in Mason, p. 125.

Foreshadowing America's "critical period" of the 1780s, the Loyalist Samuel Seabury wrote: "If we should succeed in depriving Great Britain of the power of regulating our trade, the colonies will probably be soon at variance with each other. Their commercial interests will interfere; there will be no supreme power to interpose, and discord and animosity must ensue." Ibid., p. 118.

31. *Federalist,* no. 15.

32. John Quincy Adams, *The Jubilee of the Constitution* (1839), pp. 17–18.

For a perceptive study of political thought during the Confederation period, see E. S. Corwin, "The Progress of Constitutional Theory between the Declaration of Independence and the Meeting of the Philadelphia Convention," *American Historical Review* 30 (1925): 511–36.

33. H. Niles, *Principles and Acts of the Revolution* (1876), pp. 234, 236.

34. *Federalist,* no. 1.

35. To David Humphreys, 17 March 1789. Ford, ed., V, 470.

36. To Edward Rutledge, 18 July 1788. Boyd, ed., XIII, 378.

37. Jonathan Elliot, ed., *The Debates of the Several State Constitutional Conventions on the Adoption of the Federal Constitution* (Washington: Taylor & Maury, 1836), II, 406.
38. John W. Burgess, *Political Science and Comparative Constitutional Law* (Boston: Ginn & Co., 1890), I, 105.
39. *Federalist,* no. 40.
40. Elliot, II, 426.
41. Louis Hartz, *The Liberal Tradition in America* (New York: Harcourt, Brace and Company, 1955), p. 140.
42. Jefferson to Thomas Mann Randolph, Jr., 30 May 1790. Boyd, ed., XVI, 449.
43. Phillips.

The shades of John Locke have not vanished from the councils of the judiciary. See the illuminating colloquy between Justices Douglas and Frankfurter in *Perez v. Brownell,* 356 U.S. 603, 622 (1958), and *Kingsley Pictures Corp. v. Regents of New York,* 360 U.S. 648, 699 (1960). Quoted in A. T. Mason, *The Supreme Court: Palladium of Freedom* (Ann Arbor: University of Michigan Press, 1962), p. 7.
44. *Federalist,* no. 20.
45. Ibid., no. 51.
46. Quoted in Mason, *Free Government,* p. 371.
47. Dr. Benjamin Rush, "Address to the People of the United States, 1787," in Niles, p. 234.
48. *Works,* VI, 484. See R. R. Palmer, "Notes on the Use of the Word 'Democracy,' 1789-1799," *Political Science Quarterly* 68 (1953): 203–26.
49. J. Q. Adams, *Jubilee of the Constitution,* p. 115.

"If there be any truth . . . , it is that in proportion as a government is free, it must be complicated. Simplicity belongs to those only where one will governs all, . . . where few arrangements are required because no checks to power are allowed. . . ." Joseph Story, *Miscellaneous Writings,* W. W. Story, ed. (Boston: C. C. Little and J. Brown, 1852), p. 619. Quoted in C. T. Dunne, *Justice Joseph Story and the Rise of the Supreme Court* (New York: Simon and Schuster, 1970), p. 337.
50. I am aware of only one contemporary description or definition of free government—that by James Wilson in the Pennsylvania Ratifying Convention:

> A free government has often been compared to a pyramid. This allusion is made with peculiar propriety in the system before you; it is laid on the broad basis of the people; its powers gradually rise while they are confined, in proportion as they ascend, until they end in that most permanent of all forms. When you examine all its parts, they will invariably be found to preserve that essential mark of free governments—a chain of connection with the people. [J. Elliot, ed., II, 484]

In his *Reflections on the French Revolution,* p. 121, Burke, with certain qualifications, underscored essential aspects of the system.

> To make a government requires no great prudence. Settle the seat of power; teach obedience; and the work is done. To give liberty is still more easy. It is not necessary to guide; it only requires to let go the rein. But, to form a *free government* that is to temper together these opposite elements of liberty and restraint in one consistent work, requires much thought; deep reflection; a sagacious, powerful, and combining mind.

51. Resolutions relating to the Alien and Sedition Laws, 1798. Ford, ed., *Works,* VIII, 475.
52. *Federalist,* no. 53.
53. Eliot, ed., II, 406.
54. W. Wilson, *Constitutional Government in the United States* (New York: Columbia University Press, 1907), p. 146.

55. W. C. Bruce, *John Randolph of Roanoke* (New York: G. P. Putnam's Sons, 1922), II, 211.
56. *Federalist,* no. 9.
57. Ibid., no. 69.
58. Montesquieu, *Spirit of Laws.* Quoted in Mason, *Free Government,* p. 45.
59. *Federalist,* nos. 47 and 48.
60. Ibid., no. 43.
61. Ibid., no. 26.
62. Ibid., no. 28.
63. Jefferson to Madison, 20 December 1787. Quoted in Mason, *Free Government,* p. 319.
64. *Federalist,* no. 84.

For Wilson's negative views on a bill of rights, see Elliot, ed., II, 408ff.
65. Quoted in Mason, *Free Government,* p. 168.
66. Mason, *The Supreme Court,* p. 51.
67. Said Jefferson: "In the arguments in favor of a declaration of rights, you omit one which has great weight with me, the legal check which it puts into the hands of the Judiciary." Jefferson to Madison, 15 March 1789, Boyd, ed., XII, 659.
68. *Federalist,* no. 81.
69. Ibid., no. 39.
70. Ibid., no. 78.
71. Elliot, ed., II, 503.

"A fear of popular majorities lies at the very basis of the whole system of judicial review, and indeed our entire constitutional system." E. S. Corwin, "The Supreme Court and the Fourteenth Amendment," *Michigan Law Review* 7 (1909): 643, 670.

Charles Evans Hughes expressed the same idea: "We protect the fundamental rights of minorities, in order to save democratic government from destroying itself by the excess of its own power." Hughes, *Proceedings in Commemoration of the 150th Anniversary of the First Congress,* H. R. Doc. No. 212, 76th Cong., 1st Sess. (1939), p. 32.
72. E. S. Corwin, *The Doctrine of Judicial Review* (Princeton: Princeton University Press, 1914), p. 17.
73. Elliot, ed., III, 208.
74. Ibid., 487.
75. *Annals of Cong.* [1789-90], I, 432, 439.
76. Jefferson to Madison, 15 March 1789. Quoted in Mason, *Free Government,* p. 323.
77. Justice Stone, dissenting in *United States v. Butler,* 297 U.S. 1, 79 (1936).
78. *Dred Scott v. Sandford,* 19 How. 393 (1857).
79. *Mora v. McNamara,* 389 U.S. 934, 935 (1967).
80. *Massachusetts v. Laird,* 400 U.S. 886 (1970).
81. *Marbury v. Madison,* 1 Cranch 137, 176 (1803).
82. *McCulloch v. Maryland,* 4 Wheat. 316, 415 (1819).
83. To Spencer Roane, 16 September 1819. Ford, ed., XII, 136. Quoted in Harris Mirkin, "Judicial Review, Jury Review and Right of Revolution against Despotism," *Polity* 9, no. 1 (fall 1973): 39.
84. Functioning as a "revolutionary committee," the Court may have "saved the country from a far more dangerous and disorderly change." Adolf Berle, *The Three Faces of Power* (New York: Harcourt, Brace & World, 1967), pp. vii-viii. See also Archibald Cox, *The Warren Court: Constitutional Decision as an Instrument of Reform* (Cambridge: Harvard University Press, 1968), p. v.
85. Elliot, ed., IV, 182.
86. *Federalist,* nos. 16 and 43.
87. Ibid., no. 43.

88. Madison to Edmund Randolph, 8 April 1787. Quoted in Mason, *Free Government,* pp. 192–93. Italics added.
89. *Slaughter House* cases, 16 Wall. 36 (1873).
90. Ibid., 78.
91. Ibid., 96.

In the years ahead, ironically, the Supreme Court was destined to play the role it had spurned in 1873—"perpetual censor" of state legislation under the Fourteenth Amendment. See, in this connection, A. T. Mason, *Security through Freedom: American Political Thought and Practice* (Ithaca: Cornell University Press, 1955), pp. 28–41.
92. *Texas v. White,* 7 Wall. 700, 725 (1869).
93. *Jubilee* p. 55.
94. *Missouri v. Holland,* 252 U.S. 416, 433 (1920).
95. R. Niebuhr, *The Children of Light and the Children of Darkness* (New York: Charles Scribner's Sons, 1944), p. xi. Niebuhr's thought was inspired by Paul's Epistle to the Romans 7:18–25.
96. *Federalist,* no. 51.
97. Ibid., no. 76. Madison concurred: "As there is a degree of depravity in mankind which requires a degree of circumspection and distrust, so there are other qualities in human nature which justify a certain portion of esteem and confidence. Republican government presupposes the existence of these qualities in a higher degree than any other form." Ibid., no. 55.
98. Ibid., no. 37.
99. By 1787 the injustice of state laws and other excesses had brought "more into question the fundamental principle of Republican government, that the majority who rule in such governments are the safest Guardians both of the public Good and private rights." Madison, "Vices of the Political System of the United States," quoted in Mason, *Free Government,* p. 171. See also *Federalist,* no. 10.
100. Niebuhr, p. 118.
101. *Federalist,* no. 1.
102. Ibid., no. 37. For Madison the methods of science are inappropriate in politics for three reasons: "complexity of the subject," "imperfection of the organ of perception," "inadequacy of the vehicle of ideas"—words. Rousseau, concerned lest the reader accuse him of self-contradiction, cited "poverty of language" as the excuse. *The Social Contract* (Everyman ed.; New York: E. P. Dutton & Co., 1913), p. 27.

Commenting on the mechanical approach in the context of constitutional interpretation generally, Holmes wrote: "The provisions of a constitution are not mathematical formulas having their essence in their form; they are organic living institutions transplanted from English soil. Their significance is vital, not final; it is to be gathered not simply by taking the words and a dictionary, but by considering their origin and the line of their growth." *Gompers v. United States,* 233 U.S. 604, 610 (1914).
103. Madison to Jefferson, 17 October 1788. Hunt, ed., V, 274.

For certain of the most liberal Supreme Court justices, the Bill of Rights does not draw constitutional lines with absolute precision. See Justice Holmes's qualifications, *Schenck v. United States,* 249 U.S. 47, 52 (1919); *Frohwerk v. United States,* 249 U.S. 204, 206 (1919). In a broader context, Holmes commented: "A word is not a crystal, transparent and unchanged, it is the skin of a living thought and may vary in color and content according to the circumstances and the time in which it is used." *Towne v. Eisner,* 245 U.S. 418, 425 (1918). See Justice Brandeis in *Whitney v. California,* 274 U.S. 357 (1927), dissenting, p. 373; Justice Douglas, dissenting in *Dennis v. United States,* 341 U.S. 494, 585 (1951). See also Walter Lippmann, *The Public Philosophy* (New York: Mentor Books, 1956), p. 132.

104. Quoted in A. T. Mason, "Politics: Science or Art?" *Southwestern Social Science Quarterly*, December 1935, p. 3.
105. Hamilton to Rufus King, 3 February 1802. Henry Cabot Lodge, ed., *The Works of Alexander Hamilton* (New York: Appleton, 1904), X, 439.

In *The Federalist*, no. 83, Hamilton wrote: "The truth is that the general *Genius* of a government [identified as "vibrations of power"] is all that can be substantially relied upon for permanent effects."
106. Rousseau, p. 25.

"He that wrestles with us," Edmund Burke observes, "strengthens our nerves and sharpens our skill. Our antagonist is our helper. . . . Time is required to produce that union of mind which alone can produce all the good we aim at." *Reflections*, pp. 105, 108.

For John C. Calhoun *The Federalist* highlighted divergence of opinion, accommodation, and compromise, convincing him that "this admirable constitution of ours . . . is superior to the wisdom of any or all of the men by whose agency it was made. The force of circumstance, and not foresight or wisdom, induced them to adopt many of its wisest provisions." R. K. Cralle, ed., *The Works of John C. Calhoun* (New York: Appleton, 1888), 417.
107. *Abrams v. United States*, 250 U.S. 616, 630 (1919).
108. Dissenting in *Lochner v. New York*, 198 U.S. 45, 75–76 (1905).
109. Mark DeWolfe Howe, ed., *Holmes-Laski Letters* (New York: Atheneum Publishers, 1953), I, 310–11.
110. "Justice is the end of government," Madison wrote. "It is the end of civil society. It ever has been and ever will be pursued until it be obtained, or until liberty is lost in the pursuit." *Federalist*, no. 51.
111. Niebuhr, p. 75.
112. Jefferson to Judge Roane, 27 June 1821. Ford, ed., XII, 203.
113. Besides the Civil War, notable exceptions are the deadlock between the judiciary and the political branches of government in the 1930s, and the Nixon administration's betrayals. In 1935–36 the Supreme Court, often by vote of 5 to 4 or 6 to 3, transcending the undefined line set by the separation-of-powers principle, became a superlegislature. President Franklin D. Roosevelt, impervious to Jefferson's warning against "rashly overleaping" lines of demarcation, counterattacked with his court-packing threat. Happily, the outcome was ambiguous. Both sides won; both lost. Roosevelt achieved judicial endorsement of his legislative program. Congress defeated courtpacking. If either had scored outright victory, the separation-of-powers principles would have been, by Madison's test, "subverted." The beneficiaries of this give-and-take outcome were the American people and free government.
114. Elliot, ed., III, 489.

2. Herbert J. Storing: THE CONSTITUTION AND THE BILL OF RIGHTS

1. *The Bill of Rights: Its Origin and Meaning* (Indianapolis: The Bobbs Merrill Co., 1965), p. 46.
2. (Chapel Hill: University of North Carolina Press, 1955), p. 125.
3. Bernard Schwartz, *The Bill of Rights: A Documentary History* (New York: Chelsea House Publishers, 1971), p. 527.
4. *The Birth of the Bill of Rights*, p. v.
5. Jonathan Elliot, ed., *Debates in the Several State Conventions on the Adoption of the Federal Constitution*, II, 122–23, 177.
6. See below, note 10.
7. Letter to George Eve, 2 January 1789, Gaillard Hunt, ed., *The Writings of James Madison* (New York: G. P. Putnam's Sons, 1904), V, 320.

8. *The Debates and Proceedings of the Congress of the United States* (Washington, 1834), I, 433.
9. Ibid., p. 432.
10. Amendments were proposed (1) to insure at least one representative for each thirty thousand people until the size of the House should reach a certain limit, when the proportion would be reduced; and (2) to make increases in the salaries of congressmen apply only after the next election of representatives. Versions of these two amendments were included in the twelve amendments proposed by the Congress, but failed to be ratified by a sufficient number of states.
11. Ibid., p. 441.
12. Ibid., p. 755.
13. Ibid., pp. 745, 775.
14. 13 January 1788, Isaac Leake, *Memoir of the Life and Times of General John Lamb* (Albany: J. Munsell, 1850), p. 310.
15. Letter to Thomas Jefferson, 29 March 1789, Hunt, ed., V, 336; see *Debates of the Congress of the United States,* I, 432–33.
16. Ibid., p. 746.
17. Ibid., p. 433.
18. 2 September 1789, *The Letters and Papers of Edmund Pendleton, 1734–1803,* ed. David John Mays (Charlottesville: University Press of Virginia, 1967), II, 558.
19. One of the arguments made by the Federalists was that specific restrictions might imply powers not intended to be granted and that a listing of powers might endanger rights not listed. There was enough plausibility in this argument to lead the First Congress to add and the states to ratify what is now the Ninth Amendment.
20. John B. McMaster and Frederick Stone, *Pennsylvania and the Federal Constitution* (Lancaster: Historical Society, Penna., 1888), pp. 143–44.
21. *Debates of the Congress of the United States,* vol. I, 436, 761, 767–68.
22. Paul Leicester Ford, *Pamphlets on the Constitution* (Brooklyn, N.Y., 1888), p. 360.
23. *Federalist,* no. 84. "It would be quite as significant to declare that government ought to be free, that taxes ought not to be excessive, etc., as that the liberty of the press ought not to be restrained." The state bills of rights did in fact contain many such "ought" statements which were intended to foster that "spirit of the people" on which Hamilton depends.
24. Essay by "A Farmer," *Maryland Gazette,* 15 February 1788.
25. Essay by "Aristides," *Maryland Journal and Baltimore Advertiser,* 4 March 1788.
26. Theophilus Parsons in the Massachusetts ratifying convention, Elliot, ed., II, 162.
27. 6 Cranch 87, 143 (1810).
28. 3 Dallas 386, 387 (1798).
29. *Palko v. Connecticut,* 302 U.S. 319, (1937).
30. *Federalist,* no. 84.
31. McMaster and Stone, p. 252.
32. Essay by "Atticus," *Boston Independent Chronicle,* 28 November 1787.
33. Elliot, ed., III, 448.
34. *Debates of the Congress of the United States,* I, 436.
35. Letter to George Eve, 2 January 1789, Hunt, ed., V, 318.
36. Letter to James Madison, 15 March 1789, Julian Boyd, ed., *The Papers of Thomas Jefferson* (Princeton: Princeton University Press, 1958), XIV, 660.
37. *Federalist,* no. 63.
38. Ford, pp. 359–60.
39. Elliot, ed., III, 37.

40. The main letters in this exchange are Madison to Jefferson, 24 October 1787, 17 October 1788, 8 December 1788; and Jefferson to Madison, 20 December 1787, 31 July 1788, 15 March 1789. These are conveniently available in Boyd, ed., XII–XIV, and in Schwartz.
41. *Debates of the Congress of the United States,* I, 436.
42. Jefferson to Madison, 20 December 1787, Boyd, ed., XII, p. 440.
43. Elliot, ed., IV, 137.
44. McMaster and Stone, p. 295.
45. *Virginia Independent Chronicle,* 25 June 1788. See *An Additional Number of Letters from the Federal Farmer to the Republican* (New York, 1788), p. 144.
46. Elliot, ed., III, 137; see essay by "A Delegate" in *Virginia Independent Chronicle,* 18 June, 25 June 1787.
47. Schwartz, p. 249.
48. See *Federalist,* no. 49.
49. *Debates of the Congress of the United States,* I, 435–36.
50. Ibid., pp. 433–34. Already this proposal significantly modified the language of the Virginia Declaration of Rights and the proposal of the Virginia convention, from which it was drawn, in the direction of supporting government. It does not begin, as the earlier versions do, with any declarations of natural rights of individuals; Madison's beginning point is already a society. The "inherent rights of which man cannot be divested," of the Virginia Declaration of Rights, are here converted into "benefits of the people" for the sake of which government is instituted. The right "to reform, alter or abolish government" (in the Virginia Declaration of Rights) or the rejection of the "slavish doctrine of non-resistance" (in the proposals of the Virginia ratifying convention) is moderated to a right to "reform or change government."
51. This debate appears in *Debates of the Congress of the United States,* I, 707–17.
52. It is of course significant in this connection that the First Amendment is addressed to Congress (the structure of the Bill of Rights is provided by the traditional legislative, executive, judicial sequence) and that for that reason, and because of the breadth of its terms, its interpretation and enforcement are unusually problematical.

3. David Fellman: THE NATIONALIZATION OF CIVIL LIBERTIES

1. DeLolme, *The Constitution of England* (London, 1775), bk. 1, ch. 9.
2. 1 Bl. Com. 161.
3. The Tenth Amendment provides: "The powers not delegated to the United States by the Constitution, nor prohibited by it to the States, are reserved to the States respectively, or to the people."
4. Ira Sharkansky, *The Maligned States* (New York: McGraw-Hill Book Company, 1972), p. 15.
5. U.S. Constitution, Art. I, sec. 8, para. 18.
6. See the definitive opinion of Chief Justice John Marshall in *McCulloch v. Maryland,* 4 Wheat. (U.S.) 316 (1819).
7. Art. III, sec. 2.
8. Art. I, secs. 9, 10.
9. Art. I, sec. 10.
10. Art. I, sec. 9.
11. 7 Pet. (U.S.) 243.
12. *Permoli v. New Orleans,* 3 How. (U.S.) 589 (1845).
13. Ibid., 609.
14. *Slaughter House* cases, 16 Wall. (U.S.) 36 (1873).
15. Ibid., 78.
16. 109 U.S. 3 (1883).

17. Ibid., 13 (Bradley, J.).
18. In *Colgate v. Harvey,* 296 U.S. 404 (1935) the Court discovered that the right of a citizen to invest his money outside his state on even terms with those who invest money locally was a federal right or privilege, but this decision, so out of line with over forty precedents, was quickly overruled in *Madden v. Kentucky,* 309 U.S. 83 (1940). Thus, the clause in question was restored to the state of somnolence it has always enjoyed.
19. *Chicago, B. & Q. Rr. Co. v. Chicago,* 166 U.S. 226 (1897).
20. 268 U.S. 652.
21. Ibid., 666. (Sanford, J.).
22. The first case in which the freedom of the press was explicitly absorbed into the liberty secured by the due process clause was *Near v. Minnesota,* 283 U.S. 697 (1931).
23. *Cantwell v. Connecticut,* 310 U.S. 296 (1940).
24. *Frank v. Mangum,* 237 U.S. 309 (1915). Justices Holmes and Brandeis dissented, arguing that unless the federal court itself examines the facts, the right to due process is "a barren one." Ibid., 348.
25. 261 U.S. 96.
26. See his dissenting opinions in *Hurtado v. California,* 110 U.S. 516, 538 (1884); *Maxwell v. Dow,* 176 U.S. 581, 605 (1900); *Twining v. New Jersey,* 211 U.S. 78, 114 (1908).
27. See especially the dissenting opinion of Justice Black in *Adamson v. California,* 332 U.S. 46, 68 (1948).
28. See Horace E. Flack, *The Adoption of the Fourteenth Amendment* (Baltimore: The Johns Hopkins Press, 1908); Joseph B. James, *The Framing of the Fourteenth Amendment* (Urbana: University of Illinois Press, 1956). The principal scholarly work which rejects the concept of total incorporation is Charles Fairman's famous essay "Does the Fourteenth Amendment Incorporate the Bill of Rights? The Original Understanding," *Stanford Law Review* 2 (December 1949): 5–139.
29. *Hurtado v. California,* 110 U.S. 516 (1884).
30. 287 U.S. 45.
31. The frustrating search for factors defining injustice began in *Betts v. Brady,* 316 U.S. 455 (1942).
32. *Gideon v. Wainwright,* 374 U.S. 335 (1963). For a lively account of this case see Anthony Lewis, *Gideon's Trumpet* (New York: Random House, 1964).
33. *Argersinger v. Hamlin,* 407 U.S. 25 (1972).
34. *Klopfer v. North Carolina,* 386 U.S. 213 (1967); *Smith v. Hooey,* 393 U.S. 374 (1969); *Dickey v. Florida,* 298 U.S. 30 (1970); *Moore v. Arizona,* 414 U.S. 25 (1973).
35. *In re Oliver,* 333 U.S. 257 (1948).
36. *Norris v. Alabama,* 294 U.S. 587 (1935); *Witherspoon v. Illinois,* 391 U.S. 510 (1968).
37. *Cole v. Arkansas,* 333 U.S. 196 (1948); *Lambert v. California,* 355 U.S. 225 (1957); *Wright v. Georgia,* 373 U.S. 284 (1963); *In re Ruffalo,* 390 U.S. 544 (1968).
38. *Pointer v. Texas,* 380 U.S. 400 (1965); *Brookhart v. Janis,* 384 U.S. 1 (1966); *Parker v. Gladden,* 385 U.S. 363 (1966); *Smith v. Illinois,* 390 U.S. 129 (1968); *Barber v. Page,* 390 U.S. 719 (1968); *California v. Green,* 399 U.S. 149 (1970); *Davis v. Alaska,* 415 U.S. 308 (1974).
39. *Washington v. Texas,* 388 U.S. 14 (1967).
40. The federal exclusionary rule was first announced by the Court in *Weeks v. United States,* 232 U.S. 383 (1914).
41. *Mapp v. Ohio,* 367 U.S. 643 (1961). For later decisions see: *Camara v. Municipal Court of San Francisco,* 387 U.S. 523 (1967); *Chimel v. California,* 395 U.S. 752 (1969); *Vale v. Louisiana,* 399 U.S. 30 (1970).
42. *Benton v. Maryland,* 395 U.S. 784 (1969). This decision overruled a venerable precedent, *Palko v. Connecticut,* 302 U.S. 319 (1937).

43. *Malloy v. Hogan*, 378 U.S. 1 (1964); *Garrity v. New Jersey*, 385 U.S. 493 (1967); *Spevak v. Klein*, 385 U.S. 511 (1967).
44. *Miranda v. Arizona*, 384 U.S. 436 (1966). See also *Orozco v. Texas*, 394 U.S. 324 (1969).
45. *Robinson v. California*, 370 U.S. 660 (1962).
46. *Duncan v. Louisiana*, 391 U.S. 145, 151 (1968). In *Baldwin v. New York*, 399 U.S. 66 (1970), the Court held that trial by jury was not constitutionally required in cases involving petty offenses, which were defined as offenses carrying a penalty of six months or less in jail.
47. *Mooney v. Holohan*, 294 U.S. 103 (1935). For later applications of this rule see: *Mesarosh v. United States*, 352 U.S. 1 (1956); *Alcorta v. Texas*, 355 U.S. 28 (1957); *Miller v. Pate*, 386 U.S. 1 (1967).
48. 294 U.S. 112.
49. *Brady v. Maryland*, 373 U.S. 83 (1963); *Giles v. Maryland*, 386 U.S. 66 (1967).
50. *Thompson v. Louisville*, 362 U.S. 199 (1960).
51. See, e.g., *Garner v. Louisiana*, 368 U.S. 157 (1961); *Taylor v. Louisiana*, 370 U.S. 154 (1962); *Barr v. Columbia*, 378 U.S. 146 (1964); *Shuttlesworth v. Birmingham*, 382 U.S. 87 (1965). See also *Johnson v. Florida*, 391 U.S. 596 (1968), which reversed a vagrancy conviction on the ground that the record was lacking in any evidence to support the judgment.
52. 28 U.S.C. Sec. 2241–55 (1970).
53. 28 U.S.C. Sec. 2254 (b)(c). In *Darr v. Burford*, 339 U.S. 200 (1950), the Court ruled that the exhaustion doctrine required that the state prisoner seek a writ of certiorari from the Supreme Court, even though most petitions for certiorari are denied summarily, before he is eligible to apply for a writ of habeas corpus in a federal district court. This decision was overruled, however, in *Fay v. Nola*, 372 U.S. 391 (1963), on the sensible ground that a petition to the Supreme Court for a writ of certiorari is not a state remedy.
54. *Jones v. Cunningham*, 371 U.S. 236 (1963). The petitioner had to report to his parole officer once a month, had to live with designated relatives, and could not leave the community, or change his residence, or operate an automobile, without his parole officer's permission.
55. *Carafas v. LaVallee*, 391 U.S. 234 (1968). This case overruled the 5–4 decision of the Court in *Parker v. Ellis*, 362 U.S. 574 (1960).
56. 28 U.S.C. Sec. 2244 (b).
57. *Jones v. Cunningham*, 371 U.S. 236, 243 (1963).
58. 347 U.S. 483 (Brown I).
59. Brown *v. Board of Education* (Brown II), 349 U.S. 294, 301 (1955).
60. *Griffin v. County School Board of Prince Edward County*, 377 U.S. 218, 234 (1964).
61. 396 U.S. 186.
62. *Wesberry v. Sanders*, 376 U.S. 1 (1964).
63. 351 U.S. 12.
64. For cases dealing with the free transcript problem in different situations see: *Eskridge v. Washington State Board*, 357 U.S. 214 (1958); *Lane v. Brown*, 372 U.S. 477 (1963); *Draper v. Washington*, 372 U.S. 487 (1963); *Williams v. Oklahoma City*, 395 U.S. 458 (1969); *Mayer v. Chicago*, 404 U.S. 189 (1971); *Gardner v. California*, 395 U.S. 925 (1969). See also *Burns v. Ohio*, 360 U.S. 252 (1959) (filing fees); *Williams v. Illinois*, 399 U.S. 235 (1970) (imprisonment based on inability to pay fine); *Tate v. Short*, 401 U.S. 395 (1971) (imprisonment solely because of indigency).
65. See, e.g., *Morey v. Doud*, 354 U.S. 457, 463–64 (1957).
66. *Reynolds v. Sims*, 377 U.S. 533 (1964). Here Chief Justice Warren declared that "especially since the right to exercise the franchise in a free and unimpaired manner is preservative of other basic civil and political rights, any alleged

infringement of the right of citizens to vote must be carefully and meticulously scrutinized." Ibid., 562.

67. See, e.g., *Hunter v. Erickson,* 393 U.S. 385, 391–92 (1969), where Justice White declared: "Because the core of the Fourteenth Amendment is the prevention of meaningful and unjustified official distinctions based on race, . . . racial classifications are 'constitutionally suspect,' . . . and subject to the 'most rigid scrutiny.' . . . They 'bear a far heavier burden of justification' than other classifications. . . ." See Wallace Mendelson, "From Warren to Burger: The Rise and Decline of Substantive Equal Protection," *American Political Science Review* 66 (December 1972): 1226–33.

68. See, e.g., *Williams v. Rhodes,* 393 U.S. 23 (1968).

69. See, e.g., *United States v. Guest,* 383 U.S. 239 (1966); *United States v. Price,* 383 U.S. 239 (1966). See also *Williams v. United States,* 341 U.S. 97 (1951); *Robinson v. Florida,* 378 U.S. 153 (1964); *Adickes v. S. H. Kress Co.,* 398 U.S. 144 (1970).

70. The leading decision on this point was *Hodges v. United States,* 203 U.S. 1 (1906).

71. *Jones v. Mayer Co.,* 392 U.S. 409 (1968). See also *Griffin v. Breckenridge,* 403 U.S. 88 (1951).

72. *Heart of Atlanta Motel v. United States,* 379 U.S. 241 (1964); *Katzenbach v. Ollie McClung,* 379 U.S. 294 (1964).

73. 71 *Stat.* 634.

74. 74 *Stat.* 86.

75. 78 *Stat.* 241.

76. 82 *Stat.* 73.

77. 79 *Stat.* 437.

78. See Chester J. Antieau, *Federal Civil Rights Acts* (Rochester, N.Y.: Lawyers Co-operative Publishing Co., 1971), ch. 6. There have also been a number of lawsuits under 42 U.S.C. Sec. 1985, dealing with conspiracies to deny federal rights. See Antieau, ch. 7.

79. Annual Report of the Director of the Administrative Office of the U.S. Courts (Washington: U.S. Government Printing Office, 1975), pp. 221, 191.

80. Charles Alan Wright, *Handbook of the Law of Federal Courts* (St. Paul: West Publishing Co., 1970, 2d ed.), p. 217.

81. *To Secure These Rights,* Report of the President's Committee on Civil Rights (Washington: U.S. Government Printing Office, 1947), pp. 99–100.

82. See the excellent survey of state court opinion by Bradley C. Canon, "Organizational Contumacy in the Transmission of Judicial Policies: The *Mapp, Escobedo, Miranda* and *Gault* Cases," *Villanova Law Review* 20 (November 1974): 50–79. For an interesting example of an expression of acute state court hostility to recent decisions of the U.S. Supreme Court, see *Dyett v. Turner,* 20 Utah 2d 403, 439 P.2d 266 (1968).

4. Henry J. Abraham: THE SUPREME COURT IN POLITICAL PROCESS

1. 1 Cranch 137 (1803).

2. In fourth place stands Mr. Justice Black, who served thirty-four years and a bit more than a month, at his retirement in September of 1971 falling just five months short of the all-time longevity record. Fifth is Mr. Justice John Marshall Harlan, the Elder, who served exactly thirty-four years.

3. 2 Cranch 170 (1804).

4. 19 How. 393 (1957).

5. See table 1 (appendix) for a complete roster of the instances involved.

6. See table 2 (appendix).

7. Of 128 state laws invalidated by the Court before 1888, 50 had involved the interstate commerce clause, 50 the obligation-of-contract clause, and only 1 the taking of property "without due process of law." The Fuller Court, on the other hand, ultimately concentrated on the latter point with a vengeance.
8. E.g., *Powell v. McCormack*, 395 U.S. 486 (1969); *Watkins v. United States*, 354 U.S. 178 (1957); *Oregon v. Mitchell*, 400 U.S. 112 (1970).
9. E.g., *Ex parte Merryman*, 17 Fed. Cas. 144 (1861); *Youngstown v. Sawyer*, 343 U.S. 579 (1951); *New York Times v. United States*, 403 U.S. 713 (1971); *United States v. Nixon*, 418 U.S. 683 (1974).
10. *Justices Black and Frankfurter: Conflict in the Court* (Chicago: University of Chicago Press, 1961), pp. 75-76. On this point see also the perceptive, albeit controversial, article by Robert A. Dahl, "Decision-Making in a Democracy: The Supreme Court as a National Policy Maker," *Journal of Public Law* 6 (1957): 279.
11. *Justice Holmes, Natural Law, and the Supreme Court* (New York: The Macmillan Company, 1961), p. 73.
12. See Victor G. Rosenblum, "Law as an Instrument of Social Reform: A Second Look," *Law and Liberty* 1 (winter 1975): 4.
13. E.g., S. Sidney Ulmer, "Judicial Review as Political Behavior: A Temporary Check on Congress," *Administrative Science Quarterly* 4 (March 1960): 426.
14. 385 U.S. 1.
15. *United States v. United Mine Workers*, 330 U.S. 258. Obvious illustrations are the Court's stance on proprietarian-economic problems; the congressional counterattack on the *Miranda* decision; and the passage and ratification of the Twenty-sixth Amendment.
16. See Henry J. Abraham, *Justices and Presidents: A Political History of Appointments to the Supreme Court* (New York: Oxford University Press, 1974).
17. See, for example, the actions of the 90th Congress in the Omnibus Crime Act of 1968 (*re Malloy, Wade,* and *Miranda*), and subsequent legislative action in the criminal justice realm.
18. 297 U.S. 1 (1936).
19. 297 U.S. 1 (1936), at 62. Italics added.
20. 19 How. 393 (1857).
21. 347 U.S. 783 (1954).
22. "The Case for Judicial Activism," *The Yale Review* 56, no. 2 (winter 1967): 197-211.
23. 297 U.S. 1 (1936), loc. cit. at 78. Italics added.
24. *Southern Pacific Co. v. Jensen*, 224 U.S. 205 (1916), at 221.
25. Benjamin N. Cardozo, *The Nature of the Judicial Process* (New Haven: Yale University Press, 1921), p. 169.
26. As quoted by Alpheus T. Mason and William M. Beaney in *American Constitutional Law*, 5th ed. (Englewood Cliffs: Prentice-Hall, 1972), p. xxvi.
27. For a list of sixteen "maxims" of this self-restraint, see my *The Judicial Process: An Introductory Analysis of the Courts of the United States, England, and France*, 3d ed. (New York: Oxford University Press, 1975), ch. 9.
28. *The New York Times*, 15 November 1971, p. 41. Italics added.
29. 384 U.S. 433 (1966).
30. *Roe v. Wade*, 410 U.S. 113, and *Doe v. Bolton*, 410 U.S. 179 (1973).
31. *Goss v. Lopez*, 419 U.S. 565 (1975); *Baker v. Owen*, 44 LW 3237 (1975).
32. E. g., *Downes v. Bidwell*, 183 U.S. 244 (1909), and *De Lima v. Bidwell*, 182 U.S. 1 (1901).
33. E. g., *Watkins v. U.S.*, 354 U.S. 178; *Jencks v. U.S.*, 353 U.S. 657; *Yates v. U.S.*, 354 U.S. 298.
34. E.g., *Engel v. Vitale*, 370 U.S. 421 (1962); *Abington Township v. Schempp*, and *Murray v. Curlett*, 374 U.S. 203 (1963); *Lemon v. Kurtzman*, 403 U.S. 602 (1971).
35. E.g., *Mapp v. Ohio*, 367 U.S. 643 (1961); *Gideon v. Wainright*, 372 U.S.

335 (1963); *Escobedo v. Illinois,* 378 U.S. 478 (1964); *Miranda v. Arizona,* 384 U.S. 436 (1966); *United States v. Wade,* 388 U.S. 218 (1967).

36. E.g., *Reed v. Reed,* 404 U.S. 71 (1971); *Frontiero v. Richardson,* 411 U.S. 677 (1973); *Graham v. Richardson,* 403 U.S. 365 (1971); *Norwood v. Harrison,* 413 U.S. 455 (1973).

37. E.g., *Roe v. Wade,* and *Doe v. Bolton,* supra, note 30; *Boddie v. Connecticut,* 401 U.S. 371 (1971).

38. *Brown v. Board of Education* (I), 347 U.S. 483 (1954), and ibid. (II), 349 U.S. 294 (1955); *Alexander v. Holmes County of Mississippi,* 396 U.S. 19 (1969); and *Swann v. Charlotte-Mecklenburg,* 402 U.S. 1 (1971).

39. *Marbury v. Madison,* 1 Cranch 137 (1803); *McCulloch v. Maryland,* 4 Wheat. 316 (1819); *Martin v. Hunter's Lessee,* 1 Wheat. 304 (1816); and *Gibbons v. Ogden,* 9 Wheat. 1 (1824). Among the reapportionment and redistricting decisions, see *Baker v. Carr,* 369 U.S. 186 (1962); *Reynolds v. Sims,* 377 U.S. 533 (1964); and *Avery v. Midland County,* 390 U.S. 474 (1968).

40. *Uveges v. Pennsylvania,* 335 U.S. 437 (1948), at 437.

41. *Reynolds v. Sims,* 377 U.S. 533 (1964), at 624.

42. Eugene V. Rostow, "The Democratic Character of Judicial Review," *Harvard Law Review* 66 (1952): 195.

43. Judge Hutcheson of Texas, as quoted by Eugene V. Rostow in his *The Sovereign Prerogative: The Supreme Court and the Quest for Law* (New Haven: Yale University Press, 1962), p. 110.

44. *Reynolds v. Sims,* 377 U.S. 533 (1964), dissenting opinion, at 624.

45. Anthony Lewis, *New York Times Magazine,* 17 June 1962, p. 38.

46. U.S. Court of Appeals Judge J. Skelly Wright, "The Role of the Courts: Conscience of a Sovereign People," *The Reporter* 29 (26 September 1963): 5.

47. Alexander Meiklejohn, *Free Speech and its Relations to Self-Government* (New York: Harper & Bros., 1948), p. 32.

48. Justice Holmes once stated this [his own] constitutional philosophy to the then sixty-one-years-old Stone: "Young man, about 75 years ago I learned that I was not God. And so, when the people . . . want to do something I can't find anything in the Constitution expressly forbidding them to do, I say, whether I like it or not, 'Goddammit, let 'em do it!'" As quoted in Charles P. Curtis, Jr., *Lions under the Throne* (Boston: Houghton Mifflin Company, 1947), p. 281.

49. Charles L. Black, Jr., *The People and the Court* (New York: The Macmillan Company, 1960), p. 12.

50. *The Supreme Court of the United States* (New York: Columbia University Press, 1928), p. 236.

51. Robert H. Jackson, *The Supreme Court in the American System of Government* (Cambridge: Harvard University Press, 1955), p. 23.

52. "The Logic and Rhetoric of Constitutional Law," *Journal of Philosophy, Psychology, and Scientific Method* 15 (1918): 656.

APPENDIX TO CHAPTER 4

Table 1: **Federal Laws Declared Wholly or Partly Unconstitutional by the United States Supreme Court**

Period	Number	
1789–1801	0	
1801–1836	1	1803: *Marbury v. Madison*
1836–1857	0	Taney's Court
1857–1864	1	1857: *Dred Scott v. Sandford*
1864–1873	9	1870: *Legal Tender* cases
1874–1888	8	1883: *Civil Rights* cases

1888-1910	14(15)	1895: *Income Tax* cases
1910-1921	13	1918: *Child Labor* case
1921-1930	13	1923: *Minimum Wage* case
1930-1936	14	Of these, 13 came in 1934-36! (Hughes Court)
1936-1941	0	Hughes Court moves into the New Deal.
1941-1946	2	Stone
1946-1953	1	Vinson
1953-1969	19	Warren Court
1969-	21	Burger Court

Post-1943 Cases

Tot v. United States, 319 U.S. 463 (1943).
United States v. Lovett, 328 U.S. 303 (1946).
United States v. Cardiff, 344 U.S. 174 (1952).
Bolling v. Sharpe, 347 U.S. 497 (1954).
United States ex rel. Toth v. Quarles, 350 U.S. 11 (1955).
Reid v. Covert, 354 U.S. 1 (1957), coupled with *Kinsella v. Singleton* and *Grisham v. Hagan,* 361 U.S. 234 (1960), 361 U.S. 278 (1960).
Trop v. Dulles, 356 U.S. 86 (1958).
Kennedy v. Mendoza-Martinez, and *Rusk v. Cort,* 372 U.S. 144 (1963)–same citations, but separate provisions of *two* separate statutes.
Schneider v. Rusk, 377 U.S. 163 (1964).
Aptheker v. Secretary of State, 378 U.S. 500 (1964).
Lamont v. Postmaster-General, and *Fixa v. Heilberg,* 381 U.S. 301 (1965)–same citations and same provisions of the same statute.
Afroyim v. Rusk, 387 U.S. 253 (1967).
Marchetti v. United States, 390 U.S. 39 (1968), *Grosso v. United States,* 390 U.S. 62 (1968), and *Haynes v. United States,* 390 U.S. 85 (1968)–same S.I. issue (combined), but involving provisions of two separate statutes.
United States v. Jackson, 390 U.S. 569 (1968).
Washington v. Legrant, 394 U.S. 618 (1969).
Leary v. U.S., 395 U.S. 6 (1969)–same decision and same litigants, but involving two separate statutes.
Schacht v. U.S., 398 U.S. 58 (1970).
Blount v. Rizzi, and *U.S. v. The Book Bin,* 400 U.S. 410 (1971)–same citation but two different statutes involving the same ("mail block") problem.
Tilton v. Richardson, 403 U.S. 672 (1971).
Chief of Capitol Police v. Jeannette Rankin Brigade, 409 U.S. 972 (1972).
Richardson v. Davis, and *Richardson v. Griffin,* 409 U.S. 1069 (1972)–same citations and same provisions of the same statute.
Frontiero v. Richardson, 411 U.S. 677 (1973)–two provisions in two different statutes, but same case.
United States Department of Agriculture v. Moreno, 413 U.S. 508 (1973), and *United States Department v. Murry,* 413 U.S. 528 (1973).
Jiminez v. Weinberger, 417 U.S. 628 (1974).
Weinberger v. Wiesenfeld, 420 U.S. 636 (1975).
Buckley v. Valeo, 421 U.S. 1 (1976).
National League of Cities v. Usery, 426 U.S. 833 (1976).
Califano v. Goldfarb, 97 S. Ct. 1021 (1977).
Califano v. Silbowitz, 97 S. Ct. 1021 (1977).

Table 2. **Periods of Discernible Tendencies toward Supremacy of Branches of the Government**

A. Tendencies toward Legislative Supremacy

Years	*President(s)*	*Chief Justice(s)*	*Commentary*
1809–1829	Madison, Monroe	Marshall	Supremacy facilitated and advanced by powerful Court
1837–1845	Van Buren, W. H. Harrison, Tyler	Taney Taney	Aided by strong Court and passive presidents
1849–1861	Taylor, Fillmore, Pierce, Buchanan	Taney Taney	Nadir of presidency *Dred Scott* case
1865–1885	Johnson, Grant, Hayes, Garfield, Arthur	S. P. Chase, Waite	Partially effective opposition by Johnson and Hayes
1919–1921	Wilson	White	Defeat of League; President ill
1921–1933	Harding, Coolidge, Hoover	Taft, Hughes	Cooperative Court; weak, passive presidents
1953–1959	Eisenhower	Taft, Hughes, Warren	Strong Court; passive president

B. Tendencies toward Executive Supremacy

Years	*President(s)*	*Chief Justice(s)*	*Commentary*
1789–1797	Washington	Jay, Rutledge, Ellsworth,	Cooperative Congress; weak, docile Court
1801–1809	Jefferson	Marshall	Some doubt about executive supremacy
1829–1837	Jackson	Marshall, Taney	President in high form; last years of Marshall Court
1845–1849	Polk	Taney	Underrated President
1861–1865	Lincoln	Taney, S. P. Chase	High-water mark of presidency; Civil War
1901–1908	T. Roosevelt	Fuller	Assertive Court; popular president
1913–1919	Wilson	White	President lost control to Republican Congressional majority in 1919
1933–1947	F. D. Roosevelt, Truman	Hughes, Stone, Vinson	Revolution on Court, 1937; powerful president: FDR
1963–1968	L.B. Johnson	Warren	Powerful president: L.B.J.
1969–1974	Nixon	Burger	Power-asserting President, felled by "Watergate"; resigned 9 August 1974

C. Tendencies toward Judicial Supremacy

Years	*President(s)*	*Chief Justice(s)*	*Commentary*
1801–1829	Jefferson, Madison, Monroe, J.Q. Adams	Marshall	The greatest chief justice at power's peak
1857	Pierce, Buchanan	Taney	*Dred Scott* case
1889–1910	B. Harrison, Cleveland, McKinley	Fuller	Some doubt about Cleveland's term (his second)
1935–1936	F.D. Roosevelt	Hughes	13 New Deal laws declared unconstitutional

D. Not Readily Discernible Supremacy Tendencies

1797–1801	John Adams	Ellsworth	President and Congress shared power
1885–1889	Cleveland	Waite, Fuller	Probably presidential, but uncertain
1910–1913	Taft	White	Uncertainty
1947–1953	Truman	Vinson	Divided foreign and domestic tendencies
1959–1960	Eisenhower	Warren	Sudden assertion of power by President; Democratic Congressional majority
1961–1963	Kennedy	Warren	Too brief to judge conclusively, but featured by divided foreign and domestic tendencies
1974–1977	Ford	Burger	Too brief for a definite trend
1977–	Carter	Burger	In abeyance

5. Martin M. Shapiro: THE CONSTITUTION AND ECONOMIC RIGHTS

1. The founding father of the New Deal school is E. S. Corwin. See his *Twilight of the Supreme Court* (New Haven: Yale University Press, 1934); *Court over Constitution* (Princeton: Princeton University Press, 1938). It is so dominant a school that to list its adherents would simply be to list almost all those who were prominent commentators on the Court in the 1940s, 50s, and 60s.
2. See, e.g., E. S. Corwin, *The President: Office and Powers,* 4th ed. (New York: New York University Press, 1957); Richard Lenstadt, *Presidential Power* (New York: John Wiley & Sons, 1968); James MacGregor Burns, *Presidential Government* (Boston: Houghton Mifflin Company, 1965).
3. See, e.g., Arthur Schlesinger, Jr., *The Imperial Presidency* (Boston: Houghton Mifflin Company, 1973).
4. One of the leaders of this New Deal school was a Bull Moose Republican, Learned Hand. See his *Bill of Rights* (Cambridge, Mass.: Harvard University Press, 1958); Corwin, *Twilight.* A review of this school and its premises may be found in Martin Shapiro, *Freedom of Speech: The Supreme Court and Judicial Review* (Englewood Cliffs: Prentice Hall, 1966) ch. 1.
5. See, e.g., Harold W. Chase and Craig R. Ducat, *Constitutional Interpretation* (St. Paul: West Publishing Co., 1974) pp. 446–48.
6. See. e.g., Alpheus T. Mason and William M. Beaney, *American Constitutional Law,* 5th ed. (Englewood Cliffs: Prentice-Hall, 1972) pp. 323–41.
7. See, e.g., Alpheus T. Mason, *The Supreme Court from Taft to Warren* (Baton Rouge: Louisiana State University Press, 1958); Arthur S. Miller, *The Supreme Court and American Capitalism* (New York: Free Press, 1968); Robert G. McCloskey, "Economic Due Process and the Supreme Court: An Exhumation and Reburial," *Supreme Court Review* 1962: 34.
8. See Benjamin F. Wright, *The Growth of American Constitutional Law* (Boston: Houghton Mifflin Company, 1942).
9. See E. S. Corwin, "The 'Higher Law' Background of American Constitutional Law," *Harvard Law Review* 42 (1928–29): 149, 365.
10. Two of the major pieces of nineteenth-century business regulation show this tendency clearly, the Interstate Commerce Act of 1888 and the Sherman Antitrust Act of 1890.

11. 298 U.S. 238.
12. 295 U.S. 495.
13. 317 U.S. 111.
14. 347 U.S. 483.
15. *Mapp v. Ohio,* 367 U.S. 643 (1961).
16. *Miranda v. Arizona,* 384 U.S. 436 (1966).
17. *Swift and Company v. United States,* 196 U.S. 375 (1905); *Stafford v. Wallace,* 258 U.S. 495 (1922).
18. 156 U.S. 1.
19. See *National Labor Relations Board v. Jones and Laughlin Steel Corporation,* 301 U.S. 1 (1937).
20. *Schechter Poultry Corp. v. United States,* 295 U.S. 495 (1935).
21. *United States v. Butler,* 297 U.S. 1 (1936).
22. *Mulford v. Smith,* 307 U.S. 38 (1939).
23. *Panama Refining Company v. Ryan,* 293 U.S. 388 (1935).
24. 295 U.S. 495.
25. See Theodore Lowi, *The End of Liberalism* (New York: W. W. Norton & Company, 1969), pp. 298–99.
26. 304 U.S. 144. Justice Stone himself was a pre–New Deal Republican appointee. But he voted fairly consistently in favor of the New Deal even before 1937 and was Roosevelt's choice for chief justice in 1941. In the discussion of preferred position that follows and on many other points later in this paper, my views closely parallel those of Professor Funston. Both of us have been attacking the distinction between civil rights and property rights for some time. Cf. Richard Funston, "The Double Standard of Constitutional Protection," *Political Science Quarterly* 90 (1975): 261; with Martin Shapiro and Douglas Hobbes, *Politics of Constitutional Law* (Cambridge, Mass.: Winthrop Publishers, 1974), pp. 152–53; Shapiro, "The Burger Court: A Judicial Impact Statement," paper delivered at the annual meeting, Southwestern Political Science Association, Dallas, Texas, April 1973, particularly pp. 4–5, 17–23. But see Frank R. Strong, "The Economic Philosophy of Lochner: Emergence, Embrasure and Emasculation," *Arizona Law Review* 15 (1973): 419.
27. See, e.g., Wallace Mendelson, *Justices Black and Frankfurter: Conflict in the Court* (Chicago: University of Chicago Press, 1961).
28. It must be noted that New Deal commentators on the Court almost invariably speak of judicial deference to Congress or legislative intent. But this language must be read in the more general context of New Deal political commentary that preached congressional subservience to strong presidential leadership. Thus, when one reads such commentary, one must translate "deference to the legislature" as "deference to the executive."
29. Shapiro, *Freedom of Speech,* pp. 111–72.
30. While the incorporation of the First Amendment into the due process clause of the Fourteenth is suggested in *Gitlow v. New York,* 268 U.S. 652 (1925), the actual incorporation seems to occur in *De Jonge v. Oregon,* 299 U.S. 353 (1937), and *Herndon v. Lowry,* 301 U.S. 242 (1937), both decided just the year before *Carolene Products.*
31. See his opinion in *Roth v. United States,* 354 U.S. 476 (1957).
32. 316 U.S. 535.
33. See Karst, "Individious Discrimination: Justice Douglas and the Return of the 'Natural-Law-Due-Process Formula,'" *U.C.L.A. Law Review* 16 (1969): 716.
34. Cf. *Waltz v. Tax Commission,* 397 U.S. 664 (1970) with *Comm. for Public Education v. Nyquist,* 413 U.S. 756 (1973).
35. Cf. *Tilton v. Richardson,* 403 U.S. 672 (1971), with *Lemon v. Kurtzman,* 403 U.S. 602 (1971).
36. Wallace Mendelson, "From Warren to Burger: The Rise and Decline of Substantive Equal Protection," *American Political Science Review* 66 (1972): 1226;

G. Gunther, "In Search of Evolving Doctrine on a Changing Court: A Model for a Newer Equal Protection," *Harvard Law Review* 86 (1972): 1.

37. But it has made one extension. Sex is now a suspect classification. See *Frontiero v. Richardson*, 411 U.S. 677 (1973).

38. 405 U.S. 438.

39. 406 U.S. 164.

40. Id. at 173–176.

41. 391 U.S. 68.

42. 391 U.S. 73 (1968).

43. See K. Karst, "Legislative Facts in Constitutional Litigation," *Supreme Court Review* 1960: 75.

44. 410 U.S. 179 (1973).

45. See, e.g., *United States v. Darby*, 312 U.S. 100 (1941); *Wickard v. Filburn*, 317 U.S. 111 (1942).

46. See Martin Shapiro, *Law and Politics in the Supreme Court* (New York: Free Press, 1964), pp. 77–83.

47. These cases are reviewed and commented upon in Note: "Government Employee Disclosures of Agency Wrongdoing," *University of Chicago Law Review* 42 (1975): 533.

48. See *Adler v. Board of Education*, 342 U.S. 485 (1952).

49. *Keyishian v. Board of Regents*, 385 U.S. 589 (1967).

50. 414 U.S. 632.

51. 198 U.S. 45.

52. 243 U.S. 426.

53. 261 U.S. 525.

54. See *Arnett v. Kennedy*, 94 S. Ct. 1633, 1649–50 (1974). (Justice Powell concurring); *Goss v. Lopez*, 95 S. Ct. 729 (1975). "Protected interests in property. . . are created . . . by state statutes. Accordingly a state employee who under state law has a legitimate claim of entitlement to continued employment . . . may demand . . . protections of due process."

55. See, for example, *Shelley v. Kraemer*, 334 U.S. 1 (1958), *Pennsylvania v. Board of Trusts*, 353 U.S. 230 (1957), *Evans v. Newton*, 382 U.S. 296 (1966), *Jones v. Alfred H. Mayer Company*, 392 U.S. 441 (1968), and *Lindsey v. Normet*, 405 U.S. 56 (1972).

56. 339 U.S. 629.

57. 347 U.S. 483.

58. *Vlandis v. Kline*, 412 U.S. 441 (1973).

59. *San Antonio Independent School District v. Rodriguez*, 411 U.S. 1 (1973).

60. *Goss v. Lopez*, 95 S. Ct. 729 (1975).

61. 366 U.S. 420.

62. 374 U.S. 398.

63. *Waltz*, supra, note 34. See also *Committee for Public Education v. Nyquist*, 413 U.S. 756 (1973), and *Meek v. Pittenger*, 95 S. Ct. 1753 (1975).

64. 394 U.S. 618.

65. Much of the case law, which runs across welfare, criminal procedure, voting and elections, housing, education and a number of other areas, is summarized in Michelman, "On Protecting the Poor through the Fourteenth Amendment," *Harvard Law Review* 83 (1969): 7, and "Developments in the Law: Equal Protection," *Harvard Law Review* 82 (1969): 1065. The Warren Court's use of "fundamental rights" language was nicely calculated to blur the distinction between personal and economic rights without openly abandoning it.

66. *Goldberg v. Kelly*, 397 U.S. 254 (1970).

67. *Dandridge v. Williams*, 397 U.S. 471 (1970); *Richardson v. Belcher*, 404 U.S. 78 (1971); *Jefferson v. Hackney*, 406 U.S. 535 (1972); *Graham v. Richardson*, 403 U.S. 365 (1971); *Jiminez v. Weinberger*, 94 S. Ct. 2497 (1974).

68. See, for example, *Dandridge* (supra, note 67), and *Ortwein v. Schwab*, 411 U.S. 922 (1973).
69. See supra, note 36.
70. 413 U.S. 528.
71. 6 Cr. 87.
72. 165 U.S. 578.
73. 272 U.S. 365.
74. 341 U.S. 494.
75. 402 U.S. 137.
76. *Boddie v. Connecticut*, 401 U.S. 371 (1971).
77. *Sniadack v. Family Finance Corporation*, 395 U.S. 337 (1969); *Lindsey v. Normet*, 405 U.S. 56 (1972); *Fuentes v. Shevin*, 407 U.S. 67 (1972); *Mitchell v. W. T. Grant Company*, 94 S. Ct. 1895 (1974).
78. For two recent examples see *Austin v. New Hampshire*, 95 S. Ct. 1191 (1975); *Colonial Pipeline Company v. Traigle*, 95 S. Ct. 1538 (1975).
79. *Reed v. Reed*, 404 U.S. 71 (1971).
80. *Kahn v. Shiven*, 416 U.S. 351 (1974).
81. *Cleveland Board of Education v. La Fleur*, 94 S. Ct. 791 (1974).
82. *Geduldig v. Aiello*, 417 U.S. 484 (1974).
83. *Schlesinger v. Ballard*, 419 U.S. 498 (1975).
84. *Weinberger v. Eisingeld*, 95 S. Ct. 1225 (1975).
85. *Stanton v. Stanton*, 95 S. Ct. 1373 (1975).
86. 411 U.S. 677 (preference for men over women in armed forces dependents' benefits).
87. 261 U.S. 525.
88. 208 U.S. 412.
89. 243 U.S. 426.
90. 261 U.S. 525.
91. *Griggs v. Duke Power Company*, 401 U.S. 424 (1971); *Albemarle Paper Company v. Moody*, 95 S. Ct. 2362 (1975).
92. *DeFunis v. Odegaard*, 94 S. Ct. 1704 (1974); *Morton v. Mancari*, 94 S. Ct. 2474 (1974).
93. Cf. *Food Employees Local 509 v. Logan Valley Plaza, Inc.*, 395 U.S. 575 (1969), with *Lloyd Corp. v. Tanner*, 407 U.S. 551 (1972).
94. "Chief Justice Stone's Concept of the Judicial Function," in Dillard, ed., *The Spirit of Liberty*, 3rd ed. (New York, 1963), I.
95. See Henry Abraham, "'Human' Rights vs. 'Property' Rights: A Comment on the 'Double Standard,'" *Political Science Quarterly* 90 (1975): 288.
96. Shapiro, *Freedom of Speech*, pp. 34–44.
97. 405 U.S. 538, 543–48, 551–2. Viewed narrowly, this case involves only the statutory interpretation issue of whether Congress intended to grant standing under 28 U.S.C. 1343 (3) to those with property interests. Yet the quotation from *Shelley v. Kraemer*, which is a constitutional holding, the extremely general language of the Court, and the fact that the statutory distinction attacked is exactly parallel to the constitutional one and initially came from the same inventor, Justice Stone, clearly suggests that the Court has generally abandoned the distinction and not merely decided that Congress did not intend to apply it to a particular statute.
98. *Pittsburgh v. Alco Parking Corp.*, 417 U.S. 369 (1974).
99. In the 1976 term the Court seemed deliberately to couple two cases in order to underline its greater concern for the new property than the old. *Massachusetts Board of Retirement v. Murgia*, 96 S. Ct. 2562 (1976), repeated the teaching of *Goss v. Lopez* that the Court would intervene to protect public employment interests created by state statute although it signaled that it would read such statutes narrowly. In *City of New Orleans v. Dukes*, 96 S. Ct. 2513 (1976), on the other hand, it proclaimed complete New Deal deference to legislative judgment where

government was merely depriving a private citizen of his business rather than a civil servant of his government job.

6. C. Herman Pritchett: JUDICIAL SUPREMACY

1. *History of the Supreme Court of the United States: Antecedents and Beginnings to 1801* (New York: The Macmillan Company, 1971).
2. *Vagaries and Varieties in Constitutional Interpretation* (New York: Columbia University Press, 1956), p. 14.
3. *The Supreme Court and the Constitution* (Englewood Cliffs: Prentice-Hall, 1962), p. 47.
4. *Politics and the Constitution in the History of the United States* (Chicago: University of Chicago Press, 1953), chs. 28–29.
5. *The Bill of Rights* (Cambridge: Harvard University Press, 1958), p. 15.
6. Introduction to Beard, p. 11.
7. *United States v. Burr,* 4 Cr. 470 (1807). See Raoul Berger, "The President, Congress, and the Courts–Subpoenaing the President: Jefferson v. Marshall in the Burr Case," *Yale Law Journal* 83 (1974): 1111.
8. *Ex parte Merryman,* 17 Fed. Cas. 144 (1861). See Clinton Rossiter, *The Supreme Court and the Commander in Chief* (Ithaca: Cornell University Press, 1951), pp. 18–26.
9. "Court-Curbing Periods in American History," *Vanderbilt Law Review* 18 (1965): 925.
10. For an account of this period, see C. Herman Pritchett, *Congress versus the Supreme Court, 1957-1960* (Minneapolis: University of Minnesota Press, 1961), and Walter F. Murphy, *Congress and the Court* (Chicago: University of Chicago Press, 1962).
11. The sole exception was the congressional limitation on the Court's appellate jurisdiction approved in *Ex parte McCardle,* 7 Wall. 211.506 (1896).
12. See Irving Brant, *Impeachment: Trials and Errors* (New York: Alfred A. Knopf, 1972).
13. See Henry J. Abraham, *Justices and Presidents: A Political History of Appointments to the Supreme Court* (New York: Oxford University Press, 1974).
14. *West Virginia State Board of Education v. Barnette,* 319 U.S. 1 (1943).
15. *Pollock v. Farmers' Loan and Trust Co.,* 157 U.S. 429 (1895); *In re Debs,* 158 U.S. 564 (1895).
16. *Furman v. Georgia,* 408 U.S. 238 (1972).
17. *Roe v. Wade,* 410 U.S. 113 (1973), *Doe v. Bolton,* 410 U.S. 179 (1973).
18. *Buckley v. Valeo,* 96 Sup. Ct. 612 (1976).
19. See Gerald Gunther, "In Search of Evolving Doctrine on a Changing Court: A Model for a Newer Equal Protection," *Harvard Law Review* 86 (1972): 1.
20. "Decision-Making in a Democracy: The Role of the Supreme Court as a National Policy-Maker," *Journal of Public Law* 6 (1958): 279.
21. *The Supreme Court: Its Politics, Personalities, and Procedures* (New York: Holt, Rinehart and Winston, 1960), p. 59.
22. The other, of course, is Chief Justice Warren's footnote in *Brown v. Board of Education,* 347 U.S. 483 (1954), citing certain social science studies in support of the Court's ruling against school segregation.
23. See Philippa Strum, *The Supreme Court and "Political Questions,"* (University: University of Alabama Press, 1974).

7. Louis Henkin: CONSTITUTION AND FOREIGN AFFAIRS

1. I have written on the general subject, notably a book, *Foreign Affairs and the Constitution* (Mineola, N.Y.: Foundation Press, 1972), and later a paper for the Commission on the Organization of the Government for the Conduct of Foreign Policy ("The Murphy Commission"), published as "'A More Effective System for Foreign Relations: The Constitutional Framework," *Virginia Law Review* 61 (1975): 751.

2. Of course, contemporary controversies might too readily appear to us as crises, while those of an earlier day might seem less acute. But in the pages of the historians, at least, the controversies over Washington's Neutrality Proclamation or his treatment of Citizen Genêt, or Secretary Seward's French policy in Mexico, or Theodore Roosevelt's unilateral actions in Santo Domingo and elsewhere, or Senator Bricker's attempts to amend the Constitution to limit the treaty power, while they agitated individual congressmen and some evoked congressional resolutions, do not seem to have reached dimensions of crisis.

Supreme Court cases that have involved issues of allocation of authority between president and Congress were generally brought by private parties and did not in fact confront the president with Congress, and few if any of them were, or were seen as, foreign affairs cases. E.g., the *Steel Seizure* case, *Youngstown Sheet & Tube Co. v. Sawyer,* 343 U.S. 579 (1952); compare note 41 below. The leading foreign affairs cases were "lawyers' cases" and apparently did not agitate either the political arena or the public. E.g., *Missouri v. Holland,* 252 U.S. 416 (1920); *United States v. Curtiss-Wright Export Corp.*, 229 U.S. 304 (1936); *United States v. Belmont,* 301 U.S. 324 (1937); *Banco Nacional de Cuba v. Sabbatino,* 376 U.S. 398 (1964). In an earlier day, too, cases that were close to foreign affairs also did not seem to have loomed large in national politics, e.g., *Chinese Exclusion* case, 130 U.S. 581 (1889); *Downes v. Bidwell,* 182 U.S. 244 (1901).

3. James G. Rogers, *World Policing and the Constitution* (Boston: World Peace Foundation, 1945), p. 14.

4. Compare Mr. Justice Jackson in *Youngstown Sheet & Tube Co. v. Sawyer,* 343 U.S. 579, 634–35 (1952):

> A judge, like an executive adviser, may be surprised at the poverty of really useful and unambiguous authority applicable to concrete problems of executive power as they actually present themselves. Just what our forefathers did envision, or would have envisioned had they foreseen modern conditions, must be divined from materials almost as enigmatic as the dreams Joseph was called upon to interpret for Pharaoh. A century and a half of partisan debate and scholarly speculation yields no net result but only supplies more or less apt quotations from respected sources on each side of any question. They largely cancel each other. And the court decisions are indecisive because of the judicial practice of dealing with the largest questions in the most narrow way.

5. The president and Congress also have powers of general applicability that are important for foreign affairs. Congress taxes and spends for the common defense and the general welfare, appropriates funds, raises and supports armies, establishes executive offices, and makes necessary and proper laws to carry out other powers of government. (The "spending power" of Congress, in particular, has become a principal instrument in foreign policy, providing financial aid and arms to foreign governments.(The president has claimed authority related to foreign affairs by virtue of his designation as commander in chief of the armed forces and his responsibility to take care that the laws be faithfully executed.

6. The only reference to "the Government of the United States" is buried in the "necessary and proper" clause, Article I, section 8, clause 18. Perhaps the framers were not eager to emphasize the change from league of states to nation, from decision by vote in an assembly of state delegations to government by a national, central, United States government, out of fear that attention to that radical transformation might encourage opposition to ratification of the Constitution.

Compare the resolution of the Continental Congress convening the constitutional convention, which spoke of that convention as "appearing to be the most probable means of establishing in these states a firm national government"; it called for such revisions of the articles as shall "render the federal constitution adequate to the exigencies of Government and the preservation of the Union." Farrand, *Records of the Federal Convention of 1787* (1937 rev. ed.), III, appendix A, 13-14. Those references to "government" may refer to function, to "governance," rather than to an entity conceived of as "the Government."

7. 299 U.S. 304 (1936). I restate and discuss Sutherland's thesis at length in *Foreign Affairs,* ch. 1.

8. For recent, authoritative support for the thesis that we were essentially a union from independence, see Morris, "The Forging of the Union Reconsidered," *Columbia Law Review* 75 (1974): 1056.

9. Sutherland refers to "the very delicate, plenary and exclusive power of the President as the sole organ of the federal government in the field of international relations," 299 U.S. at 320, but he does not define the president's power, does not distinguish or divide it from the powers of Congress, nor does he justify or support it in constitutional scripture or in any implications from nationhood.

10. Such arguments can be found in Philip Quincy Wright, *The Control of American Foreign Relations* (1922).

11. *Head Money* cases, 112 U.S. 580 (1884). The Supreme Court later abandoned reliance on the commerce power and found authority to control immigration to be inherent in nationhood and sovereignty. *Chinese Exclusion* case, 130 U.S. 581 (1889). That this power belonged to Congress was assumed, perhaps as a "legislative component" of the powers of the United States inherent in its sovereignty, but some authority to exclude aliens was also found in the president. See *United States ex rel. Knauff v. Shaughnessy,* 338 U.S. 537, 542-43 (1950); Henkin, *Foreign Affairs,* pp. 303-4.

12. In our early history Congress abrogated treaties with France. 1 *Stat.* 578 (1798), 2 *Stat.* 7 (1800). See Henkin, *Foreign Affairs,* 418-19, n. 136.

13. Speaking of the president's part in the distribution of federal power generally, Justice Jackson suggested that there may be a "zone of twilight in which he and Congress may have concurrent authority, or in which its distribution is uncertain." *Youngstown Sheet & Tube Co. v. Sawyer,* 343 U.S. 579, 647 (1952) (concurring opinion); see Henkin, *Foreign Affairs,* pp. 96, 104-8, 348-52.

14. For example, can the president make a treaty ending a war declared by Congress, or modifying a congressional regulation of commerce? Can Congress direct the president to withdraw troops he has deployed on his own authority? Can Congress preempt, preclude, supersede, or otherwise control or regulate presidential decisions to recognize governments or to participate in international negotiations or organizations? May Congress enact legislation inconsistent with obligations in treaties which the president has made (with the consent of the Senate), or refuse to pass legislation or to appropriate funds to carry out the international obligation? See Henkin, *Foreign Affairs,* ch. 4.

15. In the Pacificus letters, Hamilton, *Works,* ed. Hamilton (1851), VII, 76, 81; Madison's reply, signed "Helvidius," is in Madison, *Writings,* ed. Hunt (1910), pp. 138, 147-50. The Pacificus-Helvidius debate, and an early twentieth-century replay between Senators Spooner and Bacon, are reproduced in part in E. S. Corwin, *The President's Control of Foreign Relations* (Princeton: Princeton University Press, 1917). Those debates focused, respectively, on the allocation of power to proclaim

neutrality or to make treaties. I have restated, embellished, supplemented, and generalized both arguments here. See also Henkin, *Foreign Affairs,* pp. 82–85.

16. That phrase is Jefferson's: "The transaction of business with foreign nations is *Executive* altogether. It belongs, then, to the head of that department except such portions of it as are specially submitted to the Senate. Exceptions are to be construed strictly." Jefferson, *Writings,* Ford ed. (1895), V, 161 (emphasis in original). Jefferson was hardly an exponent of expansive constitutional construction, but in terms of the distinction commonly drawn Jefferson was perhaps writing only of conducting foreign relations; Hamilton seemed to consider making foreign policy also executive. Compare p. 119 below.

17. See note 15 above. Madison rejected Hamilton's thesis as inspired by notions of British royal prerogative.

The views expressed by Madison as Helvidius do not necessarily ring the same as those he expressed at the Constitutional Convention, in the *Federalist* papers, as a member of the early Congress, or later as secretary of state or President of the United States.

18. The early state legislatures developed from assemblies of representatives of freeholders, like the Virginia House of Burgesses. In most states the governor was chosen by the legislature, and the states differed in how strong and independent the governorship they established.

19. Until quite late in the convention the prevailing proposal would have had the president chosen by Congress. Compare Farrand, I, 77, II, 32, 121, 185, 403, with 497, 498, 511, 525.

20. Compare John Marshall's famous statement in a different context: "Commerce, undoubtedly, is traffic, but it is something more; it is intercourse." *Gibbons v. Ogden,* 22 U.S. (9 Wheat.) 1, 189 (1824).

21. Article I, section 10. In general, that Congress was given power to impeach and remove the president has been cited as suggesting congressional control of the president rather than an equal, separate, and independent presidency.

22. The Senate, representing the states, can be seen as simply continuing the role which the state delegations served under the articles, with two-thirds of the Senate (consisting originally of representatives of thirteen states) being essentially the equivalent of the votes of nine states needed for making treaties and adopting other important decisions under the articles. See Article IX. In this view, the president was merely inserted as a negotiating agent and diplomat-in-chief, with the essential voice in treaty making left with the state representatives.

23. See *Hearings on Separation of Powers before the Subcommittee on Separation of Powers of the Senate Committee on the Judiciary,* 90th Cong. 1st sess. 43–44 (1967); Henkin, *Foreign Affairs,* pp. 84, 335–36, n. 70.

24. The Supreme Court held that the power to remove executive officers was implied in "the Executive power" and could not be denied by Congress. *Myers v. United States,* 272 U.S. 52, 128 (1926). On the other hand, in the *Steel Seizure* case, Justice Jackson, concurring, wrote that he could not accept that clause as a "grant in bulk of all conceivable executive power but regards it as an allocation to the presidential office of the generic powers thereafter stated." *Youngstown Sheet & Tube Co. v. Sawyer,* 343 U.S. 579 641 (1952). Chief Justice Vinson dissenting, however, seemed to echo Hamilton. Id. at 681–82. See Henkin, *Foreign Affairs,* pp. 42–44, and nn. 297–99.

25. Presidents have claimed as much as, or more than, Hamilton claimed for them, not from what the Constitution says but from what it has become. See p. 120 below; Henkin, *Foreign Affairs,* ch. 2.

26. Compare note 24. It has been noted that the difference in language was the handiwork of Gouverneur Morris in the Constitutional Convention's Committee on Style; he added "herein granted" to Article I but not to Article II. See Charles C. Thach, Jr., *Creation of the Presidency 1775-89* (Johns Hopkins University Press, 1970), pp. 138–39. But there is no evidence that Morris's drafting in this regard

failed to reflect accurately what the fathers intended, and slipped by them unnoticed. Details of language were sharply scrutinized in the many writings and the sharp debates during ratification, but this one apparently drew no objection.

27. While Hamilton insisted on the president's power to proclaim neutrality, he recognized that Congress could undo it later if it chose to declare war. Perhaps, then, Congress could undo other presidential initiatives by exercising its war, commerce, or other enumerated powers. He does not suggest a general power in Congress to supersede, control, or regulate all presidential initiatives in foreign affairs.

28. Madison wrote of separation generally that "unless these departments be so far connected and blended as to give to each a constitutional control over the others, the degree of separation which the maxim requires, as essential to a free government, can never in practice be duly maintained." *Federalist* no. 48, p. 343.

29. See note 27.

30. Jefferson even took the position, when United States vessels were attacked by those of the Bey of Tripoli, that the President could order only acts of self-defense unless and until Congress declared war. Hamilton (writing as Lucius Crassus) heaped scorn on that view. *Works,* pp. 745–48; see E. S. Corwin, *The President, Office and Powers, 1787-1957,* 4th rev. ed. (New York: New York University Press, 1957), p. 199.

There is evidence, however, that Jefferson, Madison, and Monroe strained under the limitations on their power as they conceived it, and withheld information, manipulated, perhaps deceived, to justify what they wished to do.

31. Article II, section 3: The president "may, on extraordinary occasions, convene both Houses, or either of them. . . ."

32. Act of 27 July 1789, 1 *Stat.* 28–29.

33. For example, for decades presidents sought congressional endorsement of the Monroe Doctrine, without success. Dexter Perkins, *The Monroe Doctrine, 1826–1867* (Baltimore: The Johns Hopkins Press, 1933), pp. 217–23.

34. While the War of 1898, and to some extent the War of 1812, were substantially congressional wars (though only the latter followed extended debate), the Mexican War and the two World Wars were essentially the results of presidential policy.

35. See *Curtiss-Wright,* note 9 above; also *Chicago & Southern Air Lines v. Waterman S. S. Corp.,* 303 U.S. 103, 111 (1948); *Zemel v. Rusk,* 381 U.S. 1, 17 (1963). See Henkin, *Foreign Affairs,* pp. 112, 356, 60. Also *United States v. Belmont,* 301 U.S. 324 (1937); *United States v. Pink,* 315 U.S. 203 (1942); *Ex parte Republic of Peru,* 318 U.S. 578, 589 (1943); but cf. *First National City Bank v. Banco Nacional de Cuba,* 406 U.S. 759 (1972).

36. Congress's repeal of the Tonkin Gulf Resolution was clearly not intended either to direct an end to the war, or even to remove congressional authorization for continuing it, only to deny authorization for future involvements in the area. See Henkin, *Foreign Affairs,* pp. 101–3, 107–8, 351.

37. Parliamentary government is surely not the answer for those who want a greater role for the legislature, for in Western parliamentary systems today the prime minister and cabinet (with a majority in parliament) have virtually unlimited power, the parliament effectively none.

38. Pub. L. no. 93-148, 87 *Stat.* 555 (1973), 50 U.S.C.A. Sec. 1541 (Supp. 1975).

39. Congressional Budget and Impoundment Control Act, Pub. L. no. 93–344, 88 *Stat.* 297, 31 U.S.C.A. Sec. 1301 (Supp. 1975). Presidents had claimed authority to impound funds in domestic as well as foreign affairs, but the plausibility of their claims might be greater in foreign affairs. Cf. Henkin, pp. 110–11.

40. Pub. L. no. 92–403, 86 *Stat.* 619, 1 U.S.C. Sec. 112b (Supp. 1973).

41. The Court generally decided for Congress in the "big ones," e.g., *Kendall v. United States ex rel.* Stokes, 37 U.S. (12 Pet.) 524 (1838); *Youngstown Sheet &*

Tube Co. v. Sawyer, 343 U.S. 579 (1952). See also *Brown v. United States,* 12 U.S. (8 Cranch) 110 (1814); *Fleming v. Page,* 50 U.S. (9 How.) 603 (1850); cf. *Valentine v. United States ex rel. Neidecker,* 299 U.S. 5 (1936); *Kent v. Dulles,* 357 U.S. 116 (1958); *Train v. City of New York,* 420 U.S. 351 (1975); also *United States v. Nixon,* 418 U.S. 683 (1974). The President won in *Myers v. United States,* 272 U.S. 52 (1926), vindicating President Andrew Johnson a half-century earlier, but the Court took much of it back in *Humphrey's Ex'r v. United States,* 295 U.S. 602 (1935), and *Weiner v. United States,* 357 U.S. 349 (1958). *Buckley v. Valeo,* 96 Sup. Ct. 612 (1976), upheld the President's appointment power against Congressional usurpation, but the President had apparently not objected. Cf. also *United States v. Midwest Oil Co.,* 236 U.S. 459 (1915). Presidents won when an issue of separation implicated "rights" of a private complainant. Cf. the Court's vindication of the President's pardoning power in *Ex parte Garland,* 71 U.S. (4 Wall.) 333 (1867), and *United States v. Klein,* 80 U.S. (13 Wall.) 128 (1872); cf. *United States v. Lovett,* 328 U.S. 303 (1946).

42. Some lower courts have accorded, while some have denied, standing to an individual member of Congress to challenge alleged presidential interference with the legislative function. See *Holtzman v. Richardson,* 361 F. Supp. 544, 553 (E.D.N.Y. 1973), reversed *sub nom. Holtzman v. Schlesinger,* 484 F. 2d 1307, 1315 (2d Cir. 1973), cert. denied, 416 U.S. 936 (1974); compare *Mitchell v. Laird,* 488 F. 2d 611 (D.C. Cir. 1973), with *Harrington v. Schlesinger,* 528 F. 2d 455 (4th Cir. 1975); cf. *Kennedy v. Sampson,* 511 F. 2d 430 (D.C. Cir. 1974).

43. See, generally, *Baker v. Carr,* 369 U.S. 186, 211 (1962). But see Henkin, "Is There a Political Question Doctrine?" *Yale Law Journal* 85 (1976).

44. E.g., *Mora v. McNamara,* 387 F. 2d 862 (D.C. Cir. 1967) cert. denied, 389, U.S. 934 (1967), rehearing denied, 389 U.S. 1025 (1967); *Orlando v. Laird,* 443 F. 2d 1039 (2d Cir. 1971), cert. denied, 404 U.S. 869 (1971); *Sarnoff v. Connally,* 457 F. 2d 809 (9th Cir. 1972), cert. denied, 409 U.S. 929 (1972); *Holtzman v. Schlesinger,* note 42 above. *Atlee v. Laird,* 347 F. Supp. 689 (E.D. Pa. 1972), was affirmed by the Supreme Court without hearing argument or writing an opinion. *Atlee v. Richardson,* 411 U.S. 911 (1973).

45. See note 41 above; cf. *Powell v. McCormack,* 395 U.S. 486 (1969); *United States v. Nixon,* 418 U.S. 683 (1974).

46. Of course, the courts did not vindicate individual rights against the claims of our foreign relations during our first hundred years, when the Bill of Rights hardly restricted government in any respect. Before the Civil War the only case in which the Court invalidated an act of Congress under the Bill of Rights was *Scott v. Sandford,* 60 U.S. (19 How.) 393 (1857), holding that the Missouri Compromise deprived Dred Scott's master of his property without due process of law.

47. Compare *Perez v. Brownell,* 356 U.S. 44 (1958), overruled, *Afroyim v. Rusk,* 387 U.S. 253 (1967); *Frend v. United States,* 100 F. 2d 691 (D.C. Cir. 1938), cert. denied, 306 U.S. 640 (1939); *Greenberg v. Murphy,* 329 F. Supp. 37 (S.D.N.Y. 1971). Requirements of "strict scrutiny" and "compelling state interest" were established in other kinds of cases, e.g., *Korematsu v. United States,* 323 U.S. 214 (1944); *Shapiro v. Thompson,* 394 U.S. 618 (1969); *Roe v. Wade,* 410 U.S. 113 (1973); cf. *United States v. Carolene Products Co.,* 304 U.S. 144, 152 n. 4 (1938).

48. See Henkin, "Some reflections on Current Constitutional Controversy," *University of Pennsylvania Law Review* 109 (1961): 637. The courts have also been more willing to consider issues of federalism or allocation of federal powers when alleged constitutional improprieties invaded important private interests. See, e.g., *Kinsella v. United States ex rel. Singleton,* 361 U.S. 234 (1960); *Kent v. Dulles,* 357 U.S. 116 (1958); *Oregon v. Mitchell,* 400 U.S. 112 (1970).

49. See, e.g., *Aptheker v. Secretary of State,* 378 U.S. 500 (1964); *Kent v. Dulles,* 357 U.S. 116 (1958); *Afroyim v. Rusk,* 387 U.S. 253 (1967); *New York Times Co. v. United States,* 403 U.S. (1971); *Kinsella v. United States ex rel. Singleton,* 361 U.S. 234 (1960).

50. *Mandel v. Mitchell,* 325 F. Supp. 620 (E.D.N.Y. 1971), reversed *sub nom. Kleindienst v. Mandel,* 408 U.S. 753 (1972).
51. Compare *Orlando v. Laird,* 443 F. 2d 1039 (2d Cir.), cert. denied, 404 U.S. 869 (1971); *DaCosta v. Laird,* 471 F. 2d 1146 (2d Cir. 1973); the dissents from denial of certiorari in *United States v. Mitchell,* 386 U.S. 972 (1967) (Douglas, J.); *Mora v. McNamara,* 389 U.S. 934 (1967) (Douglas and Stewart, JJ.); also the dissenting views in *Massachusetts v. Laird,* 400 U.S. 886 (1970).
52. See Henkin, *Foreign Affairs,* ch. 11.

8. Walter F. Murphy: THE ART OF CONSTITUTIONAL INTERPRETATION

For careful reading and lavish criticism of earlier drafts, I am indebted to: Sidney M. Davis, Sanford V. Levinson, W. Duane Lockard, Dennis F. Thompson, and Edith Brown Weiss of Princeton University, W. E. Y. Elliott of the Claremont Colleges, Charles A. Miller of Lake Forest College, and Joseph Tanenhaus of SUNY at Stony Brook. Mrs. Lorraine Salazar typed—and edited—the final two drafts. The Center of International Studies of Princeton University has supported the larger project from which this paper was "untimely ripp'd."

1. Madison, *Federalist,* no. 37, Benjamin F. Wright, ed. (Cambridge: Harvard University Press, 1961), p. 270.
2. See Paul Brest, "The Conscientious Legislator's Guide to Constitutional Interpretation," *Stanford Law Review* 27 (1975): 585.
3. *Elements of Judicial Strategy* (Chicago: University of Chicago Press, 1964).
4. "Toward Neutral Principles of Constitutional Law," *Harvard Law Review* 73 (1959): 1.
5. See Arthur S. Miller and Ronald F. Howell, "The Myth of Neutrality in Constitutional Adjudication," *University of Chicago Law Review* 27 (1960): 661.
6. See John Rawl's brilliant reconstruction of a theory of individual contract, *A Theory of Justice* (Cambridge: Harvard University Press, 1971).
7. Canadian constitutional law before 1949, when the Judicial Committee of the Privy Council functioned as Canada's super-supreme court, offers the best set of examples of what happens when judges treat a constitution as a special statute rather than as a charter for government. The literature here is vast. Much of it is cited in W. F. Murphy and Joseph Tanenhaus, eds., *Comparative Constitutional Law: Cases, Commentaries, and Materials* (New York: St. Martin's Press, 1977), esp. chs. 4 and 8. Particularly helpful for the purposes of this paper is Ivor Jennings, "Constitutional Interpretation," *Harvard Law Review* 51 (1937): 1. For a justification of the Judicial Committee's approach, see esp. *Bank of Toronto v. Lambe,* [1887] A.C. 575. For general—though American—analyses of statutory interpretation and hints of differences with constitutional interpretation, see: Jerome Frank, "Words and Music," *Columbia Law Review* 47 (1947): 1259, and *Courts on Trial* (Princeton: Princeton University Press, 1950), ch. 21; Felix Frankfurter, "The Reading of Statutes," in Philip Elman, ed., *Of Law and Men* (New York: Harcourt, Brace, 1956), pp. 44ff.; Edward H. Levi, *An Introduction to Legal Reasoning* (Chicago: University of Chicago Press, 1948), pp. 19-72; Frank C. Newman and Stanley S. Surrey, eds., *Legislation: Cases and Materials* (Englewood Cliffs: Prentice-Hall, 1955); Julius Cohen, ed., *Materials and Problems in Legislation,* 2d ed. (Indianapolis: The Bobbs-Merrill Company, 1967); Charles B. Nutting, S. D. Elliott, and R. Dickerson, eds., *Legislation: Cases and Materials* (St. Paul: West Publishing Co., 1969); and the literature cited in W. F. Murphy and C. Herman Pritchett, eds., *Courts, Judges, and Politics,* 2d ed. (New York: Random House, 1974), ch. 13.
8. *McCulloch v. Maryland,* 4 Wheat. 316, 407 (1819).
9. "The power of searching analysis of what it is that they are doing seems rarely to be possessed by judges, either because they are lacking in the art of critical exposition or because they are inhibited from practicing it." Felix Frankfurter, "The

Judicial Process and the Supreme Court," reprinted in Elman, ed., p. 32. Justices, however, have been somewhat more candid in their writings off than on the bench. See, for instance, Frankfurter's other articles and addresses in Elman; Benjamin N. Cardozo, *The Nature of the Judicial Process* (New Haven: Yale University Press, 1921); Hugo L. Black, *A Constitutional Faith* (New York: Random House, 1969); William J. Brennan, "Developments in Constitutional Law," *New Jersey Law Journal* 99 (1976): 473; William O. Douglas's writings cited below, notes 89–95; Charles Evans Hughes, *The Supreme Court of the United States* (New York: Columbia University Press, 1928); Robert H. Jackson, *The Supreme Court in the American System of Government* (Cambridge: Harvard University Press, 1955); Owen J. Roberts, *The Court and the Constitution* (Cambridge: Harvard University Press, 1951); and for collections of off-the-bench remarks, A. F. Westin, ed., *An Autobiography of the Supreme Court* (New York: The Macmillan Company, 1963), and *The Supreme Court: Views from the Inside* (New York: W. W. Norton & Company, 1961).

10. The so-called test of "clear and present danger," although not originally so, became a rule to protect such a priority. Compare Holmes's opinion for the Court in *Schenck v. United States,* 249 U.S. 47 (1919) with his and Brandeis's opinions in *Abrams v. United States,* 250 U.S. 616 (1919), and *Whitney v. California,* 274 U.S. 357 (1927).

11. *Civil Liberties and the Vinson Court* (Chicago: University of Chicago Press, 1954), p. 201.

12. *Uverges v. Pennsylvania,* 335 U.S. 437, 449–50 (1948).

13. *Terminiello v. Chicago,* 337 U.S. 1, 11 (1949). Frankfurter's sneering reference to a kadi simply expressed his ignorance of Muslim jurisprudence.

14. *Minersville School District v. Gobitis,* 310 U.S. 586 (1940); *West Virginia v. Barnette,* 319 U.S. 624, dis. op. (1943).

15. See *Haley v. Ohio,* 332 U.S. 596, concur. op. (1948), and *Louisiana ex rel. Francis v. Resweber,* 329 U.S. 459, concur. op. (1947).

16. *Dennis v. United States,* 341 U.S. 494, concur. op. (1951).

17. *Malinski v. New York,* 324 U.S. 401, concur. op., 414 (1945).

18. *Falbo v. United States,* 320 U.S. 549, dis. op., 561 (1944).

19. See generally: Giovanni Sartori, *Democratic Theory* (New York: Praeger Publishers, 1965), esp. chs. 12–15; Charles H. McIlwain, *Constitutionalism: Ancient and Modern,* rev. ed. (Ithaca: Cornell University Press, 1947); Carl J. Friedrich's books: *Constitutional Government and Democracy,* 4th ed. (Waltham: Blaisdell Publishing Co., 1968), esp. chs. 1, 7 and part 4, *Limited Government* (Englewood Cliffs: Prentice-Hall, 1974), *Transcendent Justice* (Durham: Duke University Press, 1964), *The Impact of American Constitutionalism Abroad* (Boston: Boston University Press, 1966), and *Constitutional Reason of State* (Providence: Brown University Press, 1957).

20. *Federalist,* no. 14, p. 154.

21. See esp. *The Supreme Court from Taft to Warren,* rev. ed. (Baton Rouge: Louisiana State University Press, 1968), pp. 9–10, and more generally, *Free Government in the Making,* 3rd ed. (New York: Oxford University Press, 1965). Still more generally, see Gordon S. Wood, *The Creation of the American Republic, 1776–1787* (Chapel Hill: University of North Carolina Press, 1969).

22. *The Least Dangerous Branch* (Indianapolis: The Bobbs-Merrill Company, 1962), p. 18.

23. See esp. nos. 10, 39, 51, and 63; but cf. no. 57. In 1788 Madison wrote to Jefferson:

> Wherever the real power in a Government lies, there is the danger of oppression. In our Governments the real power lies in the majority of the Community, and the invasion of private rights is *chiefly* to be apprehended, not

from acts of Government contrary to the sense of its constituents, but from acts in which the Government is the mere instrument of the major number of Constituents. (G. Hunt, ed., *The Writings of James Madison* [New York: G. P. Putnam's Sons, 1904], V, 272)

24. "The Bill of Rights," reprinted in Irving Dilliard, ed., *One Man's Stand for Freedom* (New York: Alfred A. Knopf, 1971), p. 36. Specifically, of course, Aristotle defined a constitution as "an organization of offices in a state, by which the method of their distribution is fixed, the sovereign authority is determined, and the nature of the end to be pursued by the association and all its members is prescribed." *Politics,* bk. IV, ch. 1, sec. 9; see also bk, III, ch. 6, sec. 1. But I think Sir Ernest Barker was correct when he interpreted Aristotle's usage of the word to encompass "a way of life, or a system of social ethics, as well as a way of assigning political offices." Introduction, p. lxvi, to his translation of *The Politics of Aristotle* (Oxford: The Clarendon Press, 1948). I might add parenthetically that, as I recall Prof. Leo Strauss's seminar on book III of the *Politics,* he agreed with Barker on this point.

25. *Gray v. Sanders,* 372 U.S. 368, 381 (1963): "The conception of political equality from the Declaration of Independence, to Lincoln's Gettysburg Address, to the Fifteenth, Seventeenth, and Nineteenth Amendments can mean only one thing–one person, one vote."

26. In *Reynolds v. Sims,* 377 U.S. 533, 558 (1964), Warren quoted Douglas's sentence found in note 25 above. See, more generally, Justice Arthur Goldberg's argument about equality in "Equality and Governmental Action," *New York University Law Review* 39 (1964): 205.

27. "The Bill of Rights," in Dilliard, ed., p. 36. Although such a restriction fitted in well with Black's endorsement of a very restricted role for judges, he did not–in consistence with a hallowed tradition–explain why "the Constitution" was so limited. I suspect that if he had given more thought to the problem, his Jeffersonianism would have led him to concede that the Declaration's second paragraph provided valuable illumination of the ideals of the generation(s) of 1776 and 1787. Black would then have also had to face the much debated question of the consistency between the two documents. My argument faces a strong objection in that Black, writing for the Court in *Wesberry v. Sanders,* 376 U.S. 1, 18 (1964), also cited Douglas's passage in *Gray* but restricted himself to quoting the phrase "one person, one vote."

28. *United States v. Curtiss Wright,* 299 U.S. 304, 318 (1936).

29. *United States v. Nixon,* 418 U.S. 683 (1974).

30. 2 Dallas 419, 465 (1793).

31. 3 Dallas 386, 387–88.

32. 6 Wheat. 264, 383 (1821). See also 384: "While weighing arguments drawn from the nature of government, and from the general spirit of an instrument, and urged for the purpose of narrowing the construction which the words of that instrument seem to require, it is proper to place in the opposite scale those principles, *drawn from the same sources,* which go to sustain the words in their full operation and natural import." Italics supplied.

33. 4 Wheat. 316, 421 (1819).

34. 4 Wheat. 122, 202 (1819). In fact, the Court was not unanimous, although the disagreement had nothing to do with the legitimacy of consulting the spirit of the Constitution. See Justice Johnson's explanation in *Ogden v. Saunders,* 12 Wheat. 213, 272–73 (1827).

35. *Hepburn v. Griswold,* 8 Wall. 603, 623 (1870).

36. *Knox v. Lee,* 12 Wall. 457 (1871).

37. 209 U.S. 123. See also John Marshall's opinions in *Osborn v. Bank of the United States,* 9 Wheat. 728, 818ff. (1824), and *Cohens v. Virginia,* supra, note 32.

38. *We the Judges* (Garden City: Doubleday & Company, 1956), p. 75.

39. See, e.g., *Jacobson v. Massachusetts,* 197 U.S. 11 (1905).

40. For a discussion of some of these problems, see Murphy and Tanenhaus, ch. 9 and literature cited.
41. See esp. the preamble and Article 41.
42. There are limited exceptions. See, for example, Edward S. Corwin, *The "Higher Law" Background of American Constitutional Law* (Ithaca: Cornell University Press, 1955) (originally published in 1928 and 1929 in *Harvard Law Review* 42); Morris R. Cohen, "Jus Naturale Redivivum," *Philosophical Review* 25 (1916): 761. Corwin's study provides a historical tracing of ideas of natural law in English and American legal development, and Cohen's essay provides a jurisprudential critique of the problems in self-evident principles. Neither attempted to link natural law directly to problems of judicial decision making.
43. Holmes to John C. H. Wu, 1 July 1929, in Max Lerner, ed., *The Mind and Faith of Justice Holmes* (New York: Random House, 1943), p. 435. See also Holmes's essay "Natural Law," ibid., pp. 394–98, and Francis Biddle, *Justice Holmes, Natural Law, and the Supreme Court* (New York: The Macmillan Company, 1961).
44. "The Path of the Law," in Lerner, p. 75. Mark DeWolfe Howe does not believe that Holmes was an Austinian. Oliver Wendell Holmes, *The Common Law*, Howe, ed. (Cambridge: Harvard University Press, 1963), p. xviii. It is true that Holmes does not seek a sovereign *in* itself (himself?), but if one substitutes Holmes's "judges" for Austin's "sovereign," the two men, it seems to me, fundamentally agree. For an analysis supporting my position, see Sanford V. Levinson, "Skepticism, Democracy, and Judicial Restraint: An Essay on the Thought of Oliver Wendell Holmes and Felix Frankfurter," Ph.D. diss., Harvard University, 1969, ch. 3.
45. Quoted in Corwin, p. 45.
46. Ibid., p. 44.
47. Ibid., p. 45.
48. Ibid., p. 42. As one would expect, Jefferson was by no means an uncritical admirer of Coke.
49. Robert Allen Rutland, *The Birth of the Bill of Rights, 1776–1791* (New York: Collier Books, 1962), p. 21.
50. William Blackstone, *Commentaries on the Laws of England* (Philadelphia: Robert Bell, 1771), I, intro., sec. 2; and ch. 1.
51. *American Interpretations of Natural Law* (Cambridge: Harvard University Press, 1931), p. 11. See also Bernard Bailyn, *The Ideological Origins of the American Revolution* (Cambridge, Mass.: Belknap Press, 1967), esp. chs. 2 and 5. Some commentators on both Blackstone and Coke interpreted them to mean not that a court could invalidate an act of Parliament for infringing natural law or justice but only that a court should interpret an act of Parliament so as not to infringe natural law or justice.
52. See Wright, *American Interpretations*, p. 328 and ch. 2 generally. In this section I have obviously depended heavily on Wright's scholarship.
53. See esp. Leo Strauss, *Natural Right and History* (Chicago: University of Chicago Press, 1953).
54. Carl L. Becker, *The Declaration of Independence* (New York: Alfred A. Knopf, 1922), pp. 24–25.
55. Jefferson to F. W. Gilmer, 7 June 1816, Paul L. Ford, ed., *The Works of Thomas Jefferson* (New York: G. P. Putnam's Sons, 1905), X, 31–33. See also Virginia's Statute of Religious Liberty, largely drafted by Jefferson but adopted during his absence in 1786. Part 3 reads: "And though we know that this assembly . . . have no power to restrain the acts of succeeding assemblies . . . yet as we are free to declare, and do declare, that the rights hereby asserted are of the natural rights of mankind, and that if any act shall hereafter be passed to repeal the present [statute], or to narrow its operation, such an act will be an infringement of natural right." Henry Steele Commager, ed., *Documents of American History* (New York: Crofts, 1938), I, 126.

56. See the discussion in Robert K. Faulkner, *The Jurisprudence of John Marshall* (Princeton: Princeton University Press, 1968), esp. ch. 3.

57. As far as reason was concerned, the framers' faith was closely bounded. Their belief that it was possible to build a political system that would operate largely through peaceful persuasion attested to that faith; but, having been reared in heavily Calvinist societies, the framers were also aware of man's fallen nature and vulnerability to selfish temptations. To the extent that some of them had read and understood Hume, their faith in reason was probably further tempered, as it also was by a robust empiricism. "Experience must be our only guide," John Dickinson warned the convention. "Reason may mislead us." Quoted in Alpheus T. Mason, *The Supreme Court: Palladium of Freedom* (Ann Arbor: University of Michigan Press, 1962), p. 8. For a reconstruction of what Madison, at least, actually read during his year of "graduate" study at Princeton, see Dennis F. Thompson, "The Education of a Founding Father," *Political Theory* 4 (1976): 523.

58. James Kent, *Commentaries on American Law,* 7th ed. (New York: William Kent, 1851), I sec. 24; III, sec. 34. Wright analyzes Kent's writings at pp. 288-90.

59. Joseph Story, *Commentaries on the Constitution of the United States* (Boston: Hilliard, Gray, 1833), Sec. 1399, 1876. Wright discusses Story's views at pp. 290-91. One could, of course, add Thomas Cooley to the list of "relatively" early commentators who accepted natural rights: *A Treatise on the Constitutional Limitations Which Rest upon the Legislative Power of the States of the American Union* (Boston: Little, Brown, 1868).

60. *The Revival of Natural Law Concepts* (Cambridge: Harvard University Press, 1930), p. 85. For a view that the revolutionary ideology had weakened the doctrine of natural law in American jurisprudence well before 1820, see Morton J. Horwitz, "The Emergence of an Instrumental Conception of American Law, 1780-1820," in Donald Fleming and Bernard Bailyn, eds., *Perspectives in American History,* vol. V, *Law in American History* (Cambridge: Charles Warren Center for Studies in American History, 1971), pp. 287-326.

61. *Horne's Lessee v. Dorrance,* 2 Dallas 304, 310.

62. 6 Cranch 87, 136 (1810).

63. Ibid., at 139.

64. Ibid., at 143.

65. *Ogden v. Saunders,* 12 Wheat. 213, 346 (1827).

66. For a discussion of the cases see Robert M. Cover, *Justice Accused: Antislavery and the Judicial Process* (New Haven: Yale University Press, 1975), esp. part 2. It should become apparent that while I admire Cover's work, I think he overestimates the amount of positivism in American constitutional law during the pre-Civil War period. My reading of the cases is that the justices, like most other federal officials, were willing to accept slavery as a lesser evil than disunion. I agree that judges faced a moral dilemma, but it was not that which Cover describes as a choice between anarchy and law, though that was a convenient rationalization. Rather, I think the choice was between what the judges saw as the evil of slavery and what they saw as the greater evil of disunion.

67. See the background of *Ableman v. Booth,* 21 How. 506 (1859).

68. Article IV, sec. 2, cl. 3, conferred a right on the owner of an escaped slave, but according to the explicit terms of the Constitution that right ran against the government of the state to which the slave had fled, not against the federal government. Congress, however, passed the first fugitive slave law in 1793 and the Supreme Court rationalized it as constitutional in *Prigg v. Pennsylvania,* 16 Pet. 539 (1842). It is interesting to compare the Court's opinion there, written by Joseph Story, and more particularly Chief Justice Taney's opinion concurring in part and dissenting apart, with Taney's opinion for the Court in *Kentucky v. Dennison,* 24 How. 66 (1861). In the latter case, the Court held that a state's obligation to return a fugitive from justice was beyond the authority of Congress or the federal courts to enforce. I do not think that any theory of natural law, natural rights,

or legal positivism can explain either decision or account for the differences between them. Each was based firmly and exclusively on what a majority of the Court considered expedient for the survival of the Union.

69. 10 Wheat. 66, 120–212 (1825).

70. *La Jeune Eugénie,* 26 Fed. Cases 846 (1822).

71. Eric Foner, *Free Soil, Free Labor, Free Men* (New York: Oxford University Press, 1970), ch. 3 and esp. pp. 76–77, summarizes Chase's argument, essentially based on the due process clause of the Fifth Amendment. Foner and Merton L. Dillon, *The Abolitionists* (DeKalb: Northern Illinois University Press, 1974), make it clear that by no means did all abolitionists accept William Lloyd Garrison's and Wendell Phillips's constitutional arguments. See, for example, Lysander Spooner, *The Unconstitutionality of Slavery* (Boston: Bela Marsh, 1847).

72. Quoted in Jacobus tenBroek, *Equal under Law* (New York: Collier Books, 1965), pp. 164–65.

73. Ibid., p. 163.

74. *License Tax* cases, 5 Wall. 462, 469 (1869).

75. Their dissents in the *Slaughterhouse* cases, 16 Wall. 36 (1873), provide a fertile source of such reasoning. Field, of course, was more persistent in his pursuit of natural rights than was Bradley.

76. See, for example, his opinion for the Court in *Loan Association v. Topeka,* 20 Wall. 655, 663 (1875).

77. *Monongahela Bridge Co. v. United States,* 216 U.S. 177, 195 (1910).

78. *American Interpretations,* pp. 305–6.

79. The emphasis on social justice and duty to one's fellow man expounded by Pope Leo XIII in his encyclical "Rerum Novarum" provides an interesting illustration of the sharp contrast between traditional notions of natural law and social Darwinism's narrow focus on the natural right to acquire and use private property.

80. 332 U.S. 46 (1947).

81. E.g., *Rochin v. California,* 342 U.S. 165 (1952); *Malinski v. New York,* supra, note 17; *Ashcraft v. Tennessee,* 322 U.S. 143 (1944); *Louisiana ex rel. Francis v. Resweber,* supra, note 15; *Haley v. Ohio,* supra, note 15; testimony before the Royal Commission on Capital Punishment, supra, note 15; *Irvine v. California,* 347 U.S. 128 (1954).

82. Helen Shirley Thomas, *Felix Frankfurter: Scholar on the Bench* (Baltimore: The Johns Hopkins Press, 1960), p. 231.

83. 322 U.S. at 72, quoting *Ex parte Bain,* 121 U.S. 1, 12 (1887).

84. *Everson v. Ewing Township,* 330 U.S. 1, 8 (1947). Black, like most judges and most lawyers, was interested in using history less to find truth than to find justification. For analyses of judicial misuses of history, see: Charles A. Miller, *The Supreme Court and the Uses of History* (Cambridge: Harvard University Press, 1969); Alfred Kelly, "Clio and the Court: An Illicit Love Affair," *Supreme Court Review* 1965: 119; John Woodford, "The Blinding Light: The Uses of History in Constitutional Interpretation," *University of Chicago Law Review* 31 (1964): 502. Note Mark DeWolfe Howe's comments regarding the Court and the First Amendment: "By superficial and purposive interpretation of the past, the Court has dishonored the arts of the historian and degraded the talents of the lawyer." *The Garden and the Wilderness: Religion and Government in American Constitutional History* (Chicago: University of Chicago Press, 1967), p. 4. See also Levinson (supra, note 44), p. 275 and works cited.

85. *In re Yamashita,* 327 U.S. 1, dis. op. 26–27.

86. Cf. Aristotle, *Nicomachean Ethics,* bk. V, ch. 10.

87. 332 U.S. at 124.

88. The first draft of his dissent that Murphy circulated differed somewhat from the final version. Black apparently expressed some reservations and Murphy sent him a note on 19 June 1947, asking what changes he would like to see made. In reply Black listed several specific points, then went on to argue that "I have not

attempted to tie procedural due process exclusively to the Bill of Rights. In fact there are other constitutional prohibitions relating to procedure which I think due process requires to be observed." The Papers of Frank Murphy, Michigan Historical Collections, University of Michigan.

89. *Skinner v. Oklahoma,* 316 U.S. 535, 541. After I had written a draft of this section, I read Kenneth L. Karst, "Return of the Natural-Law-Due-Process Formula," *U.C.L.A. Law Review* 16 (1969): 716. As a result, I redrafted the section and adopted some of Prof. Karst's persuasive interpretations.

90. For example, *Rochin v. California,* supra, note 81.

91. (Garden City: Doubleday & Company, 1954), p. 5.

92. *The Right of the People* (Garden City: Doubleday & Company, 1958), p. 145.

93. *The Anatomy of Liberty* (New York: Trident Press, 1963), p. 2.

94. *Poe v. Ullman,* 367 U.S. 497, dis. op. 516 (1961).

95. Ibid., at 519; Douglas quoted Roberts, p. 80.

96. 381 U.S. 479 (1965).

97. Ibid., at 521.

98. Ibid., at 500.

99. 6 Fed. Cases 546 (1823).

100. 367 U.S., at 541.

101. *Perez v. Brownell,* 356 U.S. 44, dis. op. 64-65.

102. Most especially his concurring opinion in *Furman v. Georgia,* 408 U.S. 238 (1972), and his dissenting opinion in the second capital punishment ruling, *Gregg v. Georgia,* 428 U.S. 153 (1976).

103. See his concurring opinion in *Rosenblatt v. Baer,* 383 U.S. 75, 92 (1966). Stewart grounds his argument primarily in the Ninth Amendment, but I think the outline of the traditional argument from natural rights is present. See also his opinion in *Gregg v. Georgia,* supra, note 102.

104. *Korematsu v. United States,* 323 U.S. 214 (1944), rationalized putting American citizens of Japanese ancestry in concentration camps. For accounts of the treatment accorded the Nisei, see: Morton Grodzins, *Americans Betrayed* (Chicago: University of Chicago Press, 1949); Jacobus tenBroek, et al., *Prejudice, War, and the Constitution* (Berkeley: University of California Press, 1954); and Michi Weglyn, *Years of Infamy* (New York: William Morrow & Co., 1976).

105. Watergate is an oft-told story. For the longer-ranged and perhaps even more insidious criminal activity of the FBI, CIA, NSA, and IRS, see U.S. Senate, Select Committee to Study Governmental Operations, Final Report, 94th Cong., 2d. sess. (1976), Report no. 94-755, esp. books II and III, and vols. 2, 4, 5, and 6 of the committee's *Hearings.*

106. *United States v. Shaughnessy,* 338 U.S. 537, dis. op., 551 (1950).

107. See, for example, Walter Berns, *Freedom, Virtue and the First Amendment* (Baton Rouge: Louisiana State University Press, 1957).

108. 17 October 1788; G. Hunt, ed. (supra, note 23), V, 274.

109. Frankfurter to Stone, 27 May 1940; the entire letter is reprinted in Alpheus T. Mason, *Security through Freedom* (Ithaca: Cornell University Press, 1955), pp. 217-20.

110. *Brinegar v. United States,* 338 U.S. 160, dis. op., 180 (1949).

111. See his letter to Stone cited in note 109, and, for an even earlier view, Frankfurter's *Mr. Justice Holmes and the Supreme Court* (Cambridge: Harvard University Press, 1938), ch. 11, where, after noting "there is a hierarchy of values," p. 74, he goes on to praise Holmes for defending freedom of expression against legislative interference.

112. *Ullman v. United States,* 350 U.S. 422, 428 (1956).

113. *Kovacs v. Cooper,* 336 U.S. 77, concur. op., 90 (1949). See also his dis. op. in *West Virginia v. Barnette,* 319 U.S. 624, 648 (1943), in which he argued that, "so far as the scope of judicial power is concerned," the right to property was of the same constitutional dignity as the right to religious freedom.

114. *Nebraska Press Ass'n. v. Stuart,* 427 U.S. 539, (1976). In *Bridges v. California,* 314 U.S. 252, 260 (1941), Black wrote for the Court that "free speech and fair trials are two of the most cherished policies of our civilization, and it would be a trying task to choose between them." Twenty-one years later Black had come to a somewhat different view. He said, "I want both fair trials and freedom of the press," and added that his faith in the intelligence and integrity of the American people led him to doubt that adverse publicity could prevent a fair trial. "Justice Black and the First Amendment 'Absolutes': A Public Interview," in Dilliard, ed. (supra, note 27), pp. 474–75.
115. *Palko v. Connecticut,* 302 U.S. 319, 327 (1937).
116. *Sweezy v. New Hampshire,* 354 U.S. 234 (1957).
117. *Dennis v. United States,* 341 U.S. 494, concur. op., 540 (1951).
118. See his own accounts of his involvement, while on the Court, in executive policy making, in Joseph P. Lash, ed., *From the Diaries of Felix Frankfurter* (New York: W. W. Norton & Company, 1975), passim.
119. See, for example, his *A Constitutional Faith.*
120. "If the authors of these guarantees . . . were unwilling or unable to resolve the issue by assigning to one priority over the other, it is not for us to rewrite the Constitution by undertaking what they declined." *Nebraska Press Ass'n. v. Stuart,* supra, n. 114.
121. *Politics and the Constitution* (Chicago: University of Chicago Press, 1953), 2 vols.
122. Art. 79 (3).
123. *The South West Case,* 1 BVerfGE 14 (1951); the opinion is translated and excerpted in Murphy and Tanenhaus (supra, note 7), ch. 7.
124. *Golak Nath v. Punjab,* A.I.R. 1967 S.C. 1643. For an excellent nontechnical discussion of the decision, see H. C. L. Merillat, *Land and the Constitution in India* (New York: Columbia University Press, 1970), esp. chs. 8–12.
125. *United States v. Carolene Products,* 304 U.S. 144, 152 (1938). Alpheus T. Mason, *Harlan Fiske Stone* (New York: The Viking Press, 1956), ch. 21, provides the biography of the footnote. In *The Supreme Court from Taft to Warren,* as well as in later chapters of *Stone,* Mason develops the footnote's implications for constitutional jurisprudence.
126. 328 U.S. 549 (1946). The votes at conference are recorded, although somewhat differently, in both the Papers of Frank Murphy (supra, note 88), and those of Harold H. Burton, the Library of Congress. Stone, of course, died before the decision was announced, and Douglas persuaded Black of the errors of his ways and possibly Murphy also, since Murphy "passed" at the original vote.
127. *Loving v. Virginia,* 388 U.S. 1 (1967); see also *Skinner v. Oklahoma,* supra, note 89, at 541.
128. *Skinner v. Oklahoma,* supra, note 89.
129. *Shapiro v. Thompson,* 394 U.S. 618 (1969); *Dunn v. Blumstein,* 405 U.S. 330 (1972); *Memorial Hospital v. Maricopa County,* 415 U.S. 250 (1974).
130. *Afroyim v. Rusk,* 387 U.S. 253 (1967).
131. *Griswold v. Connecticut,* supra, note 96; *Roe v. Wade,* 410 U.S. 113 (1973); but see *Doe v. Commonwealth's Attorney,* 425 U.S. 901 (1976).
132. *Brown v. Board of Education,* 347 U.S. 483 (1954). After *Brown* but before *San Antonio v. Rodriguez,* 411 U.S. 1 (1973), I would have said "to a decent education at least equal to that afforded others in the same state." After *Rodriguez* "minimal education" seems more accurate, although less precise.
133. The term Stone used in the *Carolene Products* footnote was "more searching judicial inquiry" (supra, note 125). As far as I know, the phrase "strict scrutiny" was first used by Douglas in his opinion for the Court in *Skinner* (supra, note 89) at 541. For discussions of the various permutations of "strict scrutiny," see: Karst (supra, note 89); Gerald Gunther, "In Search of Evolving Doctrine on a Changing Court," *Harvard Law Review* 86 (1972): 1; and Owen M. Fiss, "Groups and the Equal Protection Clause," *Philosophy and Public Affairs* 107 (1976).

134. *Outline of Lectures on Jurisprudence* (Cambridge: Harvard University Press, 1943), pp. 96–97; see also *Jurisprudence* (St. Paul: West Publishing Co., 1959), III, esp. ch. 14, sec. 82.
135. "A Survey of Social Interests," *Harvard Law Review* 57 (1943): 1, 2.
136. 360 U.S. 109.
137. Ibid., dis. op., 144. For more general criticisms of balancing, see Donald Meiklejohn, "Labels and Libertarians," *Ethics* 66 (1955): 51; Thomas I. Emerson, *Toward a General Theory of the First Amendment* (New York: Random House, 1966), pp. 54–56. For a defense of balancing, see Dean Alfange, Jr., "The Balancing of Interests in Free Speech Cases," *Law in Transition Quarterly* 2 (1965): 1.
138. *The Role of the Supreme Court in American Government* (New York: Oxford University Press, 1976), p. 49.
139. Natural law/rights have no monopoly here, of course. A conventionalist could distinguish between more and less fundamental conventions and could probably do so with greater ease and objective justification than a believer in natural law/rights could distinguish the natural from the conventional.
140. Op. cit. (supra, note 7).
141. See Staughton Lynd, *Class Conflict, Slavery, and the U.S. Constitution* (Indianapolis: The Bobbs-Merrill Co., 1967), chs. 7–8.
142. As I shall show in the larger work from which this paper is excerpted, I am very dubious of our ability to divine "original intent." See William Anderson, "The Intention of the Framers: A Note on Constitutional Interpretation," *American Political Science Review* 49 (1955): 340.
143. *We the Judges,* p. 429.
144. *Miranda v. Arizona,* 384 U.S. 436, 460 (1966).
145. *Gregg v. Georgia,* supra, note 102. For a summary of the case law on human dignity up to 1968, see Bernard Schwartz, *A Commentary on the Constitution of the United States* (New York: The Macmillan Company, 1968), II, ch. 20.
146. *Miranda v. Arizona,* supra, note 144, at 460.
147. "The Philosophy of Law of the Early Sophists," *American Journal of Jurisprudence* 20 (1975): 81, 94.
148. Op. cit. (supra, note 54), p. 225.
149. *Rosenblatt v. Baer,* supra, note 103, at 92.
150. See the sentence quoted supra, note 92. Carl Friedrich found a heavy religious emphasis in the whole concept of constitutionalism; see the works cited in note 19.
151. Hans Kelsen, *General Theory of Law and State* (Cambridge: Harvard University Press, 1945), esp. chs. 1 and 11.
152. " The Supreme Court and the People's Will," *North Dakota Law* 33 (1958): 573, 577.
153. See, for example, their denial that a right to a decent reputation against false allegations is protected by the Constitution; *Paul v. Davis,* 424 U.S. 693 (1976). In a blistering dissent Brennan wrote: "I had always thought that one of this Court's most important roles is to provide a formidable bulwark against governmental violation of the constitutional safeguards securing in our free society the legitimate expectations of every person to innate human dignity and sense of worth."
154. *United States v. Butler,* 297 U.S. 1, dis. op., 79 (1936).
155. See my *Elements of Judicial Strategy,* ch. 2.

TABLE OF CASES